State Capture in the Militarized Fight Against Illegal Small-Scale Goldmining in Ghana

Jasper Abembia Ayelazuno ·
Maxwell Akansina Aziabah

State Capture in the Militarized Fight Against Illegal Small-Scale Goldmining in Ghana

palgrave
macmillan

Jasper Abembia Ayelazuno
University for Development Studies
Tamale, Ghana

Maxwell Akansina Aziabah
SD Dombo University of Business
and Integrated Development Studies
WA, Ghana

ISBN 978-3-031-82672-6   ISBN 978-3-031-82673-3   (eBook)
https://doi.org/10.1007/978-3-031-82673-3

This Palgrave Macmillan imprint is published by the registered company Springer Nature
Switzerland AG
The registered company address is: Gewerbestrasse 11, 6330 Cham, Switzerland

If disposing of this product, please recycle the paper.

For Maxwell Akansina Aziabah, co-author of this book, who passed away before it was published. You worked long hours and late into the night to meet deadlines of the publisher. And you did so while battling, in silence, the ailment that finally snuffed out your young, vibrant, and precious life. Your remarkable fortitude, sheer mental tenacity, and unwavering resolve as a scholar made this book to finally see the light of day. Hopefully, your wish for it to define the field of state capture in the governance of small-scale mining in Ghana will be fulfilled. But undoubtedly, the ideas you postulated here will survive your demise for decades. Rest in Peace! Paɛ suŋa!

FOREWORD

STATE CAPTURE AND ILLEGAL ARTISANAL AND SMALL-SCALE GOLD MINING (ASGM) IN GHANA: A CANCEROUS AFFAIR

As a journalist, I have dedicated my career to exposing the truth and shedding light on the darkest corners of our society. In Ghana, one of the most pressing issues that has caught my attention is the scourge of state capture and illegal Artisanal and Small-Scale Gold Mining (ASGM). This book is a culmination of tireless efforts to uncover the truth behind these interconnected issues, and I am honoured to write this foreword.

State capture, a phenomenon where private interests manipulate and control the state for personal gain, has become a cancer in our nation's governance. In Ghana, this has manifested in the form of corrupt government officials, politicians, and business moguls colluding to plunder our natural resources, including gold. The consequences are devastating environmental degradation, displacement of communities, and a loss of revenue that could have been used to develop our country.

ASGM, while providing a livelihood for many, has become a conduit for illegal activities, including environmental destruction and pollution of water bodies in enormous proportions. The sector's informality and lack of regulation have created a fertile ground for criminal elements to thrive, further entrenching state capture.

My experience as an embedded journalist with the Government's anti-galamsey taskforce, Galamstop, revealed the depth of corruption and state capture. I saw firsthand how influential people in government, politically exposed persons, and political actors micro-manage law enforcement agencies to undermine their own mission. Politicians, predominantly from the ruling party, own illegal mining sites in forest reserves, with the Upper Wassa and Apamprama forest reserves being stark examples.

This book meticulously uncovers the web of corruption, patronage, and deceit that has led to the capture of our state. Through rigorous research and investigative journalism, the authors expose the key players, their motivations, and the devastating impact on our nation.

The license regime, meant to regulate mining, has been hijacked by a few influential individuals, with the autonomy of approval resting in the hands of a single minister in some cases. This concentration of power determines who gets to mine and who is raided by the military.

My team and I experienced this firsthand when we were held captive in the Apamprama forest reserve by the army, who were protecting a miner ravaging the forest. The lack of transparency and accountability is a testament to the entrenched corruption and state capture that perpetuates illegal mining in Ghana.

This book is not just an exposé; it is a call to action. It demands that we, as a nation, confront the cancer of state capture and illegal ASGM head-on. We must strengthen our institutions, ensure transparency and accountability, and protect our environment.

To the policymakers, this book serves as a reminder that the people demand better. We need policies that prioritize the welfare of citizens, not just the interests of a privileged few. To the citizens of Ghana, this book empowers you to demand justice and accountability. We must reclaim our state and ensure that it serves the people, not just the powerful.

In conclusion, this book is a vital contribution to our national conversation. It is a testament to the power of investigative journalism and a reminder that the truth, no matter how uncomfortable, must be told.

Let us join forces to fight this cancerous affair and reclaim our nation.

Erastus Asare Donkor
Award-winning and Investigative/
Environmental Journalist,
Multimedia Group, Ghana

PREFACE

The main ideas of this book were incubated when the first author was commissioned by *Third World Network—Africa (TWN-Africa)* in 2017 to write a position paper on Artisanal and Small-scale Gold Mining (ASGM) in Ghana. The timing of this assignment was not mere happenstance, happening as it did at the time the Head-of-State of Ghana declared war against the calamitous destructions of the environment by illegal ASGM, known popularly in Ghana as the *galamsey menace*. It was rather precisely because of these developments that TWN-Africa commissioned the position paper to serve as the point of departure to canvass a social justice perspective on this issue, which arguably predominated political discourses in the media at the time. The paper argued then that the devastating human and environmental effects of illegal ASGM (known in Ghanaian parlance as *galamsey*) were not preordained. But rather, were created and deepened by the Ghanaian state due to its failure to play its regulatory role effectively. It then predicted gloomily that based on the history of the use of military crackdowns in Ghana and other African countries against illegal ASGM, the first military crackdown authorized by the Head-of-State of Ghana in his war against the galamsey menace— *Operation Vanguard*—would also fail. And it did. Against this backdrop, both authors started tracking the political scandals and failures that bedeviled the war against the galamsey menace by the Ghana president. The outcome of this is the present book.

This book, thus, addresses one of the most vexed questions about governance and politics in natural resources-rich, albeit poor, countries across the world. Why have most states in natural resources-rich developing countries failed to regulate their artisanal and small-scale mining (ASM) industries? With specific reference to gold, why have these states failed to regulate their artisanal and small-scale gold mining (ASGM) industries? This failure is both intellectually and politically puzzling, because these same states demonstrate capability in different functions and regulations of other sectors of the economy. Ghana is a quintessential example of this puzzle. Despite its legendary reputation as a relatively well-governed, peaceful, and democratic country, its ASGM sector is characterized predominantly by informality, criminality, and deleterious environmental and human development effects, which include the ferocious denuding of the country's vegetation cover, toxic pollution of water bodies, and serious health and safety hazards inflicted on the rural populace in mining areas.

The book draws on the insights of state capture theory to shed greater light on this puzzling failure, and in doing so, to contribute to unpick it, and ultimately to address the stubborn problem of the incapability of the state to regulate the ASGM sector in Ghana and beyond. State capture is a relatively new theory that explains the emergence of oligarchic and kleptocratic business classes in post-communist East European and Russian states, linking them and their illicit wealth to the powerful influence they exert on the regulatory functions of the state. Even though the insights of other and related state-centric theories—such as political corruption, neopatrimonialism, clientelism, and state failure—have been deployed to analyse this puzzle, this book illustrates that state capture provides more fascinating and penetrating insights into the puzzle. It is also endowed with great potential to proffer effective solutions to this stubborn problem of unsustainable, illegal, even criminal ASGM—*galamsey*.

Though related to grand political corruption, state capture provides deeper insights into the lethargy and dysfunctionality of the Ghanaian state (and other states) to regulate its ASGM sector. In a seminal paper on state capture, Joel S. Hellman, Geraint Jones, and Daniel Kaufmann illustrate the ways in which "state captors" shape and affect the formulation of rules and regulations governing the private sector to favour their interests, by paying public officials and politicians in these post-communist states to make this possible. In Sub-Saharan Africa, the unprecedented political decadence and malfeasance in South Africa under President Jacob Zuma has been analysed with the lens of state capture, providing incisive insights on the situation. Focusing, for example, on the Gupta family (Atul, Ajay, and Rajesh Gupta) as "state captors," scholars have analysed the relationship between this family and senior government officials—including President Zuma himself and his family—to illustrate the hallmarks of state capture in this country.

In this book, we demonstrate similar dynamics of state capture in the failed militarized fight against illegal ASGM—*galamsey*—in Ghana between 2017 and 2024. Though the problem of the incapability of the Ghanaian state to regulate its ASGM sector predates this period by several decades, it spiralled out of control at this historical conjuncture. For example, it was during this period that the ASGM sector of Ghana changed dramatically to mechanized/industrialized mining, making it a misnomer to refer to the industry as artisanal and small-scale mining (ASM); and more so, to refer to the operators of the industry as artisanal and small-scale miners. Tied to this change is the aggravation of the deleterious environmental and human effects of *galamsey*. Rivers and water bodies witnessed an unprecedented scale and level of poisoning, demonstrated by—to mention just one example—dangerously high turbidity levels never witnessed before. Ghana is, therefore, running out of fresh water from these rivers, bearing in mind that these are the sources of water for the Ghana Water Company Limited (GWCL), which treats and distributes water to Ghanaians. A recent case in point is the pollution of the Pra river in the Central Region of Ghana. The GWCL issued a press release in August 2024, which reported that about sixty per cent of the catchment capacity of the Pra is silted because of illegal mining. As a result of this, the river is recording an average turbidity of 14,000 NTU; this is far above the maximum of 2,000 NTU, the parameters within which the water can be treated for drinking.

Connected to the poisoning of rivers, water bodies, and soil are the unprecedented serious health and safety hazards the populace living in mining areas have experienced during the period under study. Medical Scientists have discovered serious maternal and neonatal health issues, such as hideous congenital and physical disorders of some babies born in these communities, and sadly, deaths of these babies. These scientists have curated in their laboratories, harrowing images of stillborn babies and those born with congenital disorders such as imperforate anuses, transverse deficiency, and atypical genitalia. Their research established that these horrific physical deformities are caused by the pollution of food and water with lethal chemicals like mercury and cyanide often used in galamsey. In addition to these health complications, the rural populace has lost their livelihoods because of this new mechanized/industrialized mining masquerading as ASM. By its nature, this capitalist medium-scale mining (CMM)—as it is conceptualized in this book—requires huge tracts of land. Thus, inherent to the dramatic transformation of ASM to CMM between 2017 and 2024 is the destruction of the farms of peasants in the mining areas, and in some cases, the dispossession of these peasants of their farmlands.

Yet this book argues that these are only the morbid symptoms of state capture in the ASGM sector of Ghana. It posits that the empirical context and evidence of state capture are in the action and inaction of the Ghanaian state in the face of the aggravation of the environmental and human menace caused by CMM galamsey during this period. The Ghanaian state resorted to a strongarm—even a Rambo-style—approach to fighting the "galamsey menace," as it was popularly called. First, the Head-of-State, President Akufo-Addo, vowed to put his job as president on the line to fight the problem. And in accordance with this vow, his government ordered the highest number of military crackdowns in the history of the fight against galamsey. He authorized three successive military operations and one taskforce to fight the problem, namely, Operation Vanguard, Operation Halt I, Operation Halt II, and the GALAMSTOP taskforce. These are not only the highest number of military crackdowns authorized by a single Head-of-State, but the highest number ever mobilized within such a relatively short span.

Enter state capture in the militarized fight against galamsey! Poignantly, the militarized fight against galamsey failed spectacularly, and the evidence of this is amply documented in this book. This poses a poignant question: why did the president lose the fight against galamsey despite his vow to fight it at all cost, and despite the coercive apparatuses of state he commandeered to do the fighting? Addressing this question, which is at once an intellectual and political problem, is the thrust of this book. It documents, using digital and internet sources, solid evidence of state capture as the main cause of the dismal failure of the Ghanaian state to fight the galamsey menace. This problem is neither peculiar to Ghana nor Black Africa. Military crackdowns and their dismal record of success in fighting illegal ASM, as well as its deleterious environmental and human effects, can be found in Asia, Latin America, and Oceania. This makes the *prolematique* of the book and the contribution it makes, both theoretical and in praxis, global in scope and significance.

Despite the global appeal of the book, its purpose and plot are deeply embedded and shaped by the Ghanaian local context. For one thing, it captures the zeitgeist of the declining quality of governance and political decadence in Ghana between 2017 and 2024. And for another, state capture has entered the lexicon of the political discourse of Ghana in this period. On the first point, the much-acclaimed stature of Ghana as a model of democracy is fast declining in the last eight years. Press freedom is eroding—to cite just one example—as journalists are intimidated and assaulted by state security agencies; and in one case (in the case of Mr. Ahmed Suale), a journalist was murdered, simply because of stories he had done, or was doing, which were critical of the government. Ghana is, thus, experiencing the wave of "autocratization" sweeping across the world. Its four-yearly presidential and parliamentary elections are increasingly characterized by deadly violence. And the elections management body of the country (the Electoral Commission [EC]) is increasingly distrusted because of the appointments of known supporters of the president's political party, the New Patriotic Party (NPP), to management positions of the EC.

Political corruption and mismanagement of the economy have reached all-time high in Ghana; and like the case of galamsey studied in this book, the political elites of the incumbent government indulge in these acts of bad governance with impunity. *State capture* is the term used by critics of the government, both its political opponents and opinion leaders, to capture the deteriorating state of governance in the country. A case in point is Justice William Atuguba, an eminent retired judge of the Supreme Court of Ghana. Worried about the wrong direction the country is presently headed because of the above-mentioned issues, he granted an interview to a journalist of Accra-based TV3 Network, in which he decried the hardships Ghanaians were suffering in the hands of the government. For him, the state is increasingly becoming dictatorial as it exercises power without circumspection and regard for the checks provided by the 1992 Constitution of the country. He concluded that Ghana is facing state capture: "If we are being honest, there is state capture in this country."[1]

---

[1] https://x.com/tv3_ghana/status/1836938516166594892?ref_src=twsrc%5Etfw%7Ctwcamp%5Etweetembed%7Ctwterm%5E1836938516166594892%7Ctwgr%5E022c3cb0e463afb5b65c41a9f76d991a6748d91a%7Ctwcon%5Es1_&ref_url=https%3A%2F%2Fyawanews.com%2Fthere-is-state-capture-in-this-country-justice-william-atuguba-rtd%2F

During the period under study in this book, key state institutions responsible for its core functions have been bastardized by the appointments and sackings of top state officials, both of which are often informed by the protection of the political and economic interests of the power elite rather than the promotion of the public good. For example, the former EC Chairperson, Mrs. Charlotte Kesson-Smith Osei, who managed the 2016 Ghanaian presidential and parliamentary elections—which resulted in the election of the president of Ghana for the period under study—was removed and replaced by the incumbent EC Chairperson, Ms. Jean Adukwei Mensa. It is under the leadership of the latter that the EC has lost considerable public trust, as its compilation of the voters register, and computation of election results are increasingly losing credibility; and are characterized by violence. It is important to note that one of the most potent ways of state capture is the influence by the power elite over the appointments of top government officials to protect their interests.

This resonates with the evidence of state capture documented in this book. We demonstrate that the power elite are engaged in destructive *galamsey* with impunity, in the full glare of state institutions responsible for enforcing the laws of ASGM. Indeed, they have been protected by the very state agencies responsible for enforcing the laws against galamsey. It is unsurprising, therefore, that the aggravated situation of destructive galamsey discussed above happened during the military operations authorized by the president. During these operations, 500 excavators seized from illegal miners got missing; and to date, they have not been found, and no one has been held accountable for their disappearance. All the relevant security agencies of the state, like the Ghana Police Service and the National Intelligence Bureau (NIB), were incapacitated to investigate this case because the top management and leaders of these institutions feared they would lose their jobs, to state it mildly. In stronger terms, their appointments were influenced by some of the powerful elites engaged in destructive galamsey. Thus, they were appointed not to enforce the ASGM laws, but to protect the power elite to do galamsey.

As we demonstrate elsewhere (see Ayelazuno and Aziabah, 2023), the bombshell leakage of the Frimpong-Boateng galamsey report via social media illustrates the influence of the galamsey power elite over appointments of top government officials. The famed scholar and Cardiothoracic surgeon, Professor Kwabena Frimpong-Boateng, lost his cabinet ministerial position as Minister for Environment, Science, Technology, and Innovation. Why? Because his report—which is based on information he was privy to as the government official spearheading its militarized fight against galamsey—was basically alerting the president of the complicity and direct participation of government officials in galamsey. Besides being a Minister of one of the institutions responsible for regulating mining, he was appointed by the president as the chairman of the Inter-Ministerial Committee on Illegal Mining (IMCIM). His sacking by the president illustrates that his appointments as the Minister and Chairman of the IMCIM were not for him to protect the environment and fight galamsey, but rather to protect the power elites to do galamsey. This is state capture writ large.

Our book, therefore, is situated in this broader context of the deteriorating governance and backsliding of democracy in Ghana. As critical scholars on the ground observing this situation, we write this book from a critical Social Science perspective. It is a case study of the increasing decadence of the Ghanaian society. The state capture that is documented in this book is a microcosm of the deterioration of governance in the Ghanaian democratic state in general. We hope the book will open new and exciting vistas for studying and fighting the virulent cancer of state capture spreading across various facets of the Ghanaian society regulated by the state. In line with the critical Social Science tradition, the book is a call to action by activist-scholars and radical civil society organizations: to rise and fight to liberate Ghana from the state capture of the few power elites.

Happily, as we write this preface (September 2024), this is already beginning to happen. Incensed by the aggravation of the deleterious environmental and human effects of galamsey documented in this book, a coalition of civil society organizations (CSOs) are up in arms over the dismal failure of the government to address the problem. The coalition that is made up of various CSOs, concerned about sundry issues, has issued press statements calling on the government to take decisive action to stop galamsey. The CSOs include the following: Ghana Catholic Bishops' Conference (GCBC), the Ghana Association of Medical Laboratory Scientists (GAMLS), Media Coalition Against Galamsey, The Christian Council of Ghana (CCG), the Executive Women Network (EWN), the Office of the Chief Imam, the Trades Union Congress (TUC), Ghana Journalists Association (GJA), University Teachers Association of Ghana (UTAG), The General Agricultural Workers Union (GAWU), The Centre for Climate Change and Food Security (CCCFS), and the Civil Society Organisations (CSOs) Platform on the Sustainable Development

Goals (Ngnenbe & Koomson—*Graphic Online*, 2024). In fact, Ghanaian workers unions, led by the TUC, have threatened to embark on a nationwide strike by the end of September 2024 if the government fails to take decisive action to address the escalating galamsey crisis (Citi Newsroom, 2024).

Illustrative of the emerging positive signs of resistance to state capture in the failed militarized fight against galamsey and the impunity of the power elite mining class, *Democracy Hub*, a youth-dominated CSO, embarked on a three-day protest dubbed *#OccupyJulorbiHouse demonstration*. The demonstration was aimed at drawing attention to not only the aggravated situation of galamsey, but to other serious problems of governance and socioeconomic issues such as injustice, unemployment, rising poverty, state capture, nepotism, corruption, and the need for judicial independence (Darko—Myjoyonline.com, 2024). But reminiscent of the backsliding of democracy in Ghana, over 50 of the protesters were arrested by the police; and there are credible reports of abuses of their human rights during their arrest (Mensah—The Africa Report, 2024). Even though the offences they were charged and arraigned before court were mainly misdemeanours related to breaches of the laws of public order/peace, the court refused to grant them bail. They were remanded in prison and police custody for two weeks, while the power elites who have committed more serious crimes of illegal mining are walking scot-free and actively committing the crime.

Even more interesting, but illustrative of state capture, is the action of the Ministry of Justice and Attorney General in this case. Though the protestors are alleged to have committed misdemeanour offences, it is the Attorney General's (AG) prosecutors who are leading the prosecution. Both the prosecution by the AG's department and the refusal by the court to grant bail are strange, if not bizarre, in the history of demonstrations under democratic governance in Ghana the last three decades. But as we demonstrate in this book, this is part of the contradictions of the captured state: it shows capacity where it needs to do so to promote the interests of its captors and their allies within it. But it is lethargic and dysfunctional where its effective functioning will hurt the interests of its captors and their allies within it. This is precisely what is literally unfolding before our eyes in this case: while Ghana is facing existential threat from the criminal activities of the mining power elites, the police and AG department are deploying the might of the state to deal with minor offences.

However, reminiscent of hope in political agency and resistance of Ghanaians, there is public outrage against the government because of this; and social media is rife with campaigns for the release of the protesters, with the hashtag #FreetheCitizens going viral (Mensah—The Africa Report, 2024).

Come along with us, as we walk you through, in the following pages, the dark alleys of state capture in the militarized fight against galamsey between 2017 and 2024. Thanks to the digital revolution and the Internet, we shine light on these dark alleys.

Tamale, Ghana	Jasper Abembia Ayelazuno
WA, Ghana	Maxwell Akansina Aziabah

REFERENCES

Ayelazuno, J.A. and Aziabah, M.A. (2023). "Making visible the galamsey scandals in Ghana: digital media as new technologies of democratic accountability." *The Extractive Industries and Society*, 16 (101366), 1–9.

Darko, K.A. Myjoyonline news (2024). *Democracy Hub defies injunction to protest against Akufo-Addo*. https://www.myjoyonline.com/democracy-hub-defies-injunction-to-protest-against-akufo-addo/

Citi Newsroom (2024). *Organised Labour threatens nationwide strike over galamsey crisis*. https://citinewsroom.com/2024/09/organised-labour-threatens-nationwide-strike-if-govt-fails-to-act-on-galamsey-crisis/

Mensah, K. The Africa Report (2024). Ghana: Public outrage mounts over police crackdown on protesters. https://www.theafricareport.com/363119/ghana-public-outrage-mounts-over-police-crackdown-on-protesters/

Ngnenbe, T & Koomson, J.B. Graphic Online (2024). *More groups rise against galamsey*. https://www.graphic.com.gh/news/general-news/ghana-news-more-groups-rise-against-galamsey.html

ACKNOWLEDGEMENTS

First, to God and our Ancestors be the glory for giving us good health, strength, and peace of mind to write this book. We are also grateful to our families for the support and sacrifices they gave and made, respectively, for us to write this book.

The book is the product of an initial position paper written by the first author for the Third World Network–Africa (TWN-Africa), a progressive civil society organization based in Ghana, and engaged in advocacy for social justice and good governance policies in the extractive industry sector. It is this position paper which laid the foundation for nurturing the ideas that crystalized into this book. To Dr. Yao Graham, Coordinator of the TWN-Africa, and the entire team (especially, Ms. Pauline Vande-Pallen), we are immensely indebted to you for the opportunity and resources to write this position paper, which then opened the vista for exploring this seminal work on state capture in Ghana.

We also express profound gratitude to Erastus Asare Donkor, the award-winning Investigative and Environmental Journalist with the Multimedia Group, Ghana. Erastus was the only embedded journalist in the war against illegal goldmining (galamsey), risking his life to report on the work of the Government's anti-galamsey taskforce—Galamstop. He also traversed communities, forest reserves, and water bodies that were ravaged by galamsey, and produced two documentary series—*Destruction for Gold* and *Poisoned for Gold*—which exposed the power elites and state captors engaged in criminal and destructive galasey with impunity. These documentaries served as a treasure trove of data for this book, and we are forever indebted to Erastus for this.

Our book drew heavily on secondary sources: scholarly and grey literature, as well as internet/online news media sources. It is also a book based on what anthropologists have termed "internet" and "digital" ethnography, as we have mined information from social media stories, videos, images, and news reports on the massive destruction of the environment by galamsey. The empirical analysis of the devastating effects of galamsey by the mining power elites, as well as the light shun on the dark corners of state capture, in this book are based on these sources. We are indebted to all the content creators and the news portals that we have gleaned information from for this book. They are too many to mention by names here, something we have done through the embedded citations in the book and the references we have compiled.

To Gavin Hilson, the leading scholar of ASM in Ghana and Sub-Saharan Africa generally, we acknowledge your immeasurable scholarly contributions to the field, from which this book has benefitted immensely. The first author is also grateful to Gavin for not only mentoring him on research and publication, but for the persistent prodding to do same.

We are also indebted to our respective institutions of affiliation, namely, the University for Development Studies (UDS) and the S.D. Dombo University of Business and Integrated Development Studies (SDD-UBIDS), for providing the conducive academic environment to research and write this book.

The first author wishes to thank Mr. Ismail Razak, his Graduate and Teaching Assistant, who provided research assistance, as well as helped in teaching and marking responsibilities, which provided the time needed to write this book.

This book benefitted immensely from the critical and insightful comments and suggestions of two anonymous reviewers, as well as the editors of Palgrave McMillan. To them, we express our profound appreciation for their contributions to making this book better than we could have made it.

Last, but certainly not the least, we owe Mr. Solomon Mizumah Debi (known popularly as Ali) tonnes of gratitude for painstakingly reading the whole manuscript, though on short notice and with a tight schedule. And with an eagle eye, he captured many spelling errors and awkward sentences, which we have addressed to improve the prose of the book. Thanks, Ali!

Praise for *State Capture in the Militarized Fight Against Illegal Small-Scale Goldmining in Ghana*

"This book draws attention to the mining power-elites engaged in "illegal" semi-industrialized medium-scale mining and associated state capture, in the process, nuancing further the complexities of the sector's informality. The book is an invaluable source of information for both scholars and environmental activists concerned with the environmental and human-related dimensions of informal ASM in sub-Saharan Africa, and how the sector's "illegality" is portrayed more generally."

—Gavin Hilson, *Professor and Chair of Sustainability in Business, University of Surrey, UK*

"This book provides deep insights into the puzzle of why the Ghanaian state has failed so spectacularly to tackle the issue of galamsey – informal and illicit small-scale gold mining – and its associated environmental destruction, despite stated intentions to do so. Drawing on state capture theory and class analysis, the authors evidence the operation of a shadow state in which power elites, inclusive of powerful politicians and government officials, are themselves engaged in illegal, mechanised mining with state protection, thus undermining any ostensible 'fight against galamsey'. This analysis poses serious questions about Ghana's status as a model democratic state in Africa."

—Gordon Crawford, *Research Professor in Global Development, Centre for Peace and Security, Coventry University, UK*

"This book provides a much-needed social justice perspective on artisanal and small-scale gold mining. Though rich on the political economy of Ghana and the role of the Ghanaian state in shaping illegal gold mining operations, the book is also highly relevant for understanding the challenges of small-scale mining across the globe."

—Ingrid Harvold Kvangraven, *Senior Lecturer, International Development, King's College, London*

CONTENTS

Abbreviations

AAK	Abura, Asebu, Kwamankese
AMV	Africa Mining Vision
ASGM	Artisanal and Small-Scale Gold Mining
AU	Africa Union
CABuD	Centre for Agroforestry Business Development
CAN	Community of Andean Nations
CCCFS	Centre for Climate Change and Food Security
CCG	Christian Council of Ghana
CDD	Center for Democracy and Development
CDS	Chief of Defense Staff
CMM	Capitalist Medium-Scale Mining
CMS	Community Mining Schemes
COCOBOD	Ghana Cocoa Board
CSOs	Civil Society Organizations
DISEC	District Security Councils
DOLTA	Domestic Lumber Trade Association
DSRA	Day of Scientific Renaissance of Africa
EC	Electoral Commission
EPA	Environmental Protection Agency
EWN	Executive Women Network
FC	Forestry Commission
FFP	Fund for Peace
FIMS	Foreigner Identification Management System
FOBs	Forward Operating Bases
GAF	Ghana Armed Forces
GAMLS	Ghana Association of Medical Laboratory Scientists

GAWU	General Agricultural Workers Union
GBC	Ghana Broadcasting Corporation
GCBC	Ghana Catholic Bishops' Conference
GFP	Global Firepower
GIF	Ghana Institute of Foresters
GJA	Ghana Journalists Association
GWCL	Ghana Water Company Limited
ICC	Interstate Commerce Commission
IGP	Inspector General of Police
IMCIM	Inter-Ministerial Committee on Illegal Mining
JTF	Joint Task Force
MCAG	Media Coalition Against Galamsey
MDD	Madre de Dios
MLNR	Ministry of Lands and Natural Resources
MMDAs	Metropolitan, Municipal, and District Assemblies
MMIP	Multilateral Mining Integrated Project
MNCs	Multinational Mining Companies
MP	Member of Parliament
NDC	National Democratic Congress
NIA	National Identity Authority
NIB	National Investigation Bureau
NPP	New Patriotic Party
OM	Operation Mercury
OSP	Office of the Special Prosecutor
PAID	Appraisal and Implementation Document
PNDC	Provisional National Defence Council
PPE	Personal Protective Equipment
REGSEC	Regional Security Council
SCC	State Capture Commission
SMGHL	Shaanxi Mining (Ghana) Limited
SOEs	State-Owned Enterprises
TAM	Traditional Artisanal Mining
TUC	Trades Union Congress
UGBS	University of Ghana Business School
USD	United States Dollars
UTAG	University Teachers Association
VPSHR	Voluntary Principles on Security and Human Rights
WRC	Water Resources Commission

LIST OF FIGURES

Introduction: Ghana's ASGM Industry and the Intractable Problem of "Galamsey"

The Ghanaian state has failed to regulate its artisanal and small-scale mining (ASM) sector; particularly, the burgeoning artisanal and small-scale gold mining (ASGM) component. Rather than a well-regulated, sustainable, poverty-reducing, and gender-balanced industry envisaged by the Africa Mining Vision (AMV, 2009: 32), it is a chaotic ASGM sector. It is dominated by informal and "illegal" mining and sale of gold, popularly known in Ghanaian parlance as "galamsey": a local vernacular word used to describe not just its informality, but also its illegal and criminal characteristics (McQuilken & Hilson, 2016; Ayelazuno & Mawuko-Yevugah, 2021: 556). It is difficult to get the accurate number of people engaged in the industry; however, some authoritative sources estimate that between 70 and 85 per cent of small-scale miners are operating illegally in the country (University of Ghana Business School [UGBS] 2017; McQuilken & Hilson, 2016; Eduful et al., 2020). Inherent in galamsey are negative environmental and health effects such as "mercury contamination, land degradation, water deterioration, habitat destruction, air pollution, and the destruction of farmland" (Eduful et al., 2020: 1–14; Ayelazuno & Mawuko-Yevugah, 2021: 556). In addition to these are horrific human and social effects such as "deadly mining accidents, child labour, exploitation of women, violent crimes, smuggling and illicit financial flows" (Ayelazuno & Mawuko-Yevugah, 2021: 556).

This problem is not peculiar to Ghana, nor to gold and diamond mining. In most minerals-rich countries in Sub-Saharan Africa (see Hilso et al., 2017), in Asia (see Verbrugge, 2015), and in Latin America (see Zabyelina and van Uhm, 2020), informality, illegality, and criminality characterize the ASM industry; illustrating the general failure of states in developing countries to regulate this important component of their economies. As observed about Ghana, what is even more disturbing is the horrendous environmental and socioeconomic destruction wrought on the inhabitants of mining areas, especially women and children. In Sub-Saharan Africa (henceforth, Africa), the core concern of the continental development blueprint on mining—the Africa Union's (AU's) Africa Mining Vision (AMV)—is to sanitize ASM and turn it to a sustainable livelihood for the rural poor in the continent. As we will illustrate in this book, perhaps, nowhere in Africa is this needed more than in Ghana, an influential member of the AU. The ASM sector of this country is a quintessential example of informality, chaos, and the environmentally and socially ruinous nature of the industry across the continent and other regions of the Global South.

This situation raises a poignant and fundamental question why a relatively capable state as Ghana is incapable of governing its artisanal and small-scale mining (ASM) industry in general, and the ASGM in particular. As this is a problem in most minerals-rich developing countries, the question is also germane to, for example, Peru and Columbia in Latin America and the Philippines and Indonesia in Asia. And this is a question that scholars have grappled with in these countries (see, for example, Verbrugge, 2015; Benites, 2023; Rodríguez-Novoa and Holley, 2023). This book seeks to address this question, at once an intellectual and political puzzle: that is the unsuccessful efforts of the Ghanaian state to address the problem of galamsey, including the use of the military to fight it, but with little success. We argue and demonstrate in this book that the Ghanaian state has been captured by the power elite mining class who are doing, *not* ASM as we know it, but capitalist mechanized mining (CMM).

We shall return to this argument later to flesh it out in more detail. But at this juncture, a bit more information on the militarized fight against galamsey in Ghana is needed to establish the context of the argument of the book. Represented and widely known in Ghana as the galamsey menace—that is the environmentally and socially ruinous effects of illegal mining—the Ghanaian state has periodically deployed the police and the military to fight operators of the industry (Ayelazuno & Mawuko-Yevugah, 2021: 556; Eduful et al., 2020: 1–14; Hilson, 2017: 54; Bansah & Acquah, 2022; Ayelazuno & Mawuko-Yevugah, 2019: 1, 26). So the militarized fights against galamsey predate the period 2017-2024, the focus of analysis of this book. But this period is purposefully selected for scrutiny because it is unique: it represents the era during which the Head of the Ghanaian state, President Akufo-Addo, vowed to put his job as president on the line to fight galamsey (Ayelazuno & Mawuko-Yevugah, 2021: 570). And in accordance with this vow, his government ordered the highest number of military crackdowns in the history of the fight against galamsey. Between 2017 and 2024, he authorized three successive military operations and one taskforce to fight the problem: Operation Vanguard, Operation Halt I, Operation Halt II, and the GALAMSTOP taskforce.

But before proceeding further, it is important to note that militarized fights against illegal ASM are not peculiar to Ghana. They have been used in South Africa against the zama zamas in *Operation Prosper* (Panchia, 2023); in Zimbabwe, the government launched a nationwide operation against gold panners, miners, and traders—called *Operation Chikorokoza Chapera*—in November 2006 (Spiegel 2015); the government of Peru authorized a military operation, *Operation Mercury* (OM, *Operación Mercurio* in Spanish), against illegal ASM in the region of Madre de Dios (MDD) in February 2019 (Dethier et al., 2023); the cabinet of the government of Papua New Guinea authorized a joint military and police operation against illegal ASM in the Porgera Valley (Department of Prime Minister and National Executive Council, 2023), and the Colombian government has since 2012 "led police and military operations against ASM under the Community of Andean Nations (CAN) authority, a regional body composed of Colombia, Peru, Ecuador, and Bolivia" (Benites, 2023: 2).

In Ghana, these military operations are often managed and supervised by high civilian government officials made up of the ministers of relevant ministries. Often preceding these military operations is the setting up of inter-ministerial committees. In 2017, the president set up the Inter-Ministerial Committee on Illegal Mining (IMCIM), made up of the ministers of the following ministries: Environment, Science, Technology, and Innovation (Chairman); Lands and Natural Resources; Monitoring and Evaluation; Local Government and Rural Development; Chieftaincy and Religious Affairs; Regional Re-Organisation and Development; The Interior; Defence; Information; and Water and Sanitation (Frimpong-Boateng, n.d.: 27). As illustrated by Figure I.1, in September 2024, the president again established a five-member ministerial ad hoc committee on galamsey, made up of the following ministers: National Security Minister—Albert Kan-Dapaah (Chairman); Lands and Natural Resources Minister—Samuel Abu Jinapor; Defense Minister—Dominic-Nitiwul; Employment and Labour Relations Minister—Ignatius Baffour Awuah; and Information Minister—Fatima Abubakar. The committee was "to evaluate the government's ongoing efforts to combat illegal mining" (Arhinful –Myjoyonline, 2024). But as this book will illustrate, the government's efforts to combat illegal mining have failed disastrously because of state capture by the power elite mining class engaged in capitalist medium-scale mining (CMM). Like the IMCIM—which the president bizarrely dissolved in January 2021 without any reasons (Wiafe - Citi Newsroom, 2021)—this ad hoc committee is not only useless but is symptomatic of the contradictions of state capture in the failed militarized fight against galamsey documented in this book.

Small wonder, therefore, that these inter-ministerial committees and the military crackdowns have, at best, accomplished insignificant successes. At worst, they have failed; and as correctly observed by Ampaw et al. (2023), despite these interventions, nothing out of the ordinary has happened to illegal ASGM, as it continues unabated, ravaging the environment.

As we type these words in September 2024, Ghana's ASGM sector is a crime scene of unprecedented environmental menace engendered by CMM galamsey, a heinous crime committed with impunity by the power elite mining class. A case in point is the pollution of rivers and water bodies. In 2017, it was the spectacle of brown-milky colours of major rivers in Ashanti, Western, and Central Regions—their high turbidity levels (see Frimpong-Boateng, n.d.: 14-17)—that the media (led by Citi FM's *Breakfast Show*) used to mobilize public opinion, angst, and anger against galamsey. The famous *#StopGalamseyNow* campaign, started by Benard Avle—a journalist with Accra-based Citi FM—and his team in April 2017, used this spectacle to good effect (Adogla-Bessa - Citifmonline.com, 2017); of which the president's vow to fight and defeat galamsey at all cost is the clearest example.

But almost eight years into the government's militarized fight against galamsey, the turbidity levels of these rivers have worsened. The ad hoc ministerial committee mentioned above was formed because of this worsening state of the pollution of these rivers by CMM galamsey. In fact, it was formed because of the press statement of Ghana Water Company Limited (GWCL), as illustrated by Figure I.2, informing its customers in

MINISTRY OF INFORMATION

P. O. Box M41, Accra - North
Digital Address : GA-076-8230

Kindly quote this number and date on all correspondence
My Ref. No. PB126/168/02
Your Ref. No.
Date 13 - 09 - 2024

ADHOC MINISTERIAL COMMITTEE TO ENGAGE STAKEHOLDERS ON ILLEGAL MINING

On the instruction of the President of the Republic, Nana Addo Dankwa Akufo-Addo, an adhoc Ministerial committee has been set up to engage all stakeholders to assess government's efforts in dealing with illegal mining in Ghana.
The five-member committee is led by the

1. National Security Minister, Hon. Albert Kan-Dapaah

Other members of the committee are:

2. Minister for Lands and Natural Resources, Hon. Samuel A. Jinapor

3. Minister for Defense, Hon. Dominic Nitiwul

4. Minister for Employment, Labour Relations and Pensions, Hon. Ignatius Baffour Awuah

5. Minister for information, Fatimatu Abubakar

FATIMATU ABUBAKAR
MINISTER

Tel: +233 (0) 302 909 609
Email : info@moi.gov.gh
Website : www.moi.gov.gh

Fig. I.1   Ministry of Information Letter Announcing the Formation of an Inter-Ministerial Adhoc Committee

GHANA WATER LTD.

Main Bankers: GCB Bank Limited
Societe Generale Ghana
National Investment Bank

Central Regional Office
Post Office Box 377
Cape Coast - Ghana
West Africa

My Ref. No.: CR/P.A/CMT/VS/SEA/64

Your Ref. No.: ....

3rd August, 2024

DISTRIBUTION

THE MEDIA

WATER SUPPLY CHALLENGES EMANATING FROM ILLEGAL MINING ACTIVITIES

The Management of Ghana Water Limited (Central Region) wishes to inform all its cherished Customers of water supply challenges within Cape Coast, Elmina and surrounding communities in recent times.

The recent Demand-Supply gap is as a result of inadequate raw water received at the Sekyere Hemang Water Treatment Plant (WTP) as a result of galamsey. Pollution of the Pra River along its course and most especially at the catchment for abstraction has reduced water embarkment to the bearest minimum.

About Sixty percent (60%) of the catchment capacity is silted as a result of illegal mining (galamsey) compromising the quality of raw water. We are currently recording an average turbidity of 14,000 NTU instead of 2000 NTU designed for adequate treatment.

Currently the plant is able to produce only about (7,500m³/day), a quarter of its installed capacity.

This situation has caused severe inconveniences to our Customers and Consumers and we sincerely apologize for this.

The company is engaging all stakeholders to find a lasting solution to this.

We are by this announcement entreating all interest groups to join the fight against galamsey on the River Pra especially during this festive period.

Kindly report any form of illegal mining activity to your community leaders, local assembly etc. and support our initiatives to protect our water bodies, and promote sustainable water use practices.

Your assistance is crucial in helping us restore the quality of the raw water and ensure a reliable water supply of clean drinking water especially as we celebrate our most cherished festival.

WE WISH YOU A HAPPY FESTIVAL

Afehyia Paa oooo!!!

BY MANAGEMENT

Board of Directors: Hon. Patrick Yaw Boamah (Chairman), Ing. Dr. Clifford A. Braimah (Managing Director),
Mr. Noah Tumfo, Mr. Michael Ayesu, Hon. Akwasi Konadu, Chief Kabachewura Ewuntomah Zakaria, Hon. Kwame Anporfo Twumasi
Surv. Prof. Forster Kum-Ankama Sarpong, Mrs. Vida Dati, Mr. Joseph Acalatse, Ing. Hadisu Alhassan
Registered Office: 28th February Road, (Near Independence Square)
Telephone: 233-508-300-537
Website: www.gwcl.com.gh   E-mail: info@gwcl.com.gh

Fig. I.2   Press Statement of Ghana Water Company About the Pollution of River Pra

the Central Region of Ghana that there is water shortage because of the pollution of River Pra by galamsey. This press statement went viral and aroused public outrage and backlash against the government for its failed promise to fight and defeat galamsey. Embarrassed by this, the government hurriedly formed this ministerial ad hoc committee, which, for this book, is a useless and knee-jerk response by the captured Ghanaian state.

It is against this backdrop that the University of Ghana (UG) made the environmental menace of galamsey the subject of a panel discussion to climax its 2024 edition of the Day of Scientific Renaissance of Africa (DSRA) celebration. Titled "Galamsey: Preserving the Environment, Protecting Our Future," the keynote speakers and panelists all elaborated the huge environmental catastrophe that galamsey has engendered in Ghana. For example, the Vice Chancellor of the University of Ghana, Prof. Nana Aba Appiah Amfo, stated that the event was "aimed to provide a clear understanding of the current state of Ghana's distressed water bodies and forest vegetation, reminding all of the imminent danger the country faces and calling for immediate action to halt the pervasive practice of galamsey in the society" (University of Ghana [UG], 2024). The latest documentary of Erastus Asare Donkor, *Poisoned for Gold* (Part 1 and 2), demonstrates clearly the devastating extent to which many rivers across the country have been polluted, as well as the horrific destruction of Ghana's pristine and beautiful forests (Donkor, 2023), almost eight years into the militarized fight against galamsey.

This apocalyptic galamsey-driven environmental destruction flourishes despite, irrespective of the above-mentioned vow of the Ghanaian president to root out galamsey at the cost of his presidency; that is, if doing this will lead to him voted out of office by aggrieved operators of galamsey. Yet it continues to flourish despite the several millions of United States dollars (USD) spent on the above-mentioned military operations and task forces. In the words of his former minister responsible for the Ministry of Lands and Natural Resources, Mr. John-Peter Amewu— the minister at the time he launched these military crackdowns—the "Government of Ghana has invested huge resources, political and socioeconomic capital, to arrest the distressingly disastrous effects of ASM activities in the country" (The Republic of Ghana, 2017: 9). The opposition party members of Lands and Forestry Committee in Parliament claim that the government spent $30 million, per quarter of a year, for three years, on the above-mentioned IMCIM. Three million US dollars, according to Erastus Asare Donkor, was spent by the government of

Ghana in 2017 on drones to be used to fight galamsey (Donkor, 2022a). Considering the huge political investment in and the colossal sums of money spent on the militarized fight against galamsey, it is confounding that the fight has been unsuccessful. And to date (September 2024), the worsening environmental damage of galamsey continue to dominate the public discourse in the Ghanaian media landscape (see, for example, Ghana Broadcasting Corporation [GBC], 2024; Graphic Online, 2024; Ghanaweb, 2024; Ngnenbe, T & Koomson, J.B.—Graphic Online, 2024; Citi Newsroom, 2024; Darko—Myjoyonline, 2024).

To return to the argument of the book, and situated in this context, we seek to address a poignant question: why is the Ghanaian state unable to fight galamsey, even when it deploys the Ghana armed forces (GAF) against operators of the industry? This is puzzling for one major reason: the enemy the state was in battle with is weak, being unarmed civilians, and operating in plain sight of the state and its overwhelming coercive apparatuses. This book seeks to contribute a fresh state-theoretical perspective to unravelling this puzzle: that is the state capture theory. Even though there is voluminous literature offering state-inflected analysis of the worsening illegal ASGM situation and its deleterious ecological effects in Ghana, to date, state capture theory and its insights on the class dynamics of the problem have been lacking; at least, to the best of our knowledge. A great deal of the existing studies on the state-centric causes of illegal ASGM in Ghana focuses on a myriad of institutional shortcomings and the informalization of the industry (Hilson & Hilson, 2015; McQuilken & Hilson, 2016; Hilson & Maconachie, 2017; Kumah, 2022), elections and competitive elitism (Bebbington et al., 2018), political and petty corruption (Teschner, 2012; Crawford et al., 2017; Ampaw et al., 2023), and neopatrimonialism and clientelism (Ayelazuno and Mawuko-Yevugah, 2021).

Our book demonstrates that these state-centric theories, though insightful, have not posed the above question, let alone address it. Indeed, as the book will illustrate, this is the first time that the Commander-in-Chief of the GAF has gone as far as to, not only declare war on galamsey. But, as mentioned above, to put his presidency on the line to do so. Yet this did not make any difference in moving the needle in the successful fight against galamsey. This is a stunning failure like no other in the long history of Ghana's efforts to fight galamsey. Our book is, thus, the first to frame this failure in a novel way that illuminates the dysfunctionality and hollowness of the Ghanaian state at the highest level, by throwing light on its highest echelons of power or its most powerful organs: the president/Commander-in-Chief and his military.

Drawing on the theoretical insights of state capture—which have been usefully deployed in South Africa to explain the erosion and decadence of the real state—the book argues that the use of coercive agencies of the state, such as the army and police, is one of the modalities of creating and protecting the "shadow state" (Reno, 2000; Chipkin & Swilling, 2018). The shadow state—that is the informal institutional architecture of state capture—is more powerful and effective than the real state and its organs deployed to fight galamsey. Thus, the militarized fight against galamsey is both a mechanism and symptom of state capture and its class underpinnings. Indeed, the resort to the use of the military and other security agencies is signal evidence of a captured state, because there is a myriad of laws and institutions designed to regulate the ASGM sector (McQuilken & Hilson, 2016). As such, the chaotic ASGM sector and the menace of galamsey are not caused by the lack of institutions and laws governing the sector. As observed by the leading expert of this field, Ghana "has in place some of the most comprehensive and dynamic ASM laws in the world." (Hilson, 2017: 111).

As we will demonstrate in this book, the failed militarized fight against galamsey illustrates the great extent the Ghanaian state has been captured by the galamsey capitalist class; namely, the Ghanaian and foreign businesswomen and businessmen, alongside their complicit political elites, who are engaged in galamsey to accumulate wealth. Because of this deep state capture, rather than a fight against galamsey and the horrendous damage it inflicts on the environment, we are witnessing a beautiful façade in which the businesses of the galamsey capitalist classes are flourishing at the expense of the protection of the environment and livelihoods of the subaltern classes.

Symptomatic of state capture, the class that is not politically connected suffers in terms of the performance of its business or livelihood strategies. The Ghanaian subaltern classes, who have engaged in traditional artisanal mining (TAM) as an alternative means of livelihood, have been battered by the militarized fight against galamsey (Eduful et al., 2020; Bansah, 2019; Dery Tuokuu et al., 2020: 52–65). To be added to this violence is the unprecedented havoc wrought on their ecosystem (Boakye et al., 2020), dispossessing them of one of the most essential thing of life: water, provided them by mother nature through the rivers and streams that are their only sources of water. There is a sense, therefore, in which the militarized fight against galamsey is a class war by the captors of state against the powerless subaltern classes engaged in galamsey for survival.

The professional, powerful Ghana Armed Forces (GAF) is captured? We argue that the GAF has failed to win the war against galamsey, a failure that illustrates that the state is, indeed, captured. Because the GAF is part of the captured state, and its deployment to fight the war against galamsey is a charade to hide the political elites promoting and benefitting from galamsey. For these reasons, the GAF will forever lose the war against galamsey. This failure has nothing to do with the weakness, unprofessionalism, and incompetence of the Ghana Armed Forces (GAF). The GAF is a strong and professional army, but it has been deployed to fight an enemy that is complex and well-hidden; thus, very difficult to be identified by the officers and other ranks deployed to fight it. The real enemy is the shadow state (Chipkin & Swilling, 2018), made up of a network of powerful actors of the galamsey industry who have captured the real state, yet remain amorphous, elusive, and invisible relative to the enemy the military personnel are trained to fight.

As we have tried to demonstrate with examples from other African countries, as well as others in Latin America and Oceania, militarized fights against illegal ASM are not limited to Ghana. In the same vein, the insignificant successes—if not total failure—of these operations seem also to be a common feature of these operations. For example, "Operation Mercury" seemed to have failed to address the problem of illegal ASM in Peru (Damonte, 2018; Espin and Perz, 2021; Detheir et al., 2023), and same may be said about *Operation Chikorokoza Chapera* in Zimbabwe (Mkodzongi, 2020). Perhaps, the analysis of state capture in this book may provide theoretical and policy lessons for addressing the intractable problem of illegal ASM, with potential broader traction beyond Ghana.

Internet and Digital Media Sources of Material

The material presented and analysed in this book are collected from secondary sources: both internet sources and scholarly sources such as books, journal articles, and academic conference papers. For clarity of exposition, a bit more description of the internet sources is in order here. These are news stories, documents, audios, and videos that are shared, available, and easily accessible through the World Wide Web. These forms of media content are enriched with information on illegal artisanal and small-scale gold mining (ASGM) or galamsey. For example—and as Erastus Asare Donkor's documentary series "Destruction for Gold" (Donkor 2022a, b, c) illustrate—these media sources show not just the flourishing of illegal mining activities and the unprecedented environmental havoc they are causing. They also show—and illustrative of state capture—that they exist side-by-side the military operations and taskforces designed to fight galamsey. The media content is also rich with pieces of evidence that expose the power elites hiding behind the militarized fight against galamsey to engage in it with impunity. As such, the media content on galamsey brings under the floodlight and magnify the contours of the shadow state. For this book, media content on galamsey is a veritable source of information on the power elites engaged in galamsey and the ways in which the state is captured.

Indeed, the media content and the internet can capture and make easily accessible, for example, the attitude and behaviour of the political/power elites through interviews they grant to the mass media, as well as press statements and speeches they give. This information would have been almost impossible to get from these elites through traditional qualitative methods of collecting data, such as key informant interviews and in-depth personal interviews. For example, some of the evidence we document in the words of the president of Ghana to illuminate state capture, would have been near impossible to get from him using an interview guide; because one may not even get access to him, let alone interview him.

Yet, digital and internet sources are not accepted as one of the canonical social science methods; specifically, the qualitative methods that this book adopts. For qualitative methodological purists (Johnson & Onwuegbuzie, 2004), our book may not pass as work in social science. To them, we plead guilty to their charges; because, to write this book, we did not undertake any ethnographic fieldwork to do a (non-) participant observation, in-depth personal interviews, and focus groups discussion. The subject of the book—state capture in the fight against galamsey—is difficult to study with traditional ethnography, considering the complexity of the phenomenon and the shadowy nature of the actions and actors which shape it. For example, galamsey is a criminal offence, which means its culprits will try to hide their activities (the crime) as much as they can to avoid arrest. And in the case of the powerful people who may not be arrested because of the political offices they occupy or their connections to those who occupy these offices, they hide their criminal activities to avoid being named and shamed. Another layer of complexity is the political elites who leverage on their power to promote galamsey: not only do they have to do this discreetly but must simultaneously be seen to be genuinely fighting galamsey. All these are not easy to study with the classical ethnographic methods.

However, we now live in the era of the advancement of the internet from web 1.0 to web 3.0; even to 4.0. (Aghaei et al., 2012). It is an era of digital revolutions and new media; in which advances in communication technologies have dramatically transformed the landscapes of the social laboratory that social scientists undertake their studies. The milieux people live and interact with each other in situ is now digitized to a greater or less extent, with people interacting and relating on virtual platforms across space and time. In this era of digital revolutions, "mobile communication profoundly affects the tempo, structure, and process of daily life" (Katz, 2008: 3). The technology of digital media makes it possible for people who have access to it (and can use it) to enact actions and interactions with other people across the world, and in real time. The digital revolution provides the possibility of mediated interaction in which, for example, the internet makes it possible for a great number of people to meet and interact online platforms in real time and across space. This has compressed the time and space in face-to-face interaction; and thus, eliminated the spatial and temporal barriers in face-to-face interaction between people, something that requires co-presence of the actors (Thompson, 2005).

The nature of the internet makes it a powerful influential factor that shapes the virtual social world in which many social phenomena may be studied; including the complex, slippery, and shadowy phenomena of state capture and shadow state examined in this book. A key characteristic of the internet is its global nature, with the "capacity to link up and encompass other media" (Qiu, 2019: 4) across the globe. It is also mobile and can be connected to many mobile devices such as laptops, mobile phones, tablets, and iPads in remote corners of the world, including the Global South (Donner, 2015; Qui, 2019). Once connected to the internet, one has the world in their palms because, for example, they can send and receive information across the world with their mobile devices from whichever corner of the world they are located (Gralla, 1998: 2). "The diffusion of the internet, wireless communication, digital media and a variety of tools of open source social software," Manuel Castells writes, "have prompted the development of horizontal networks of interactive communication that connect local and global in chosen time" (Castells, 2019: 88). Another feature of the internet is the autonomy people have over how they use it; thus, "it is self- generated in terms of content, self-directed in emission, and self-selected in reception by many that communicate with many" (Castells, 2019: 90; Schejter & Tirosh, 2014: 76). Other features of the internet, according to Schejter and Tirosh (2014: 76) are: most content over the internet "is cheap and quick to both produce and reproduce"; the cost of content creation is low or non-existent; sharing of content over internet is instant and "can travel over the network virtually infinite"; and feedback is "immediate and personal and in fact can go directly and unmediated to the producer/distributor of content ... from its consumer/receiver."

The characteristics of the internet touched on above are inextricably linked to the characteristics of mobile ICT infrastructure needed to access the internet such as smartphones, tablets, laptops, notebooks, pocket PCs, and personal digital assistant (PDA) devices, as well as wireless communication technologies like LTE networks. Smartphones, to take as one example, have various features that not only provide mobile internet service, but also for capturing and uploading photos, videos, and audios on the internet. Some of these features, which vary by the type of smartphone and its operating system include digital camera, Bluetooth Wireless technology, instant-messaging, memory card slot, mobile office applications, picture and video multimedia messaging, and live TV capability (Kroski, 2008).

Parallel to the increasing internet-driven social life and "hypermedia" nature of our world (Dicks et al., 2005) is the digitization of sources of information that social scientists rely on to collect qualitative data. For example, qualitative data such as documents, photos, audios, and videos are now available and accessible in digital form on the internet; a development that is making hard copies and analogue forms of these data increasingly obsolete or rarely used. In the era of the digital revolution, various hi-tech devices, software, and apps have been invented that can capture and digitize documents, audio, and video recordings. And characteristic of the digital revolution, not only is data digitized—for example, taking pictures with a smart phone and saving them in its storage space—but the pictures can be easily shared through the internet. For example, they can be uploaded on a social media platform such as Facebook or Twitter and shared across the world. The digital revolution has created "a digital environment in which multiple types of information can be captured, stored, retrieved, edited and distributed in highly versatile ways and with considerable speed" (Dicks et al., 2005: 6–7). And thanks to the increasing availability of cheap mobile and portable digital recording devices as smartphones, live audio and video recordings of aspects of a social phenomenon can easily be done by onlookers and shared on social media platforms. For example, a local inhabitant of a community in which galamsey is prevalent, can do a live video recording of heavy earthmoving equipment doing surface mining and share it widely on the internet.

Galamsey and the militarized fight against it, the failure of this fight, and the dynamics of state capture have all been documented digitally and shared on the internet. The militarized fight against galamsey has engendered voluminous online literature, scholarly and grey, documenting the dynamics and characteristics of the criminality, informality, illegality, and the deleterious socioeconomic effects of the industry. Also documented and analysed in this media content are acts of corruption, facilitation, and participation of state actors—politicians and public servants—in galamsey. There is also voluminous multimedia content on these issues, created, stored, and shared on the internet. Specifically, the organization of different military operations to fight galamsey during the period under study (between 2017 and 2022), the successes, challenges, failures, and contradictions have all been watched and reported in real time by journalists and ordinary citizens, using digital devices and on online portals and social media platforms. There is rich media content on these military operations: textual, audio, and video information on how these operations are executed, their successes and failures; as well as the end of one operation and the beginning of another in its place, and so on.

As demonstrated by Donkor's documentary series, the worsening environmental menace in the thick of the anti-galamsey military operations—the result of which has led to the state launching successive anti-galamsey military operation—has also engendered news media reportage and the production, storage, and sharing of multimedia content on the worsening environmental menace. Similarly, the actions and reactions of scholars and influential actors in Ghana such as politicians, journalist, netizens, social media influencers, civil society organizations (CSOs), traditional leaders, and opinion leaders and other stakeholders in the fight against galamsey have been documented in the form of media reportage on the Ghanaian mass media portals and on websites and social media handles. For example, the content of Ghana web and Erastus Asare Donkor's Facebook, YouTube, and Twitter (X) contents are a treasure trove of information about galamsey; with videos and news stories on the subject that provide information that would have been difficult to obtain or costly to do so with traditional qualitative data-collection methods.

The behaviour and attitude of the political elites and their cronies in the militarized fight against galamsey—their actions and inactions, the internal contradictions thereof, as well as the interpretations given to all these by key stakeholders and the public—constitute the core of our analysis of state capture and the shadow state. Some of these or even most of them—for example, the ways by which the power elites participate in galamsey—are surreptitious. Thus, are intended to be hidden from public scrutiny because, first they are illicit in nature; second, they give negative press that damages the political brand of the politicians involved; and third, they are morally repugnant. All of which make the citizens, especially those in the middle class, angry, and with serious negative political implications in votes against the governing party in the next elections or even a revolt against the government.

However, the above-mentioned features of the internet and mobile ICT, along with the increasing diffusion and adoption of these technologies, have unleashed the potential of both traditional mass media and "mass self-communication" (Castells, 2019) to expose clandestine acts as the mechanics of state capture and shadow state. The internet and the digital technologies of communication have given rise to new possibilities of making the invisible and clandestine visible (Thompson, 2000; 2020). The new social media is a signal case in point. As captured correctly by Castells (2019: 89), people have appropriated these new forms of communication to build "their own system of mass communication, via SMSs, blogs, tweets, podcasts, wikis and a whole range of social networking spaces, that have come to be known as social media." The new social media is a veritable tool for exposing clandestine acts and scandals—as those documented in this book—by ordinary people. Schejter and Tirosh (2014; 2015), have done a good job of delineating and conceptualizing the key features of social media, which invest them with the affordances that ordinary citizens need to capture and expose political scandals such as the participation of the political elites in illegal ASGM. Social media provides interactive platforms for their users (interactive); they allow for mobility in access and use (mobility); they have the potential for their users to get access, deliver, and store infinite data (abundance); and their users can express themselves in written words in multiple ways (multi-mediality).

There is a sense in which the internet and digital revolution have transformed the fieldwork context and scope of the qualitative researcher. With the invention and advancement of digitized information, communication, and technology—particularly the internet and social media apps and platforms—the repertoire of data-collection methods of social sciences have advanced beyond the traditional methods usually deployed. The internet and media content are a big domain of qualitative research by social scientists. It would, therefore, border on anachronism in the understanding of the social world for a social scientist to confine fieldwork to the conventional notion of a physical social milieux (a village, community, or a street corner of a city) that the researcher immerses herself to do observation, make field notes, and interview her interlocutors (Dicks et al., 2005; Hine, 2020).

Only a few people will disagree with the point that in the present world of ICT/digital revolution, social life, and the interaction between people are increasingly taking place in the virtual space or online. Similarly, the dynamics that shape social phenomena such as galamsey and the characteristics that they display manifest on the internet. They manifest, for example, on social media platforms such as Facebook, Twitter, and WhatsApp. This has made it possible, easy, and cheap for the social scientists to observe and analyse social phenomena vividly and sometimes, live and in real time.

In keeping pace with the fast and revolutionary transformation of the space, scale, and scope of the manifestation of social relationships and phenomena, qualitative researchers "are increasingly documenting the everyday realities of social actors whose social relationships are mediated by and through the internet." In addition, the "internet has itself created various kinds of 'virtual community,' who not only exist in 'cyberspace' but can be studied via the internet itself" (Dicks et al., 2005: 1; see also Hine, 2020: 22). In the case of the subject at hand here, debates and discussions on the galamsey menace and the failed militarized fight against it have gained currency in Ghana to the extent that, one can imagine a "virtual community" of environmental conservationists or activists against galamsey in general, using the networking resources of the internet to undertake their activism.

Internet and media content are, thus, good sources of information on the clandestine phenomena under study in this book. Through desk research, we gleaned information from these internet sources for the thick description and analysis of the subject at hand in the pages that follow below. The internet links to our sources of information have been fully compiled in the reference section for ease of crosschecking, validation, and further research. We draw mainly on these sources of data to describe the militarized fight against galamsey between 2017 and 2024, to analyse the dynamics of state capture and shadow state at play in this fight, and finally, to conclude that the fight failed because of state capture.

Order of Presentation and Exposition of the Book

In the rest of the book, we flesh out our arguments in the following order: in Chapter One, we set up the empirical context and *problematique* of the book by providing an overview of the ASGM sector in Ghana. We try in this chapter to demonstrate the evolution of the industry from relatively sustainable and ecologically friendly livelihoods strategy of the subaltern classes to a capitalist and money-making enterprise, with irreversible ecological damage. Focusing on the class dynamics of state capture, we will show the ways in which the subalterns have been dispossessed of their livelihood strategies or how the organization of their social reproduction has been violently disrupted by the capitalist, semi-industrial mining by the power elites.

In Chapter Two, we document the laws and policies designed to govern the ASGM industry in Ghana, to illustrate that galamsey is caused by a captured state. The chapter illustrates that Ghana's ASGM, as observed by Gavin Hilson, is one of the well-governed ASGM in the world, with a panoply of laws regulating it, as well as corresponding institutions to enforce them. But redolent of state capture, these institutions are dysfunctional and cannot implement and enforce these policies and laws. The shadow state, we will argue is rather actively functioning; hence, the worsening of galamsey and its deleterious social and environmental effects, despite the deployment of the military to fight it.

Chapter Three is a critical engagement with the dominant theories proffered by scholars of the mainstream literature to explain the emergence and endurance of galamsey in Ghana. Specifically, we provide a panoramic overview of the state-centric theories, for example, political corruption, that have been deployed to account for the enduring existence and worsening of galamsey despite the military operations. We argue that, even though these theories help to shed light on this problem, they do not illuminate state capture; as such, miss the deeper roots of the incapability of the state to fight galamsey, even with its military might.

Situated in this theoretical context, we then present our alternative theory of state capture and the shadow state in Chapter Four. We will draw on the extant theoretical and empirical literature on state capture and the shadow state to distil the core theoretical insights and features of these phenomena. The chapter concludes with a summary of the key analytical tools it offers for the analysis of state capture in the failed militarized fight against galamsey in Ghana.

The empirical core of the book is Chapters Five and Six. In Chapter five, we document the successive military operations organized by the Ghanaian state against galamsey between 2017 and 2024. This period encompasses two four-year full terms of President Akufo-Addo, the Commander-in-Chief of the Ghana Armed Forces (GAF), who promised in 2017 to fight galamsey at the cost of losing his presidency in the next election in 2020. We show that at the end of his second four-year term as president of Ghana, galamsey and the menace it engenders have worsened under his watch. This foregrounds a puzzle, at once intellectual and political, that needs unravelling: why the president and Commander-in-Chief of the military of a state is unable to win a war he has declared against a relatively weak enemy?

Chapter Six continues with the empirical analysis of the book began in the preceding chapter, focusing on the presentation and analysis of evidence of state capture in the militarized fight against galamsey. Using internet sources such as Erastus Asare Donkor's documentaries, we describe and analyse key themes of state capture that are visible in the military operations discussed in the above chapter. We then address the question whether the strong, professional military of Ghana—the Ghana Armed Forces (GAF)—has also been captured, concluding that, indeed, it has been captured. This, we argue, illustrates the deep nature of the capture of the Ghanaian state by the power elites engaged in galamsey to make more and more money.

In conclusion, we restate and highlight the key arguments of the book and the evidence provided to support them. We then state and explain the contribution the book makes, theoretically, methodologically, and politically. Theoretically, we argue that the book advances the state-centric theories offered to explain the stubborn and chronic problem of illegal artisanal and small-scale gold mining (ASGM) —popularly known as galamsey—in Ghana. Situated in the context of the emergence and advancement of the internet (from Web 1.0 to 4.0), the digital revolution, and the virtual world, the book contributes to the advancement of qualitative social science methods. Specifically, the book illustrates that, in the era of the digital revolution and the advancement of the internet, virtual ethnographic methods are valid and potent social scientific approaches to collecting reliable qualitative data to analyse various, albeit complex, social phenomena. Politically, we posit that the lessons teased out from the state capture and shadow state theories point to more effective tools for addressing this problem. Furthermore, the class lens of the book throws into sharp relief the question of agency and resistance of the subaltern classes to the injustices that state captors inflict on them.

REFERENCES

Adogla-Bessa, D.- Citifmonline.com (2017). Citi FM launches #StopGalamseyNow campaign. https://citifmonline.com/2017/04/citifm-launches-stopgalamseynow-campaign/

Aghaei, S., Nematbakhsh, M. A., and Farsani, H. K. (2012). Evolution of the world wide web: From WEB 1.0 TO WEB 4.0. *International Journal of Web & Semantic Technology, 3*(1), 1–10.

Ampaw, E. M., Chai, J., Jiang, Y., Dumor, K., & Edem, A. K. (2023). Why is Ghana losing the war against illegal gold mining (Galamsey)? An artificial neural network-based investigations. *Environmental Science and Pollution Research, 30*(29): 73730–73752.

Arhinful, E.K. - Myjoyonline (2024). Akufo-Addo sets up 5-member ministerial ad-hoc committee to assess galamsey fight. https://www.myjoyonline.com/akufo-addo-sets-up-5-member-ministerial-ad-hoc-committee-to-assess-galamsey-fight/

Ayelazuno, J.A & Mawuko-Yevugah, L. (2021). Between the Africa Mining Vision and the neo-patrimonial state: The agency gap in Ghana's regulation of artisanal and small-scale gold mining, *South African Journal of International Affairs, 28*(4): 555–582.

Ayelazuno J. A. and Mawuko-Yevugah, L. (2019). Large-scale mining and ecological imperialism in Africa: the politics of mining and conservation of the ecology in Ghana. *Journal of Political Ecology, 26* (1): 243–62.

Benites, G. V. (2023). Natures of concern: The criminalization of artisanal and small-scale mining in Colombia and Peru. *The Extractive Industries and Society, 13*, 101105.

Castells, M., 2019. Communication power: mass communication, mass self-communication and power relationships in the network society. In: Curran, J., Hesmondhalgh, D. (Eds.), *Media and Society*. Bloomsbury Publishing Inc., London, pp. 83–100.

Chipkin, I., Swilling, M., Bhorat, H., Buthelezi, M., Duma, S., Friedenstein, H., Mondi, L., Peter, C., Prins, N., Qobo, M., Jonas, M., & Haffajee, F. (2018). *Shadow State: The Politics of State Capture*. Wits University Press. https://doi.org/10.18772/22018062125.

Citi Newsroom (2024). Organised Labour threatens nationwide strike over galamsey crisis. https://citinewsroom.com/2024/09/organised-labour-threatens-nationwide-strike-if-govt-fails-to-act-on-galamsey-crisis/

Damonte, G. H. (2018). Mining Formalization at the Margins of the State: Small-scale Miners and State Governance in the Peruvian Amazon. *Development and Change*, 49(5): 1314–1335.

Darko, K.A. Myjoyonline news (2024). Democracy Hub defies injunction to protest against Akufo-Addo. https://www.myjoyonline.com/democracy-hub-defies-injunction-to-protest-against-akufo-addo/

Department of Prime Minister and National Executive Council (2023). Prime Minister Marape Announces Military-Police Operation in Porgera Valley Amid Rising Illegal Mining Activities. https://pmnec.gov.pg/prime-minister-marape-announces-military-police-operation-inporgera-valley-amid-rising-illegal-mining-activities/ (Accessed 3 August 2024).

Dethier, E. N., Silman, M. R., Fernandez, L. E., Espejo, J. C., Alqahtani, S., Pauca:, & Lutz, D. A. (2023). Operation mercury: Impacts of national-level armed forces intervention and anticorruption strategy on artisanal gold mining and water quality in the Peruvian Amazon. *Conservation Letters*, 16(5), e12978.

Dicks B, Mason B, Coffey A, Atkinson P. (2005). *Qualitative research and hypermedia: Ethnography for the digital age*. London: Sage Publication.

Donkor, E.A., (2022a). *Destruction for gold, part 1*. https://www.youtube.com/watch?v=8wE8ya-po_c&t=57s (20 May 2023).

Donkor, E.A., (2022b). Destruction for gold, part 2. https://www.youtube.com/watch?v=0NC7ALzpYEM&t=620s (Accessed 20 May 2023).

Donkor, E.A., (2022c). Destruction for gold, part 3. https://www.youtube.com/watch?v=2roPsklYJew (Accessed 20 May 2023).

Donner, J., 2015. *After Access: Inclusion, Development, and a More Mobile Internet*. MIT press.

Eduful, M., Alsharif, K., Eduful, A., Acheampong, M., Eduful, J., and Mazumder, L. (2020). The illegal artisanal and small-scale mining (galamsey) 'menace'in Ghana: is military-style approach the answer? *Resources Policy*, 68: 101732, 1–14.

Espin, J., and Perz, S. (2021). Environmental crimes in extractive activities: Explanations for low enforcement effectiveness in the case of illegal gold mining in Madre de Dios, Peru. *The Extractive Industries and Society*, 8(1): 331–339.

Espin, J., and Perz, S. (2021). Environmental crimes in extractive activities: Explanations for low enforcement effectiveness in the case of illegal gold mining in Madre de Dios, Peru. *The Extractive Industries and Society, 8*(1): 331–339.

Frimpong-Boateng, K. (n.d.). Illegal mining (galamsey) in Ghana. https://www.wrforum.org/wp-content/uploads/2019/11/ASM-IN-GHANA.pdf (Accessed 14 July 2024).

GBC (2024). *GJA to spearhead strong media campaign for protection of the environment from "Galamsey"- Kwabena Dwumfuor.* https://www.gbcghanaonline.com/general/gja-to-spearhead/2024/ (Accessed 14 July 2024).

Ghana Broadcasting Corporation (2024). *GWCL attributes water supply challenges to galamsey activities.* https://www.gbcghanaonline.com/general-news/gwcl-attributes-water-supply-challenges-to-galamsey-activities/2024/ (Accessed 15 July 2024).

Ghanaweb (2024). *Captain Smart lists government officials allegedly involved in galamsey.* https://www.ghanaweb.com/GhanaHomePage/NewsArchive/Sue-me-if-I-m-telling-lies-Captain-Smart-as-he-lists-government-officials-allegedly-involved-in-galamsey-1940423 (Accessed 15 July 2024).

Gralla, P. (1998). *How the Internet works.* 4th ed. Indianapolis: Que Corporation.

Graphic Online (2024). *Galamsey impact: Experts call for decisive action to save nation.* https://www.graphic.com.gh/news/general-news/ghana-news-galamsey-impact-experts-call-for-decisive-action-to-save-nation.html (Accessed 14 July 2024).

Hilson, G., Hilson, A., Maconachie, R., McQuilken, J., & Goumandakoye, H. (2017). Artisanal and small-scale mining (ASM) in sub-Saharan Africa: Re-conceptualizing formalization and 'illegal'activity. *Geoforum, 83*: 80–90.

Hine C. (2020). *Ethnography for the internet: Embedded, embodied and everyday.* London: Bloomsbury Academic.

Johnson, R. B., & Onwuegbuzie, A. J. (2004). Mixed methods research: A research paradigm whose time has come. *Educational researcher, 33*(7): 14–26.

Katz, J. E. (2008*). Handbook of mobile communication studies.* The MIT Press.

Kroski, E., 2008. On the move with the mobile web: libraries and mobile technologies. *Libr. Technol. Rep.,* 44 (5): 1–48

Ministry of Information (2024). *Adhoc Ministerial Committee to engage stakeholders on illegal mining.* https://moi.gov.gh/newsroom/2024/09/adhoc-ministerial-committee-to-engage-stakeholders-on-illegal-mining/ (Accessed 15 July 2024).

Mkodzongi, G. (2020). The rise of 'Mashurugwi' machete gangs and violent conflicts in Zimbabwe's artisanal and small-scale gold mining sector. *The Extractive Industries and Society, 7*(4): 1480–1489.

Ngnenbe, T & Koomson, J.B. Graphic Online (2024). More groups rise against galamsey. https://www.graphic.com.gh/news/general-news/ghana-news-more-groups-rise-against-galamsey.html

Panchia, Y. (2023). Unearthing a crisis: South Africa's battle against illegal mining. *Mining Review Africa*. https://www.miningreview.com/gold/south-africas-battle-against-illegal-artisanal-mining/

Qiu, J.L. (2019). The global internet. In: Curran, J., Hesmondhalgh, D. (Eds.), Media and

Society. London: Bloomsbury Publishing Inc.: pp. 3–20.

Rodríguez-Novoa, F., and Holley, E. (2023). Coexistence between large-scale mining (LSM) and artisanal and small-scale mining (ASM) in Perú and Colombia. *Resources Policy, 80*, 103162.

Schejter, A., and Tirosh, N., (2014). New Media Policy: The Redistribution of Voice. In: Liu, Y., Picard, R.G. (Eds.), *Policy and marketing strategies for digital media*. Routledge, London, pp. 73–86.

Schejter, A.M., Tirosh, N., 2015. Seek the meek, seek the just: social media and social justice. *Telecomm Policy, 39* (9): 796–803.

Spiegel, S. J. (2015). Shifting formalization policies and recentralizing power: The case of Zimbabwe's artisanal gold mining sector. *Society and Natural Resources, 28*(5): 543–558.

The Republic of Ghana (2017). *Artisanal and Small-Scale Mining Handbook for Ghana.* Available at: https://www.delvedatabase.org/uploads/resources/Artisanal-and-Small-Scale-Mining-Handbook-for-Ghana-with-a-regional-perspective.pdf (Accessed 4 August 2024).

University of Ghana (2024). *UG Climaxes 2024 DSRA Celebration with a Focus on Galamsey and the need to Preserve the Environment.* https://ug.edu.gh/news/ug-climaxes-2024-dsra-celebration-focus-galamsey-and-need-preserve-environment (Acessed 27th July 2024).

Verbrugge, B. (2015). The economic logic of persistent informality: artisanal and small-scale mining in the southern Philippines. *Development and Change, 46*(5): 1023–1046.

Wiafe, S. Citi Newsroom (2021). Akufo-Addo dissolves Inter-ministerial Committee on Illegal Mining. https://citinewsroom.com/2021/01/akufo-addo-dissolves-inter-ministerial-committee-on-illegal-mining/

Zabyelina, Y., and van Uhm, D. (Eds.). (2020). *Illegal mining: Organized crime, corruption, and ecocide in a resource-scarce world.* New York: Palgrave Macmillan: Springer Nature.

CHAPTER 1

The Evolution of ASGM and Its Negative Ecological and Socioeconomic Effects

Abstract In this chapter, we set the stage for the book by outlining the empirical context and main problems of the ASGM sector in Ghana. We show that the alarming galamsey menace, which, by 2017, triggered widespread public outrage, particularly from the media and civil society organizations (CSOs), was the direct result of the dramatic transformation of the country's ASGM industry over a long period of time. This was a revolutionary change that saw ASGM evolve from a relatively rudimentary and environmentally friendly mining activity to a semi-industrialized mining enterprise. We conceptualize the earlier form as traditional artisanal small-scale mining (TAM) and the newer form as capitalist medium-scale mining (CMM). The chapter contends that TAM is the time-honoured livelihood activity of the rural people of Ghana, the subaltern classes; while CMM is operated by the power elites in the country to accumulate ill-gotten wealth. We argue further that the mechanisms through which the industry has transformed from a relatively sustainable and ecologically friendly livelihoods strategy of the subaltern classes to a capitalist and money-making enterprise is what has wreaked irreversible ecological damage to the Ghanaian environmental landscape. Two related factors have been identified to account for the evolution of TAM to CMM: first (and in the context of the hikes in demand and gold prices in the global economy) is the onrush of the capitalist classes

J. A. Ayelazuno and M. A. Aziabah, *State Capture in the Militarized Fight Against Illegal Small-Scale Goldmining in Ghana*, https://doi.org/10.1007/978-3-031-82673-3_1

1

into ASGM and second, (and flowing from the first) the use of sophisticated heavy mining equipment. Though distinct in the technology used
and logic driving them, TAM and CMM are often lumped together as
ASGM, while the illegal and criminal components are lumped together as
galamsey. In terms of defining attributes, TAM is marked out from CMM
by three main characteristics: its operators use rudimentary mining tools,
it is labour-intensive, and it is driven by the imperatives of basic needs
and alternative livelihoods. In contrast, CMM is undertaken by the capitalist classes with heavy mining equipment, acquisition of huge tracks of
land as mining concessions, and hiring workers to work on their mining
concessions with the core motive to accumulate wealth. We establish that,
intrinsic to the evolution from TAM to CMM has been the dispossession
of land from subaltern classes and the destruction of their basic livelihood
sources. Additionally, the transition has led to deleterious ecological and
socioeconomic effects, although of varying magnitude relative to the type,
methods, scale, and technology used in mining and processing the mineral
mined, in this case, gold. Even though the negative environmental effects
of ASGM are not new, they have worsened in the last two decades, in
correlation with the transition from TAM to CMM.

Keywords Ghana · Gold · Galamsey · Class · Traditional artisanal
mining · Capitalist medium-scale mining · Environmental menace ·
Human insecurity

The alarming galamsey menace that aroused the ire of the media and civil
society organizations (CSOs) discussed above was the direct result of the
dramatic transformation of the country's artisanal and small-scale gold
mining (ASGM) industry over a long period of time. This was a revolutionary change that saw ASGM evolve from a relatively rudimentary and
environmentally friendly mining activity to a semi-industrialized mining
industry. In this book, we conceptualize the former as traditional artisanal
and small-scale mining (TAM), while the latter is capitalist medium-scale
mining (CMM). We claim, also, that TAM is the time-honoured livelihood activity of the rural people of Ghana, the subaltern classes; while
CMM is operated by the power elites in the country to accumulate
ill-gotten wealth. By 2017, this evolution seemed to have reached its
apocalyptic heights when CMM caused the unprecedented devastation

of the environment; and combined with what we see as dynamics of state capture, a perfect storm of vilification and demonization of galamsey led the president of Ghana, (President Akufo-Addo) to vow to fight it at all cost, including losing his presidency. The purpose of this chapter is to describe the evolution of ASGM and analyse the negative impacts of this, as well as the negative impacts of the president's military crackdown on the subaltern operators of galamsey.

Though distinct in the technology used and logic driving them, TAM and CMM are often lumped together as ASGM, while the illegal and criminal components are lumped together as galamsey. The CSOs and the media organizations that mounted the campaign against the galamsey menace in 2017, as well as the Ghanaian state that responded by mounting a military crackdown on it, are all guilty of lumping TAM and CMM together. As correctly observed by Ofori and Ofori, (2018), the Ghanaian state and the elite CSO and the media have the power to define and represent operators of galamsey, including the subaltern classes doing TAM, in negative stereotypes and brands. Lumped together with operators of CMM, the subaltern classes doing TAM are misrecognized, misrepresented, and stigmatized as an environmental menace, "hard-core criminals," "a grievance," "unimportant," "a threat," "wicked," and "dangerous" (Ofori and Ofori, 2018, p. 365). But this way of rendering the issues is informed by class-blindness, which allows violence to be done to the livelihoods of the subaltern classes "digging for survival" and "digging for justice" (Andrews, 2015, p. 5; see also Ofori and Ofori, 2018).

Traditional Artisanal Mining (TAM) and the Livelihoods of the Subaltern Classes

In this chapter, we will disaggregate and "unbundle" TAM from CMM to bring class analysis to bear clearly on the militarized fight against galamsey and the discourses it engendered. TAM is marked out from CMM by three main characteristics: its operators use rudimentary mining tools, it is labour-intensive, and it is driven by the imperatives of basic needs and alternative livelihoods. A bit more on this: blessed with gold in their land, TAM is an integral component of the organization of the (re)production of rural populace in the ecosystem they were born. An organization of (re)production that revolves around the inextricable relationship between culture, technology, and the environment. The point is, before modern day ASGM came to being, TAM was a means of survival in gold-rich communities. It existed side-by-side with and supplemented farming as their modes of production and social reproduction. Viewed this way, it is not anymore naïve to say TAM is illegal in poverty-stricken rural communities—with gold buried in the belly of their lands—than it is to say farming and blacksmithing are illegal in these communities.

Aligned to these features of TAM are the oft-cited definitions of ASGM as the low-tech, labour-intensive mineral extraction and processing found across the developing world (Hilson and McQuilken, 2014). It is also defined as mining by individuals, groups, families, or cooperatives with minimal or no mechanization, often in the informal (illegal) sector of the market (Hentschel et al. 2002). So defined, TAM has a long history in Ghana (formerly, Gold Coast) spanning several centuries before the European explorers arrived. By some accounts, mining of gold in the Gold Coast can be traced as far back as the sixth century when gold was the magnet that attracted the Arab traders to some parts of the country as early as the seventh and eighth centuries (Kwao, 2024, p. 2).

Before the arrival of the Portuguese in the Gold Coast in 1471, the natives, particularly the inhabitants of the Akan Forest area of modern Ghana, devised simple, but effective and sustainable technologies of mining gold. In fact, "gold mining in Ghana was one of the mainstays of the economies of Bono Manso, Adanse, Denkyira, Assin, Wassa, Akyem and many other Akan states" (Ofosu-Mensah, 2011, p. 006). Thus, TAM served as the major good traded in the trans-Saharan trade through which gold reached Europe between the thirteenth and nineteenth century (Hilson, 2017; Ofosu-Mensah, 2017; Ofosu-Mensah, 2010). Even though the technology used by the Akan gold-miners was rudimentary, it was effective and sustainable; and "the gold diggers of Gyaman, Denkyira, Wassa, Asante and Akyem Abuakwa, among others, supplied Europe with enormous quantities of gold" between the fifteenth and the nineteenth century (Ofosu-Mensah 2011, p. 012; Ofosu-Mensah, 2017, p. 1).

To date, ASM endures as a livelihood activity; a means of reproduction by the rural poor across minerals-rich countries in the Global South. So, despite the Ghanaian state's actions to criminalize, dislocate, and cut the subaltern classes adrift from their time-honoured livelihood activities, they have remained resilient and managed to continue to engage in TAM throughout the colonial era to the post-independence period, and to the present era of the war against galamsey. On this, Ghana resembles closely other developing countries in Asia and Latin America where the subaltern classes have demonstrated strikingly similar resilience in the face hostilities inflicted them in the name of fighting "green crimes" (Nurse, 2017); something informed by the theory of "green criminology" (Espin and Perz, 2021), and executed through "green militarization" (Ofosu et al., 2024). Though operating in different social contexts, the subalterns view ASM as a legitimate livelihood strategy. This view from "below" about mining is held by subaltern classes across many minerals-rich countries in the Global South; encompassing, for example, the galamseyers of Ghana, the garimpeiros of the Brazilian Amazon (Lahiri-Dutt, 2018; Massaro et al., 2022), the "gurandils" of Indonesia (Lahiri-Dutt, 2018; Fashya and Suseno, 2023), the Barranquilas in Bolivia, and the Ninjas of Mongolia (Lahiri-Dutt, 2018).

This view from "below" is also held and advocated by scholars and activists concerned about the wellbeing of poor people. In its authentic artisanal form, the advocates of ASM argue and defend it as a livelihood activity of the poor (Hilson and Garforth, 2012; IGF, 2017; Schwartz et al., 2021). They support their position with ample, concrete evidence showing its critical role in the social (re)production of this segment of the populace. Thus, across the world and Africa, ASM plays a critical role in economic development generally, and specifically, in jobs-creation, income-generation, and poverty-reduction in the countries endowed with mineral resources; especially gold, diamond, and coltan. It is even viewed as not only "the most indispensable—if not the most important—rural nonfarm activity in the developing world," but as well, "fundamental to achieving all 17 Sustainable Development Goals (SDGs)" (World Bank, 2019, p. vii, 1). We must bear in mind all the time, that this crucial role of ASM is not an attribute of the legal, licensed, and formal ASM alone—a relatively small component of the industry. The informal, unlicensed, and even criminalized component—which predominates the industry across most countries in the Global South (IGF, 2017)—contributes mightily to the flourishing of the livelihoods of the rural poor.

Dr. Kevin Telmer, the Founder of the The Artisanal Gold Council (AGC), is perhaps one of the most unrelenting and passionate advocates of the view from "below" on ASM; and he makes the poverty-reduction case for the defence of ASM so convincing, only a few people may doubt it. In an interview granted to the producer of The Money Stone film (Harmon, 2018; see also O'Neill and Telmer, 2017, p. 27)—a documentary on galamsey in Ghana—he observed felicitously that ASM is not engaged by people in poverty. It is rather engaged by people taking the first step to escape poverty. He believes that ASM is a reliable source of income for a lot of impoverished people, and this is the main reason why it persists. He argues further that ASM is an effective agent of delivering wealth to poor people directly. According to him, in most cases the people mining in the middle of the jungle get 70%, or even 80% in some cases, of the international price for the minerals they get. ASM, he argues, is a vehicle for delivering or transferring wealth from the rich to the poor or from rich countries to poor countries. He thinks that it is hard to find any other industry, enterprise, or policy intervention that can deliver or redistribute wealth directly to the poor as ASM does. Most poverty interventions, according to Telmer, require huge sums of money that is always hard to come by, and are often donor dependent. In contrast, ASM has the potential of becoming a viable, self-sustaining, independent, enterprise-based economy that doesn't need hand-out from donor-countries.

As illustrated by Table 1.1, the ASM sector, both licensed and informal/criminal, "employs tens of millions of people directly and creates millions more jobs in the upstream and downstream industries it spawns; and has become a driver of economic development in numerous rural economies" (Hilson and Maconachie, 2017: 443). In Sub-Saharan Africa alone, there are "at least 20 million people employed directly in the sector, and an additional 100 million individuals who depend upon its activities indirectly for their livelihoods" (Hilson, 2017, p. 80). And these numbers have been increasing: "an estimated 40.5 million people were directly engaged in ASM in 2017, up from 30 million in 2014, 13 million in 1999 and 6 million in 1993" (IGF, 2017, p. iv). In Ghana, despite being largely informal and "illegal," ASM contributes mightily to the creation of wealth and employment, and the overall economic growth of the country, making it one of Ghana's most important livelihood activities. It employs "an estimated one million people and supporting approximately 4.5 million more" (McQuilken and Hilson, 2016, p. 16).

Considering its centrality in the organization of the (re)production of the subaltern classes—its centrality in their livelihood strategies—it is unsurprising that informal ASM endures in Ghana and other countries. To fight the environmental ills of ASM across the world will require, first and above any other thing, the distinction between TAM and CMM. The latter, as we will illustrate below, is the main driver of the destruction of the environment in Ghana.

Table 1.1   Employment estimates for artisanal and small-scale mining, and minerals extracted, in selected developing countries

Country	Directly working in artisanal and small-scale mining	Estimated number of dependents	Main minerals mined on a small and artisanal scale
Angola	150,000	900,000	Diamonds
Argentina	5800	34,800	Gold
Bolivia	72,000	432,000	Gold
Brazil	250,000	1,500,000 .	Gold, diamonds, gemstones
Burkina Faso	200,000	1,000,000	Gold
Central African Republic	400,000	2,400,000	Gold, diamonds
Chad	100,000	600,000	Gold
Chile	12,000	72,000	Gold, copper, silver
China	15,000,000	90,000,000	Gold, coal, construction materials (sand)
Colombia	200,000	1,200,000	Gold, gemstones
Cote d'Ivoire	100,000	600,000	Gold, diamonds
Democratic Republic of the Congo	200,000	1,200,000	Diamonds, gold, coltan
Ecuador	92,000	552,000	Gold
Eritrea	400,000	2,400,000	Gold
Ethiopia	500,000	3,000,000	Gold
French Guiana	10,000	60,000	Gold
Ghana	1,100,000	4,400,000	Gold, diamonds, sand
Guinea	300,000	1,500,000	Gold, diamonds
Guyana	20,000	120,000	Gold, diamonds
India	500,000	3,000,000	Gold, tin, coal, gemstones
Indonesia	109,000	654,000	Gold
Liberia	100,000	600,000	Gold, diamonds
Madagascar	500,000	2,500,000	Coloured gemstones, gold
Malawi	40,000	240,000	Coloured gemstones, gold
Mali	400,000	2,400,000	Gold
Mongolia	120,000	720,000	Gold, fluorspar, coal

(continued)

Table 1.1 (continued)

Country	Directly working in artisanal and small-scale mining	Estimated number of dependents	Main minerals mined on a small and artisanal scale
Mozambique	100,000	1,200,000	Coloured gemstones, gold
Myanmar	14,000	84,000	Gold, tin, jade, coloured gemstones
Niger	450,000	2,700,000	Gold
Nigeria	500,000	2,500,000	Gold
PNG	60,000	360,000	Gold
Peru	30,000	180,000	Gold
Philippines	300,000	1,800,000	Gold
South Africa	20,000	120,000	Gold
Sierra Leone	300,000	1,800,000	Gold, diamonds, coltan
South Sudan	200,000	1,200,000	Gold
Sri Lanka	165,000	990,000	Gold, coloured gemstones
Suriname	20,000	120,000	Gold
Tanzania	1,500,000	9,000,000	Gold
Uganda	150,000	900,000	Coloured gemstones, gold, diamonds
Venezuela	40,000	240,000	Gold
Zimbabwe	500,000	3,000,000	Gold, coltan, diamonds, coloured gemstones

Source Hilson and Maconachie (2017, p. 444)

CAPITALIST, MEDIUM-SCALE, AND SEMI-INDUSTRIALIZED MINING (CMM)

Traditional artisanal mining (TAM) described above has evolved over the years to capitalist, medium-scale, and semi-industrialized mining (CMM). Two related factors may account for this: first (and in the context of the hikes in demand and gold prices in the global economy) is the onrush of the capitalist classes into ASGM and second, (and flowing from first) the use of sophisticated heavy mining equipment. The latter has transformed TAM to semi-industrial mining or mechanized and semi-mechanized mining (MLNR, 2017, p. 2). Rather than artisanal and small-scale mining, we are presently witnessing CMM. Undertaken with heavy mining equipment, CMM marks a turning point in the long history of TAM in Ghana. It marked the historical conjuncture of the dispossession of the subaltern classes (engaged in TAM for survival) by the capitalist classes, engaged in CMM to accumulate wealth. The power elites invest money in CMM to make more of it: they invest it in buying heavy mining equipment, acquiring huge tracts of land as mining concessions, and hiring workers to work on their mining concessions. It is, therefore, disingenuous for the Ghanaian state officials to discursively frame CMM as small-scale mining (ASM), and then issue licence to the capitalist class as ASM operators. Similarly, it is dubious for the capitalist class to apply for and consider themselves as ASM operators, even as their contiguous concession stretch for several kilometres (Hausermann et al., 2020, p. 194).

Based on the quantum of the contribution of ASGM to gold production in Ghana, this evolution happened circa the 2000s, the period that the contribution of ASGM to the total amount of gold produced by Ghana witnessed astronomical and continuous rise, specifically between 2000 and 2018 (Adu-Baffour et al., 2021; MLNR, 2017; Bansah et al., 2016). In the 1990s, gold produced by ASGM was tiny relative to production in the 2000s. "Gold production from ASGM in 1990," one authoritative source reports, "was below 20,000 ounces, and this accounted for less than 5% of the total gold produced that year. Over the years [between 2000 and 2016], there was a steady increase in gold production, peaking at 1,578,440 ounces with a corresponding contribution of 35% [by ASGM] to total gold production in the country." (Owusu et al., 2019 p. 1, 18, 38–44; DeLeo et al., 2021, p. 1–3). Figure 1.1 illustrates this increasing trend of gold production by ASGM in Ghana: prior to the 2000s, the relative contribution of ASGM to gold production was insignificant, but this changed between 2000 and 2018 when gold produced by ASGM relative to large-scale mining increased significantly.

The low production of gold by the ASGM sector in the 1990s was a problem of the non-mechanized, low tech, labour-intensive, and ineffective methods used in TAM to extract and process gold. In contrast, CMM—with its use of mining machines—led to the increase in output of ASGM in the 2010s. Bansah and his co-authors provide a good description of the mining methods and the equipment used in CMM;

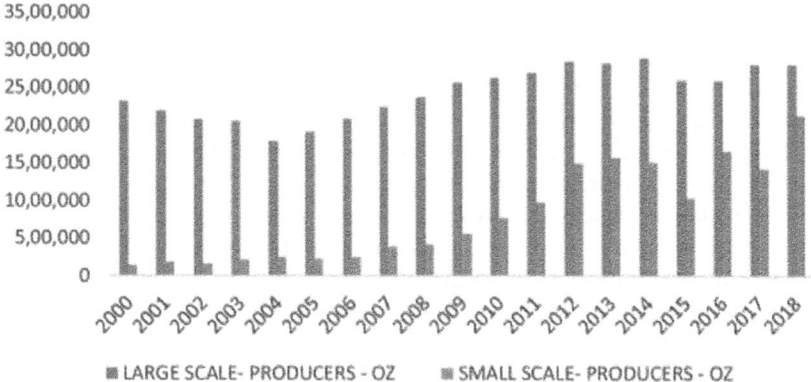

Fig. 1.1 Trends of the relative contribution of ASM to gold production in Ghana. 2017 (*Source* Adu-Baffour et al. 2021, p. 4; see also MLNR, p. 8; Bansah et al., 2016, p. 39)

namely, the "Changfa method" which uses a Chinese made (changfa) diesel powered rock crusher; the "more blade method," involving the use of excavators to mine in pits; the "dredge method," which involves the use of changfa motors and suction hose; and the "alluvial washing plant" method, which uses excavators and mini washing plants (Bansah et al., 2016, p. 12–13).

A key feature of the evolution of ASGM in Ghana is the influx of foreigners, especially the citizens of China, into the industry. This has happened in blatant disobedience of the Small-Scale Gold Mining Law (PNDC Law 218) and the Minerals and Mining Act 2006 (Act 703) make ASMG the preserve of only Ghanaians. But following this evolution—and reminiscent of the state capture argued in this book—the law is honoured rather in breach than in compliance. As a result, foreigners have invaded the industry and are operating with impunity. As correctly observed by Crawford and Botchwey (2017, p. 449), "the influx of large numbers of foreign miners into the small-scale sector, most notably from China" is a recent phenomenon of the last decade. Though Chinese nationals dominate the foreigners engaged in galamsey in Ghana, some also come from other neighbouring African countries—such as Togo, Burkina Faso, and Mali—and non-African countries such as India, Serbia, Armenia, Russia, and Ukraine. The involvement of foreigners in ASGM, especially the nationals of China, is linked directly to the mechanization and semi-industrialization that it has witnessed during the 2000s. Crawford and Botchwey (2017) are on solid ground when they argued that it is misleading to describe present-day ASGM as artisanal, because, with the involvement of the citizens of China, the rudimentary methods of mining that it used to be associated has been replaced with the use of sophisticated, mechanized methods.

Changes in Organization of Labour and Labour Process

From a class perspective of the evolution from TAM to CMM, one of the prominent noticeable changes in ASGM in Ghana is in the organization of labour, the labour process, and labour relations, as well as the inequality in the distribution of the benefits and costs of mining (see Kwao, 2024). In the case of TAM—and akin to classical peasant farming—the organization of production revolved on the family or household, with obvious gendered division of labour and exploitative power relations between men and women (Yakovleva, 2007; Dinye and Erdiaw-Kwasie, 2012; Arthur-Holmes and Busia, 2020; Arthur-Holmes, 2021). Typical of non-capitalist mode of production as peasant farming, the predominant characteristic of the organization of production in TAM is that, there is no separation between owners of means of production and labourers working for wages. In TAM, the subaltern classes work for themselves with their own rudimentary tools.

However, in the case of CMM galamsey, the organization of labour, process of labour, and labour relations resemble closely a capitalist mode of production. An organization of production marked by class formation and exploitative relationship between the capitalists, who own the means of production on one hand; and on the other, the working class with only their labour power to sell to the former for survival. To state the obvious, the mechanized mining and processing of gold in CMM galamsey need and involve the use of the labour power of workers. With their access and control of resources (such as land and capital), the power elites operating CMM galamsey—both Ghanaians and foreigners—hire workers, including those they have dispossessed of their land, to work in their mines for wages. Typical of the exploitative nature of the relations between the owners of mines and the workers, the former pays the latter low wages and subjects them to terrible working conditions of drudgery and long working hours, insecurity of jobs, and dangerous and life-threatening labouring activities; with women workers relatively more exploited than men (Calys-Tagoe et al., 2015; Arthur-Holmes and Busia, 2020; Kwao, 2024).

The capitalist organization of production in CMM is illustrated by some studies on Ghana. For example, van de Camp's (2016) study of underground mining in the Tongo area, in the Upper East Region, illustrates that the industry is organized in teams. A team is made of the "sponsor, ghetto owner, gang leader, blast man, drill man (moyee man), chisel man (chiseler), security man and local boy" (van de Camp 2016, p. 275). In terms of class and class relations of production, the sponsor, ghetto owner (or mine owner), and the gang leader constitute the capitalist class—especially when, as van de Camp has documented, they are rolled in one person. The blast man, drill man (moyee man), chisel man (chiseler), security man, and local boy constitute the working class, working for wages. Based on van de Camp's description, the organization of production of underground mining in the study area is gendered: it is an all-men thing. Baddianaah's (2024) analysis of the impact of the ban of ASM on galamsey operators in Nadowli-Kaleo District, Upper West Region, depicts a similar relation of production between the ghetto owner or financier, and the mineworkers who work for daily wages.

Like van de Camp's study, Kwao (2024, p. 4) illustrates the exploitative organization of labour and relations of production in the ASM sector of Ghana with a hierarchical structure. At the top of the hierarchy are the chiefs, traditional leaders, and elites who control land and provide protection to both legal and galamsey operators. The capitalist class, comprising owners of mines and mining machines, occupies the middle level; and typical of this class, and above anything else, they own capital and takes the risks involved in chasing profits in mining. The working class is at the bottom of the hierarchy, comprising the diggers, chisellers, transporters, washers, and sundry of workers who work for wages. The class position of the workers places them in an exploitative relationship with the capitalist class, who exploit surplus value from their labour by paying them below the value of their contribution to the production of gold. But as Kwao (2024, p. 6) reminds us, the working class is not gender-neutral, and women workers are more marginalized and exploited than men, both in terms of the types of jobs and wages they get.

The working conditions of mining are important in understanding the class dynamics of ASGM, both TAM and CMM. On this, the working conditions for the subaltern classes working for themselves in TAM and those working for wages in CMM are toxic, characterized by drudgery and high occupational hazards (University of Ghana Business School [UGBS], 2017). Studies on the health and safety of mining in the ASGM sector in Ghana and elsewhere in the world have documented ample evidence of mine accidents and health hazards, with life-threatening injuries and diseases; and even deaths (Calys-Tagoe et al., 2015; Arthur et al., 2016; Aram, 2021; Schwartz et al., 2021; Stemn et al., 2021). But because the subaltern classes working for themselves lack the capital to buy mining machines and personal protective equipment (PPE), they use low-tech methods to mine; methods that expose them to many hazards, including fatal mining accidents. In their study of ASM accidents in Ghana, Stemn et al. (2021) report 36 identified accidents that resulted in 622 fatalities from 2007 to July 2020. These may be accidents that happened in both TAM and CMM. But regardless of where they happened, the victims are mostly the subaltern classes, either working for themselves or for the capitalist class for wages. Yet driven by the survival instinct, they are compelled to engage in the most life-threatening, indecent and demeaning livelihood strategy that can only begin to make sense when one is struggling for survival—especially, with highly limited better alternatives for making a living.

Interestingly, evocative of the gendered nature of this survival strategy, women face discrimination in this work, extremely risky as it is (Dinye and Erdiaw-Kwasie 2012). Yet by some estimations, they constitute about 50% of the ASM workforce in Sub-Saharan Africa, an estimation that may reflect the situation in Ghana (Yakovleva 2007). They usually "work as ore haulers and washers, and as service providers (supplying food, clothing, water and light mine supplies)" (World Bank, 2019, p. 17). Relative to men, "women are largely confined to low-paid and labour-intensive roles, struggle to access bank loans without the signature of a male relative, and face gender-based discrimination in owning land, becoming license holders, and managing concessions" (World Bank, 2019, p. 19). Some studies have found that women are also more exposed to occupational hazards as mineworkers than men. In Ghana, they are less likely to wear PPE compared to their male counterparts, partly because they are not paid enough to afford personal protective equipment (PPE), and the companies they work for do not provide them with PPE. Because they presume that the jobs of women are not "dangerous" enough to warrant providing women miners with PPE (World Bank, 2023, p. 107).

Negative Ecological and Socioeconomic Effects of the Transformation of TAM

Intrinsic to the evolution from TAM to CMM are its deleterious ecological and socioeconomic effects. Even though mining of all shades is inherently polluting and socially-dislocating (Bell and Donnelly 2006), the magnitude of these effects varies by the type, methods, scale, and technology used in mining and processing the mineral mined, in this case, gold. For instance, because of the small-scale and low-tech nature of TAM, it cannot cause the same magnitude of destruction to vegetation cover or raise the turbidity levels of rivers as CMM does; because the latter uses heavy earthmoving equipment such as excavators and dozers (Bansah et al., 2016; Crawford and Botchwey, 2017; Eduful et al., 2020). Even though the negative environmental effects of ASGM are not new, they have worsened in the last two decades, in correlation with the transition from TAM to CMM.

But there is a sense in which this is not a mere correlation, because there is a causal relationship between the expansion and intensification of mechanized ASGM and the worsening environmental menace of galamsey; to a degree that water bodies and forests in mining areas are facing existential threats. These unprecedented ecological footprints of CMM are caused by heavy mining equipment such as excavators, with the capacity to cause huge destruction in a short time (Eduful et al., 2020, p. 2), something that the rudimentary equipment used in TAM cannot do. In particular, the Chinese foreign miners are notorious for their deployment of semi-mechanized and mechanized technologies in galamsey. They operate with excavators, crushing machines, wash plants, and platforms and suction equipment for river dredging. These resources enable them to mine on a larger scale and at a faster rate, causing extensive damage to land and forest, as well as serious pollution to water bodies (Crawford and Botchwey, 2017).

It is unsurprising that good scientific research, using the technology of remote sensing and satellite imaging, has clearly established the causal relationship between the expansion of mechanized ASGM and the galamsey menace in Ghana (Snapir et al., 2017; Forkuor et al., 2020; Nyamekye et al., 2021). Using a British multi-spectral imaging satellite, Snapir and his co-author found that, between 2011 and 2015, there was expansion of ASGM in cocoa-growing areas in southern Ghana. In their own words, "The rate of expansion [of galamsey] has increased from +

12,376 ha (+113%) for 2011–2013 to + 13,414 ha (+58%) for 2013–2015. So, the galamsey area has more than tripled from 10,907 ha in 2011 to 36,696 ha in 2015" (Snapir et al., 2017 p. 229). The study also measured the relative impact of this expansion on the destruction of the environment. For example, it reported that "Several protected forest reserves, in vicinity of a river, are directly encroached on by galamsey. The Anhwiaso East, the Tano Ofin Extension, the Upper Wassaw, the Oda River, the Subin Shelterbelt, the Denyau Shelterbelt, the Tano Nimiri, the Pra Anum, and the Atewa Range are among the most affected reserves," noting that the destruction of these forest reserves "significantly increased from 53 to 603 ha between 2011 and 2015 within the change area" (Snapir et al., 2017, p. 230).

Focusing on land use changes along a portion of the Offin River, another excellent study used remote sensing techniques to assess changes in land use, driven by mechanized mining by foreign operators. The study discovered not only a dramatic change in the tracts of land acquired for mining, but also the environmental damage this change caused. Whereas "just over 33 ha of mining existed in 2008," the researchers observed, by 2013, mining expanded to nearly 800 ha, a 2300% increase. Furthermore, the amount of "mine water"—stagnant water in abandoned pits—expanded from 1.52 ha in 2008 to 200 ha in 2013, an increase of more than 13,000%. Stagnant water exists because when mining operations move on, concession holders do not reclaim land despite requirements ensured during the licensing processes (Hausermann et al., 2018, p. 107).

The pollution of water bodies such as rivers, basins, sub-basins, and tributaries/streams is one of the most serious and life-threatening menace of mechanized and medium-scale mining. This is noticeable in the alarming rate of the pollution of rivers and drying up of water bodies (Hilson, 2017; Eduful et al., 2020). As Fig. 1.2 illustrates, the major rivers across Ghana are affected. This is so alarming that the Director for Natural Resources at the Environmental Protection Agency (EPA), Carl Fiati, warned in 2017 that Ghana may soon lose all its water bodies if the government does not arrest the galamsey problem (Citifmonline.com, 2017). He raised this alarm because of reports about the closure of the Abessim Water Treatment Plant in the Brong-Ahafo Region by the Ghana Water Company Limited (GWCL). The closure was necessitated by the reduction in water levels in the Tano River because of galamsey. As captured in the news report just cited, this problem predated 2017, as the Kyebi Water Treatment Plant was also shut down in August 2016 because the water had been rendered untreatable by galamsey.

Other relevant organizations have expressed similar grave concerns. The Executive Secretary of the Water Resources Commission (WRC), Ben Yaw Ampomah, observed gloomily in 2020 that Ghana was facing a perilous situation of shortage of water because galamsey has polluted the rivers, the sources of fresh water that GWCL treats for drinking. He elaborated on this with scientific research that used the water quality

Fig. 1.2   List of Major Rivers in Ghana Polluted by Galamsey. (*Source* Donkor 2024: https://web.facebook.com/story.php?story_fbid=10162328092458676& id=538173675&mibextid=WC7FNe&rdid=jgFp9Mf9joU9kr40)

index—comprising ten parameters including turbidity, nitrate content, and solid particles in the water—to measure the worsening pollution of rivers (Rivers Offin, Pra, and Bia) between 2016 and 2020 (*The Ghana Report*, 2020). The evidence shows that the levels of pollution were lower in the period preceding 2017, much lower during the period of the ban on ASGM between 2017 and 2018 and started getting worse in 2019. In 2022, the Director of Planning at the WRC, Dr. Bob Alfa, warned "that if illegal mining activities are not dealt with within the next six months, the Ghana Water Company Limited will not be able to provide treated water for various households" (*The Ghana Report*, 2022).

The GWCL itself has confirmed this looming threat of the shortage of fresh water for their treatment plants to process to drinkable water. Participating in Citi TV's roundtable discussion on Galamsey in November 2022—The Citi Galamsey Dialogue titled "Galamsey and Ghana's Water Security"—the Managing Director of the GWCL, Dr. Clifford Braimah, expressed grave concern about the damage that the pollution of the rivers was causing to their water processing plants, as well as the mounting high cost of treating the polluted water. He reminded the public that their "system is not made for wastewater, but for fresh water. If we do not take the issue of illegal mining seriously enough and address it, our systems may break down, and we may not be able to produce water for Ghanaians anymore" (Boakye—Citinewsroom.com, 2022). As touched on above, it was the GWCL that re-ignited the recent public angst, backlash, and anger against the government for its failure to fight galamsey. The GWCL issued a press release in August 2024, which reported that about sixty per cent of the catchment capacity of the Pra is silted because of illegal mining. As a result of this, the river is recording an average turbidity of 14,000 NTU; far above the maximum of 2000 NTU, the parameters within which the water can be treated for drinking (see Fig. I.2 of the Introduction).

As already noted, galamsey and its deleterious effects predate the period under study (2017–2024), but it was during this period (and beyond) that these problems witnessed unprecedented deterioration, despite the war declared by the incumbent president against them. Yet the failure of the war is so palpable, the incumbent president's appointees and party officials cannot deny it. Instead, they try to shift some of the blame onto their political opponents: the NDC party and its government. Thus, they engage in spurious comparison of the state of pollution of rivers by galamsey in the past and the period under study. Some of them do this a bit reasonably, to illustrate that the problem is not peculiar to the incumbent government and the presidency of Mr. Akufo-Addo. Others are not just ridiculous, but they belittle the judgement and intelligence of Ghanaians. For example, in the face of the overwhelming evidence of the deteriorating state of pollution of rivers in the period under study, a high-ranking member of parliament of the president's party—the Majority Chief Whip, Mr. Frank Anooh Dompreh—said that the opposition party, the NDC, performed worst in controlling the galamsey menace when it was in government. "If we are to look and investigate both sides of the House," he argued contemptuously on the floor of parliament, "I can tell you that the NDC polluted the water more than us. So let's get matters straight" (Myjoyonline.com, 2024).

Besides the pollution of rivers, the destruction of farms is another serious negative effect of CMM galamsey in Ghana. The production of cocoa, Ghana's third leading export commodity and foreign exchange earner, is also under threat from mechanized galamsey. Switzerland, whose chocolate industry depends on more than half of its cocoa bean imports from Ghana, has expressed its worry over "the damage illegal gold mining is inflicting on local communities and on supplies of this key raw material" (Chandrasekhar and Adogla-Bessa, 2022). This threat is in two ways: the destruction of cocoa farms and the negative effects of the above-mentioned environmental pollution on the trees and quality of cocoa produced. Land used for farming cocoa is lost to mechanized and medium-scale galamsey because of its requirement and capacity to destroy huge tracts of land with heavy mining equipment. This means more land is needed for galamsey, bringing about a stiff competition between galamsey and cocoa farming for land, in which "illegal miners have priced cocoa farmers out of the market" (Chandrasekhar and Adogla-Bessa, 2022).

Cocoa farmers have been enticed by money to sell their cocoa farmlands to the rich elite class to mine gold, both voluntarily and subtle coercion (Siaw et al. 2023). For example, in the cocoa farming village of Denkyira Asikuma, near Dunkwa in the Central Region, about 30 cocoa farmers sold their land to "miners who quickly excavated, pumped in water and chemicals, and abandoned their pits when the work was done or when soldiers chased them away" (Taylor and Taylor, 2018). These farmers took rational economic decisions; because, whereas the average amount a cocoa farmer makes annually from selling cocoa beans is between GH¢548 and GH¢1000 per acre, the rich mining class is prepared to pay between GH¢6000 and GH¢40,000 per acre of farmland (Chandrasekhar and Adogla-Bessa 2022; Snapir et al., 2017, p. 454). The cost of cocoa farmlands varies by the estimated value of the cocoa trees on it and the proximity of the farmland to an existing gold mine (Chandrasekhar and Adogla-Bessa, 2022). It is, therefore, the power of money that is causing the loss of cocoa farmlands to galamsey, because when it comes to money, "cocoa cannot compete with gold" (Chandrasekhar and Adogla-Bessa, 2022).

The Ghana Cocoa Board (COCOBOD)—the state enterprise responsible for facilitating the production, processing, and marketing of good quality cocoa—did a survey on the impact of galamsey on cocoa production in the country. It found out that the quantum of cocoa farmlands lost to galamsey is quite significant: about "19,000 hectares of cocoa plantations were taken over or damaged by illegal gold mining from 2019 to 2020, an area more than twice the size of Zurich" (Swissinfo.ch, 2022). Little wonder that, between 2017 and 2020, the area of land under cocoa cultivation reduced by 21%: from a peak of 1.9 million ha in 2017 to 1.5 million ha in 2020 (Chandrasekhar and Adogla-Bessa, 2022).

Any efforts to curate evidence on the ecological and socioeconomic ravages of illegal capitalist medium-scale mining (that is CMM galamsey) will be superficial without pieces of it from Erastus Asare Donkor's award-winning documentaries on the subject. His "Destruction for Gold" series (Part 1, 2, and 3) and "Poisoned for Gold" series (Part 1 and 2) provide overwhelming evidence of highly polluted rivers, gutted forest reserves, and expanse of devastated land cleared of its vegetative cover and littered with deep and wide pits. Poisoned for Gold (Part 1 and 2) is the latest documentary, released towards the end of 2023 (Donkor 2023a; Donkor, 2023b). The central motif of this documentary is straightforward: the ecosystem and biodiversity of the communities under the incessant attack by operators of CMM galamsey are poisoned with deadly chemicals used in or released by this criminal hunt for gold. Showing milky-brown water of rivers, Donkor introduces Poisoned for Gold, Part 1 with the aphorism, "water is life" (Donkor, 2023a) and then narrates the story of the extent to which the major rivers of Ghana such as Oda, Ankobra, Tano, and Offin—and many other rivers—are poisoned by what he described as "irresponsible mining"—what we term in this book as CMM galamsey.

The rivers are poisoned with dangerous levels of Mercury, Lead, Arsenic, Chromium, and Cadmium; and these poisons find their way into the veins of the inhabitants of the communities plagued by CMM galamsey. They are then exposed and subjected to deadly ailments, as well as reproductive, maternity, and natal health care issues. The documentary zeros in on the maternity and natal health issues, detailing the hideous congenital and physical disorders and the inescapable morbidity of some babies born in these communities. He narrates the harrowing images of stillborn babies and physical deformities such as babies born with one leg and without anus and sex organs (MyjoyOnline.com, 2023). The medical and geology experts that Erastus Asare Donkor interviewed—such as Professors Paul Sampene Osei and Emmanuel Arhin—confirm that these horrific health hazards are caused by the poisonous pollution of CMM galamsey (Donkor, 2023a; Donkor, 2023b).

The destruction of forest reserves and pollution of water bodies are the foci of Donkor's Destruction for Gold series, Parts 1, 2, and 3. We are told by Donkor early in Part 1 of the documentary that "with the introduction of heavy earthmoving equipment and water-polluting gold mining technologies, the country's forests and water bodies came under attack. Regime after regime saw the pillaging of forest and the pollution of water bodies. Large tracts of forest cover, like this one in the Western Region, were reduced to waste land" (Donkor, 2023a). The three-documentary series show active mining ongoing in the prestine forests (including forest reserves) in various parts of Western and Ashanti Regions. The narrative of Erastus Asare Donkor in the documentaries and the videos show that this destruction of the ecosystem by CMM galamsey happened (was happening) in the midst of the ban on ASM and when the Galampstop inter-ministerial taskforce and the military-cum-police Operation Vanguard were alive and active.

The documentaries take us deep into the dark underworld of CMM galamsey in the remote and deep jungles in the Ashanti and Western Regions, where it is causing havoc to Ghana's ecosystem. For example, they show destruction caused to the Tano Nimiri and Apamprama forest reserves in Ashanti Region, as well as the vegetative forests in Dompem in the Tarkwa-Nsuaem municipal area of the Western Region. Similar to the Poisoned for Gold series, the Destruction for Gold series also show the milky-brown water of the major rivers in Western and Ashanti Regions, illustrating the high pollution that CMM galamsey has caused (is causing) to beautiful rivers of Ghana.

The devastation of the environment by CMM galamsey has shocked many Ghanaians, who wonder why this happens; especially, that it happens through the actions of Ghanaians. A retired One-Star General of the Ghana army, Brigadier General Dan Frimpong, is one of the leading Ghanaians shocked by this devastation. After watching Erastus Asare Donkor's documentary, Poisoned for Gold, he wrote a feature story published on Graphic Online titled, "Poisoned for Gold! Scorched-earth policy?" The General deployed the military term and strategy, "scorched-earth policy," to analyse what he described as "the unbelievable impunity of destruction of lands, the pollution of our surface water bodies…, [and] the denuding of our forest vegetation" (Frimpong, 2023). The term refers to the strategy of a retreating army in a war, involving the destruction of things, including those belonging to them or within their own territory. Brigadier General Frimpong (Rtd) correctly likens the destruction of the environment by the power elites of Ghana, through their operations in CMM galamsey, to the "scorched-earth policy" of the military. But unlike the military, the self-destruction inflicted by CMM galamsey is not driven by any strategic sensibilities. It is "scorched-earth policy" informed and shaped by corruption, arrogance, impunity, and disrespect (Frimpong, 2023).

Dispossession of the Subalterns and Destruction of Their Livelihoods

ASGM (and TAM specifically) is widely acknowledged to play a central role in the livelihoods of the rural poor—the powerless subaltern class. Given this, only a few people will disagree with our argument that CMM is inherently and directly in conflict with the survival or social (re)production of this class. The point is that, both TAM and CMM require one key resource, land; and because CMM involves the acquisition of huge tracts of land, this inescapably involves the grabbing of land the subaltern classes farm or mine on. They are, thus, not only dispossessed, but their livelihoods are destroyed. Dispossession or grabbing applies to landed or landless peasants and TAM operators. Because they are alienated from their land, and their ability to access and use it have been directly or indirectly interdicted by the activities of CMM operators. This is distinct from landowner-farmers who voluntarily sell their lands to CMM operators because, rationally, it is more profitable to sell than to farm on them. As observed by Siaw et al. (2023: 4) in their study of galamsey and cocoa farming in Atiwa, Atiwa West, and East Akim districts in the Eastern Region, "the allure of an immediate lump sum of money persuades some landowners to sell their lands to galamsey operators."

But there is a clear case of dispossession and land grabbing when land-less peasants and TAM operators are denied access to land because, either the owners of the lands have sold or leased it out to CMM operators or because the methods of mining have endangered their farms and health. For example, the above-mentioned study revealed that "proximity to sold lands and the negative effects of ASM ... had coerced the farmers to sell their lands" (Siaw et al. 2023: 5). A quote from the story of one of their interlocutors captures a quintessential case of dispossession by coercive sale or lease of one's farmland.

> I observed that the activities of the illegal miners nearby had negative effects on my cocoa farm. The farm got flooded regularly by the tailings from the mining sites. I believe they use some chemicals in the mining operations. The leaves of the cocoa plants were getting yellowish, and the crops were wilting. When I confronted one of the managers of a neighbouring mine, he told me that they had acquired the land "legally" from the landowner and therefore had the right to mine. Thus, if I felt aggrieved, that was my problem, not theirs. Afterwards, the mine manager contacted one of my uncles and asked him to talk to me so that I could sell the land to them. I contemplated and came to the realisation that I could lose my farm and land without compensation. I therefore sold the land to them. (Siaw et al., 2023, p. 5)

Another study done in two cocoa-growing communities in Ashanti Region, Antoakrom, and Atoborakrom, in the Amansie West District, made similar findings of dispossession of cocoa farmers. CMM Galamsey had several adverse effects on them, major among them were "competition for land, flooding of farms, destruction of parts of farms, difficulty in accessing farms, and pollution of water source for farming" (Osman et al., 2022, p. 75). The study noted that because of the quest of landowners to make money very fast, they seize land from tenant-farmers and sell to operators of galamsey. The corollary of this is the dispossesion of these landless farmers of their farms and the cutting down of their cocoa trees for mining to take place. Rather than cocoa trees, their farms are turned to galamsey mines. The cocoa farmers in the study area also complained about unprecedented flooding of their cocoa farms when rain falls, because the water collects in the uncovered pits of galamsey filled with water. This, according to the farmers, "causes black pods disease and this lowers output since a significant proportion of pods rot even before they mature in some cases" (Osman et al., 2022, p. 75).

Considering that cocoa farmers depend on their farming for their liveli-hood, being dispossessed of the land they farm on inevitably denies them of their means of survival—especially the tenant-farmers who do not benefit from the lease or sale of their farmlands by their landlords to CMM galamsey operators. The violence of dispossession impacts nega-tively on the produce of the farmers, because of three reasons: their farm sizes have reduced drastically, they have no farmlands at all, and the low yield of their cocoa trees. The cumulative effect of this is the drop in income from the sale of cocoa. And in the case of the landless farmers whose land have been grabbed, they lose their income completely because of the interdiction of their access and use of it for farming cocoa and staple food.

But this problem is not limited to only cocoa-growing communities and cocoa farmers. It seems rather widespread across the country. And unsurprising at that, because rural livelihood activities and diversification seem similar across Ghana. Being agrarian communities, their livelihoods revolve on land and water, and any disruption of access to these resources will engender similar negative impacts on rural livelihoods across the board. In the northern part of Ghana, the ban on ASGM and its mili-tarized enforcement had similar negative impact on the livelihood of the subaltern classes such as the peasants. For example, in the Nanga and Takpo communities of the Nadowli-Kaleo District, Upper West Region, the study of Baddianaah (2024) found serious hardships inflicted on the inhabitants whose livelihoods depend on both farming and galamsey. In summary, the negative impacts of the ban on the inhabitants of Nanga and Takpo were the loss of income from work, by both women and men; and the decline in their purchasing power, leading to the shortage of necessi-ties of life like food for the household. It also constricted their access to essential health services because of inability to pay for them. In addition, they could not pay the school fees of their children, as well as water and electricity bills (Baddianaah, 2024, pp. 5–8).

But it is not only farmers in mining communities whose livelihoods were crushed. The livelihoods of other subaltern classes who depend mainly on TAM galamsey, licensed operators of ASGM and their depen-dents, and others whose livelihood activities are connected directly or indirectly to the industry, were battered by the ban on ASGM and the militarized fights mounted by the government against galamsey. For example, a study by Tuokuu et al. (2020) vividly illustrates this claim. The study was done in three communities in Tarkwa-Nsuaem Municipality, in the Western Region—Tarkwa, Iduapriem, and Teberibe. It reports varied ways the livelihoods of subaltern classes were dislocated by the ban on ASGM. The whole local economy of the district was adversely affected, because livelihood activities linked to galamsey—such as food vendoring and blacksmithing—diminished considerably. Put in the words of one of the interlocutors of the study, "Take away galamsey, and you'll take away people's lives. The economy of Tarkwa-Nsuaem Municipality has collapsed because of the ban on galamsey" (Tuokuu et al., 2020, p. 59). Little wonder, therefore, that poverty in the study area seemed to have worsened, and in the words of one of the respondents of the study, "abolishing [or the ban on] galamsey is tantamount to execution" (Tuokuu et al., 2020, p. 60).

This chapter has provided a panoramic view of the evolution of traditional artisanal mining (TAM), the time-honoured livelihood activity of rural people in Ghana, to its present-day capitalist medium-scale and industrialized mining (CMM): an environmentally and socially ruinous industry operated by the power elites to accumulate illicit wealth. Concomitant to this evolution, the ban on ASGM, and the militarized enforcement of the latter by the Akufo-Addo-led government of Ghana, is the devastation of the livelihoods of the subaltern classes in the mining communities. In sum, therefore, this chapter not only covers the ferocious destructions of the ecosystem by CMM galamsey, but it also documents evidence of the devastation of livelihoods of local communities by CMM galamsey, as well as the ban on ASGM by the Ghana government in 2017.

References

Adu-Baffour. F., Daum, T., and Birner, R. (2021). Governance challenges of small-scale gold mining in Ghana: Insights from a process net-map study. *Land Use Policy*, (*102*), 105271.

Andrews, N. (2015) Digging for survival and/or justice? The drivers of illegal mining activities in Western Ghana. *Africa Today*, *62*(2), 3–24.

Aram, S. A. (2021). Managing occupational health among goldminers in Ghana: Modelling the likelihood of experiencing occupational related health problems. *PLoS ONE*, *16*(7), e0254449. https://doi.org/10.1371/journal.pone.0254449

Arthur, F., Agyemang-Duah, W., Gyasi, R. M., Yeboah, J. Y., and Otieku, E. (2016). Nexus between Artisanal and Small-Scale Gold Mining and

Livelihood in Prestea Mining Region, *Ghana Geography Journal*, *2016*(1), 1605427.

Arthur-Holmes, F., & Busia, K. A. (2020). Household dynamics and the bargaining power of women in artisanal and small-scale mining in sub-Saharan Africa: A Ghanaian case study. *Resources Policy, 69*, 101884.

Arthur-Holmes, F. (2021). Gendered division of labour and "sympathy" in artisanal and small-scale gold mining in Prestea-Huni Valley Municipality, Ghana. *Journal of Rural Studies, (81)*, 358–362.

Baddianaah, I. (2024). Reflecting on the impact of an artisanal and small-scale mining ban on impoverished agrarian communities in northern Ghana. *The Extractive Industries and Society, (19)*, 101502.

Bansah, K. J., Yalley, A. B., and Dumakor-Dupey, N. (2016). The hazardous nature of small scale underground mining in Ghana. *Journal of Sustainable Mining, 15*(1), 8–25.

Bell, F. G., & Donnelly, L. J. (2006). Mining and its Impact on the Environment. London: CRC press.

Boakye, E.A. Citinewsroom.com. (2022). *GWCL risks shutdown due to turbidity of water processed—MD warns.* https://citinewsroom.com/2022/11/gwcl-risks-shutdown-due-to-turbidity-of-water-processed-md-warns/ (Accessed 30 December 2022).

Calys-Tagoe, B. N., Ovadje, L., Clarke, E., Basu, N., and Robins, T. (2015). Injury profiles associated with artisanal and small-scale gold mining in Tarkwa, Ghana. *International journal of environmental research and public health, 12*(7), 7922–7937.

Chandrasekhar, A., and Adogla-Bessa, D. (2022). *How gold mining in Ghana is threatening Swiss chocolate.* https://www.swissinfo.ch/eng/how-gold-mining-in-ghana-is-threatening-swiss-chocolate/47870756 (Accessed 25 October 2022).

Citifmonline.com. (2017). *Ghana may soon import water over galamsey—EPA.* https://citifmonline.com/2017/02/ghana-may-soon-import-water-over-galamsey-epa/ (Accessed 30 December 2022).

Crawford, G., and Botchwey, G. (2017). Conflict, collusion and corruption in small-scale gold mining: Chinese miners and the state in Ghana. *Commonwealth & Comparative Politics, 55*(4), 444–470.

DeLeo R.A., Taylor K., Crow D.A., Birkland T.A. (2021). During disaster: refining the concept of focusing events to better explain long-duration crises. *International Review of Public Policy, 3*(1), 5–28.

Dinye, R. D., and Erdiaw-Kwasie, M. O. (2012). Gender and labour force inequality in small-scale gold mining in Ghana. *International Journal of Sociology and Anthropology, 4*(10), 285–295.

Donkor, E. A. (2023a). *Poisoned for gold (Part 1).* https://www.youtube.com/watch?v=wrhPscbb_Cc (Accessed 8 August 2024).

Donkor, E. A. (2023b). *Poisoned for gold (Part 2).* https://www.youtube.com/watch?v=CXhAIKm7uS0 (Accessed 8 August 2024).

Eduful, M., Alsharif, K., Eduful, A., Acheampong, M., Eduful, J., and Mazumder, L. (2020). The illegal artisanal and small-scale mining (galamsey) 'menace'in Ghana: is military-style approach the answer? *Resources Policy, (68),* 101732, 1–14.

Espin, J., & Perz, S. (2021). Environmental crimes in extractive activities: Explanations for low enforcement effectiveness in the case of illegal gold mining in Madre de Dios, Peru. *The Extractive Industries and Society, 8*(1), 331–339.

Fashya, I., and Suseno, B. D. (2023). Illegal Gold Mining Grandil: Empirical Trail In South Citorek Lebak Regency, Indonesia. *International Journal of Information, Business and Management, 15*(3), 7–21.

Forkuor, G., Ullmann, T., and Griesbeck, M. (2020). Mapping and monitoring small-scale mining activities in Ghana using Sentinel-1 Time Series (2015–2019). *Remote Sensing, 12*(6), 911.

Frimpong, D. (2023). "Poisoned for Gold!" - "Scorched-earth" policy? https://www.graphic.com.gh/features/opinion/poisoned-for-gold-scorched-earth-policy.html (Accessed 15 July 2024).

Harmon, S. (2018). The money stone film. *Continental Drift Media.* https://www.imdb.com/title/tt4247182/; http://www.moneystonefilm.com (Accessed 7 August 2024)

Hausermann H., Adomako J., and Robles M. (2020) Fried eggs and all-women gangs: the geopolitics of Chinese gold mining in Ghana, bodily vulnerability, and resistance. *Human Geography, 13*(1), 60–73.

Hentschel, T., Hruschka, F., and Priester, M. (2002). *Global report on artisanal and small-scale mining.* International Institute for Environment and Development (IIED) and World Business Council for Sustainable Development (WBCSD). Available online https://pubs.iied.org/sites/default/files/pdfs/migrate/G00723.pdf (Accessed 21st September 2022).

Hilson, G.M. (2017). Shootings and burning excavators: Some rapid reflections on the Government of Ghana's handling of the informal 'galamsey' mining 'menace'. *Resources Policy, (54),* 109–116. https://doi.org/10.1016/j.resourpol.2017.09.009

Hilson, G., and Garforth, C. (2012). "Agricultural poverty" and the expansion of artisanal mining in sub- Saharan Africa: experiences from southwest Mali and southeast Ghana. *Population Research and Policy Review, 31*(3), 435–464.

Hilson, G., and McQuilken, J. (2014). Four decades of support for artisanal and small-scale mining in sub-Saharan Africa: a critical review. *The Extractive Industries and Society, 1*(1), 104–118.

Hilson, G. M., and Maconachie, R. (2017). Formalising artisanal and small-scale mining: Insights, contestations and clarifications. *Area, 49*(4), 443–451. https://doi.org/10.1111/area.12328

Intergovernmental Forum on Mining, Minerals, Metals and Sustainable Development (IGF). (2017). *Global trends in artisanal and small-scale mining (ASM): A review of key numbers and issues.* Winnipeg: IISD: https://www.iisd.org/system/files/publications/igf-asm-global-trends.pdf (Accessed on 6 August 2024).

Kwao, B. (2024). Labour control through risk and profit-sharing: Social inequalities and exploitation through artisanal and small-scale mining in Ghana. *Geoforum, (154)*, 104070.

Lahiri-Dutt, K. (Ed.). (2018). *Between the plough and the pick: informal, artisanal and small-scale mining in the contemporary world.* Canberra: ANU Press.

Massaro, L., Calvimontes, J., Ferreira, L. C., and De Theije, M. (2022). Balancing economic development and environmental responsibility: Perceptions from communities of garimpeiros in the Brazilian Amazon. *Resources Policy, (79)*, 103063.

McQuilken, J., and Hilson, G. (2016). *Artisanal and small-scale gold mining in Ghana: Evidence to inform an 'action dialogue'.* IIED: http://pubs.iied.org/16618IIED (Accessed 14 March 2018).

Ministry of Lands and Natural Resources (MLNR). (2017). *Project appraisal & implementation document (PAID) for the mul- tilateral mining integrated project (MMIP).* Accra: MLNR. https://mlnr.gov.gh/wp-content/uploads/2019/06/MMIP-PROJECT-DOCUMENT.pdf (Accessed 26 August 2022)

MyjoyOnline.com. (2023). *More research on galamsey's effect on women crucial—Erastus Asare Donkor advocates.* https://www.myjoyonline.com/more-research-on-galamseys-effect-on-women-crucial-erastus-asare-donkor-advocates/# (Accessed 9 August 2023).

Myjoyonline.com. (2024). *Galamsey: NDC polluted water more than us—Annoh Dompreh.* https://www.myjoyonline.com/galamsey-ndc-polluted-water-more-than-us-annoh-dompreh/

Nurse, A. (2017). Green criminology: Shining a critical lens on environmental harm. *Palgrave Communications, 3*(1), 1–4.

Nyamekye, C., Ghansah, B., Agyapong, E., & Kwofie, S. (2021). Mapping changes in artisanal and small-scale mining (ASM) landscape using machine and deep learning algorithms.-a proxy evaluation of the 2017 ban on ASM in Ghana. *Environmental Challenges, 3*, 100053.

Ofosu, G., Siaw, D., Sarpong, D., and Danquah, S. (2024). Ban mining, ban dining? Re (examining) the policy and practice of 'militarised conservationism'on ASM operations. *The Extractive Industries and Society, 17*(01432), 1–8.

O'Neill, J. D., and Telmer, K. (2017). *Estimating mercury use and documenting practices in artisanal and small-scale gold mining (ASGM)*. Geneva, Switzerland: UN Environment. ISBN 978-0-9939459-8-4: Available at https://wedocs.unep.org/handle/20.500.11822/22892 (Accessed on 7 August 2024).

Ofori, D. R., and Ofori, J. J. (2018). Digging for gold or justice? Misrecognition and marginalization of "illegal" small-scale miners in Ghana. *Social Justice Research, 31*(4), 355–373.

Ofosu-Mensah, A. E. (2010). Traditional gold mining in Adanse. *Nordic Journal of African Studies, 19*(2): 124–147.

Ofosu-Mensah, E. A. (2011). Historical overview of traditional and modern gold mining in Ghana. *International Research Journal of Library, Information and Archival Studies, 1*, 006–22.

Ofosu-Mensah, E. A. (2017). Historical and modern artisanal small-scale mining in Akyem Abuakwa, Ghana. *Africa Today, 64*(2), 69–91.

Osman, N., Afele, J. T., Nimo, E., Gorleku, D. O., Ofori, L. A., and Abunyewa, A. A. (2022). Assessing the impact of illegal small-scale mining (Galamsey) on cocoa farming and Farmer livelihood: A case study in the Amansie West District of Ghana. *Pelita Perkebunan (a Coffee and Cocoa Research Journal), 38*(1), 70–82.

Owusu O, Bansah KJ, Mensah AK. (2019). "Small in size, but big in impact": socio-environmental reforms for sustainable artisanal and small-scale mining. *Journal of Sustainable Mining, 18*(1), 38–44.

Schwartz, F. W., Lee, S., and Darrah, T. H. (2021). A review of the scope of artisanal and small-scale mining worldwide, poverty, and the associated health impacts. *GeoHealth, 5*(1), e2020GH000325.

Siaw, D., Ofosu, G., & Sarpong, D. (2023). Cocoa production, farmlands, and the galamsey: Examining current and emerging trends in the ASM-agriculture nexus. *Journal of Rural Studies, 101*, 103044.

Snapir, B., Simms, D. M., Waine, T. W. (2017). Mapping the expansion of galamsey gold mines in the cocoa growing area of Ghana using optical remote sensing. *International Journal of Applied Earth Observation and Geoinformation, (58)*, 225–233.

Stemn, E., Amoh, P. O., and Joe-Asare, T. (2021). Analysis of artisanal and small-scale gold mining accidents and fatalities in Ghana. *Resources Policy, (74)*, 102295.

Swissinfo.ch (2022). How gold mining in Ghana is threatening Swiss chocolate. https://www.swissinfo.ch/eng/business/how-gold-mining-in-ghana-is-threatening-swiss-chocolate/47870756 (Accessed 18 April 2025).

Taylor, M. S., and Taylor, K. (2018). *Illegal gold mining boom threatens cocoa farmers (and your chocolate)*. https://www.nationalgeographic.com/science/article/ghana-gold-mining-cocoa-environment (Accessed 25 October 2022).

The Ghana Report. (2020). *Figures reveal how Ghana may run out of potable water soon due to Galamsey.* https://www.theghanareport.com/figures-reveal-how-ghana-may-run-out-of-potable-water-soon-due-to-galamsey/ (30 December 2022).

The Ghana Report. (2022). *Galamsey: GWCL may not be able to Supply water in next 6 months—WRC warns.* https://www.theghanareport.com/galamsey-gwcl-may-not-be-able-to-supply-water-in-next-6-months-wrc-warns/ (Accessed 30 December 2022)

Tuokuu, F. X. D., Idemudia, U., Bawelle, E. B. G., and Baguri Sumani, J. B. (2020). Criminalization of "galamsey" and livelihoods in Ghana: Limits and consequences. *Natural Resources Forum, 44*(1), 52–65.

University of Ghana Business School (UGBS). (2017). The Galamsey Menace in Ghana: A political problem requiring political solutions? *Policy Brief*, No. 5. https://ugbs.ug.edu.gh/ugbs-policy-briefs (Accessed 20 December 2022).

Van de Camp, E. (2016). Artisanal gold mining in Kejetia (Tongo, Northern Ghana): a three-dimensional perspective, *Third World Thematics: A TWQ Journal, 1*(2), 267–283, https://doi.org/10.1080/23802014.2016.1229132

World Bank (2019). *2019 State of the artisanal and small- Scale mining sector* Washington, DC: World Bank.

World Bank (2023). *2023 State of the artisanal and small- Scale mining sector.* Washington, DC: World Bank.

Yakovleva, N. (2007). Perspectives on female participation in artisanal and small-scale mining: A case study of Birim North District of Ghana. *Resources Policy, 32*(1–2), 29–41.

CHAPTER 2

The Paradox of Galamsey: Comprehensively Regulated, yet Characterized by Chaos and Criminality

Abstract This chapter describes the policies, laws, and regulations which govern Ghana's artisanal and small-scale gold mining (ASGM). The illegal, ungovernable, chaotic, and destructive ASGM sector being witnessed in Ghana today foregrounds a fundamental question of governance: whether laws and institutions exist to steer the sector in the direction of law and order; to steer it to a regulated, formal, and sustainable livelihood activity or otherwise. In this chapter, we argue that the horrendous environmental damage that Ghana has witnessed in the ASGM sector, especially between 2017 and 2024, did not happen because the industry lacks a governance system to regulate it. Instead, it happened in the context of comprehensive regulation, with a panoply of policies, laws, and institutions governing it. Indeed, Ghana has put in place some of the most comprehensive and dynamic ASM laws in the world, yet impunity characterizes the ASGM sector. Both the colonial state of the Gold Coast and post-independence Ghanaian state designed a panoply of laws and regulations for the comprehensive governance of minerals and mining in the country. A good number of these laws cover the regulation of the artisanal and small-scale mining (ASM) sector, particularly gold mining. For example, PNDC Law 217 regulated the use of mercury in ASM; PNDC Law 218 (The Small-Scale Gold Mining Law 1989) legalized ASM and introduced a licensing process; and PNDC Law 219,

© The Author(s), under exclusive license to Springer Nature Switzerland AG 2025
J. A. Ayelazuno and M. A. Aziabah, *State Capture in the Militarized Fight Against Illegal Small-Scale Goldmining in Ghana*,
https://doi.org/10.1007/978-3-031-82673-3_2

created the Precious Minerals Marketing Corporation, a state enterprise authorized to buy gold, including gold produced from ASM. In addition, there are state institutions designed specifically to enforce the laws and regulations governing mining and to take administrative measures to ensure order and sanity in the sector. These have been augmented by the presence of generic state institutions like the Ghana Police Service and the Judicial Service of Ghana which enforce and adjudicate the laws of Ghana, including those related to mining. Against this background, this chapter demonstrates that the informality and criminality that characterize the sector, particularly in the capitalist medium-scale mining (CMM), happen not because of the lack of a governance system, but rather despite the existence of it. There is a quintessential paradox at hand here: Ghana has a well-governed ASGM industry which is characterized by chaos, criminality, and catastrophic environmental destruction and human development atrocities. State capture, as we illustrate in this book, is characterized by paradoxes and internal contradictions like this one.

Keywords Ghana · Gold · Galamsey · Mining regulations · Mining laws · Mining institutions · Paradox of ungovernable ASM

The preceding chapter portrayed an eerie situation of an illegal, ungovernable, chaotic, and destructive artisanal and small-scale gold mining (ASGM) sector in Ghana: galamsey. This foregrounds a fundamental question of governance: whether laws and institutions exist to steer the sector in the direction of law and order; to steer it to a well regulated, formal, and sustainable livelihood activity, as envisaged by the African Mining Vision (AMV). This is the question that this chapter sets out to address. We argue that the horrendous environmental damage that Ghana has witnessed in the ASGM sector, especially between 2017 and 2024, did not happen because the industry lacks a governance system to regulate it. It is rather the contrary: it happened in the context of comprehensive regulation, with a panoply of policies, laws, and institutions governing it. As correctly noted by Hilson (2017, p. 111) "Ghana has in place some of the most comprehensive and dynamic ASM laws in the world."

As Textbox 2.1 illustrates, Ghana has enacted several laws and regulations, more than enough, to govern and make the ASGM industry environmentally sustainable and mutually beneficial to the poor and the overall economy of the country. In addition, and as Textbox 2.2 illustrates, there are adequate relevant oversight state institutions to enforce these regulations and to take administrative measures to ensure order and sanity in the sector. For example, there are several relevant state agencies and departments which oversee the ASGM industry and implement these regulations. Apart from the agencies and departments directly related to mining, there are other generic state institutions such as the Ghana Police Service and the Judicial Service of Ghana which enforce and adjudicate the laws of Ghana, including those related to mining.

Both the colonial and postcolonial state had political and economic interests in gold and how it is mined and distributed; and in pursuit of these interests, both designed and implemented policies on mining and minerals in the Gold Coast and Ghana respectively (Tsikata, 1997; Ayelazuno and Mawuko-Yevugah, 2019). After gaining independence from Britain, the Ghanaian state took over ownership of gold found anywhere in the country and passed the first set of laws to regulate the industry. It passed The Minerals Act 1962 (Act 126) that vested the ownership of minerals in "the President on behalf of the Republic and in trust for the People of Ghana (Section 1)" (Tsikata, 1997). This law laid the foundation of the regalian minerals ownership system that the 1992 Constitution of Ghana has stipulated; namely, that all minerals in their natural state within the territory of Ghana [are] the property of Ghana and [are] vested in the president on behalf of and in trust for the people of Ghana (Ngaanuma, 2021).

In the rest of the chapter, we describe the policies, the laws, and regulations which govern Ghana's ASGM, doing so to illustrate the paradox of a well-governed industry that is characterized by chaos, criminality, and catastrophic environmental destruction and human development atrocities.

LAWS AND REGULATIONS GOVERNING ASGM IN GHANA

The paradox of galamsey, particularly of the type described in capitalist medium-scale mining (CMM), is that it happens in the context of several laws and regulations designed to prevent or check it, and to punish those who flout them. As illustrated by Textbox 2.1, both the colonial state of the Gold Coast and post-independence Ghanaian state designed a panoply of laws and regulations for the comprehensive governance of minerals and mining in the country. A good number of these laws cover the regulation of the artisanal and small-scale mining (ASM) sector, particularly gold mining (ASGM). In the 1980s, the military government of Ghana, The Provisional National Defence Council (PNDC), passed three pieces of laws to regulate and streamline all activities directly and indirectly related to ASM. These laws were: PNDC Law 217, which regulated the use of mercury in ASM; PNDC Law 218 (The Small-Scale Gold Mining Law 1989), which legalized ASM and introduced a licensing process; and PNDC Law 219, which created the Precious Minerals Marketing Corporation, a state enterprise authorized to buy gold, including gold produced from ASM (Tsikata, 1997, 1, pp. 2–13).

To keep pace with new developments in the ASM industry, these laws have been amended and updated with new laws. For example, the Minerals and Mining Amendment Act 475 has been amended and replaced with the Minerals and Mining Law of 2006 Act 703 (Aubynn, 2017) and further amended to the Minerals and Mining Amendment Act 2019, Act 995. This new law consolidated all the laws on mining, including the procedures for the lawful operations of ASM. It allows "artisanal miners to apply for a maximum of 25 acres concession in designated areas through the Minerals Commission, and then to obtain a licence to mine" (Republic of Ghana 2006: 10–11). This law defined the key characteristics of ASM. Sections 81–99 of the law cover a wide range of elements of the ASM industry; encompassing the licensing procedures; the qualification to operate as a small-scale miner; the procedures for acquisition of land for small-scale mining; the institutions governing ASM; the use of explosives and mercury; the sale and purchase of gold from ASM; and the penalties for various offences committed by breaching the relevant sections of the law mentioned above. For example, Section 93 states with clarity the commitment of the Ghanaian state to ensure that small-scale mining is done sustainably in the country: "A person licensed under Section 82 may win, mine and produce minerals by an effective and efficient method and shall observe good mining practices, health and safety rules and pay due regard to the protection of the environment during mining operations" (Republic of Ghana, 2006, pp. 10–11).

Textbox 2.1 Panoply of Laws and Regulations Governing the Ghanaian Mining and Minerals Sector

The fundamental Law

The 1992 Constitution of Ghana

General Mining Laws

- Minerals and Mining Law (PNDCL 153)
- Minerals and Mining (amendment) Act, 1994, (ACT 475)
- Minerals Commission Act, 1993 (Act 450; formerly PNDCL 153)
- Small-Scale Gold Mining Law, 1989 (PNDCL 218)
- Diamonds (Amendment) Law (PNDCL 217)
- Environmental Protection Council Decree, 1974 (NRCD 239)
- Precious Minerals Marketing Corporation Law, 1989 (PNDCL 219)
- Diamonds Decree, 1972 (NRCD 32)
- Additional Profit Tax Law, 1985
- Minerals and Mining Act, 2006 (Act 703)
- Minerals and Mining (Amendment) Act, 2015 (Act 900)
- Minerals Development Fund Act, 2016 (Act 912), the Minerals
- Income Investment Fund Act, 2018 (Act 978) as amended by the Minerals Income Investment Fund (Amendment) Act, 2020 (Act 1024)
- Kimberley Process Certificate Act, 2003 (Act 652).

Regulations

- Minerals and Mining (General) Regulation, 2012 (L.I. 2173)
- Minerals and Mining (Support Services) Regulations, 2012 (L.I. 2174)
- Minerals and Mining (Compensation and Resettlement) Regulations, 2012 (L.I. 2175)
- Minerals and Mining (Licensing) Regulations, 2012 (L.I. 2176)

- Minerals and Mining (Explosives) Regulations, 2012 (L.I. 2177)
- Minerals and Mining (Health and Safety) Regulations, 2012 (L.I. 2182)
- Minerals and Mining (Tracking of Earth Moving and Mining Equipment) Regulations, 2020 (L.I. 2404)
- Minerals and Mining (Local Content and Local Participation) Regulations, 2020 (L.I. 2431)
- Minerals and Mining (Ground Rent) Regulations, 2018 (L.I. 2357)
- Environmental Assessment Regulations, 1999(LI 1652) ('Environmental Regulations');
- Minerals (Royalties) Regulations, 1987

Small-scale Mining Enactments

- Diamond Mining Concessions Ordinance, 1939 (c.136, Laws of G.C. 1951 Revision), s.38 and Form of Schedule
- Gold Mining Products Protection Ordinance (c.149, Laws of the Gold Coast, 1951 Revision)
- Mining Health Areas Ordinance (c. 150, Laws of the Gold Coast 1951 Revision)
- Mining Health Areas Regulations, 1935 (Vol. VIII, 1954 Laws of the Gold Coast p. 1123)
- Prospecting & Digging License Regulations, 1950 (Vol. VIII, 1954 Laws of the Gold Coast, p. 1032)
- Minerals Regulation, 1962 (L.I. 231), especially regulation 1 and Form 5 of the first schedule
- Minerals Regulations, 1963 (L.I. 253)
- Mining Regulations, 1970 (L.I. 665), especially regulations 4,6,10 and 194–205
- Explosives Regulation, 1970 (L.I. 666)
- Diamonds Decree, 1972 (NRCD 32) (as amended by the PNDCL 216)
- Minerals and Mining Law, 1986 (PNDCL 153, especially Part X – s.73–76, and s.77)
- Mercury Law, 1989 (PNDCL 217)

- Small-Scale Gold Mining Law, 1989 (PNDCL 218)
- Precious Minerals Marketing Corporation Law, 1989 (PNDCL 219)
- Minerals Commission Act, 1993 (Act 450)
- Environmental Protection Agency Act, 1994 (Act 490)
- Water Resources Commission Act, 1996 (Act 552)

Other laws

- The Lands Act, 2020 (Act 1036);
- The Local Governance Act, 2016 (Act 936)
- The Land Use and Spatial Planning Act, 2016 (Act 925).
- The Companies Act, 2019
- The (Act 992); the Incorporated Partnership Act, 1962 (Act 152);
- The Ghana Investment Promotion Centre Act, 2013 (Act 865);
- The Income Tax Act, 2015 (Act 896); the Labour Act, 2003 (Act 651);
- The Workmen's Compensation Act, 1987 (PNDCL 187)

Source S Hilson (2001); McQuilken and Hilson (2016)

Sections of the law were amended by Act 900 of 2015, key among them is Section 99 on mining offences and penalties. As a deterrent to illegal ASM, the amended section stipulated harsher penalties for both Ghanaians and foreigners found guilty by a competent court for engaging in illegal ASM. A person engaging in ASM without a valid licence, if convicted, will be liable to a minimum fine of three thousand penalty units (up from the previous one thousand) or to a term of imprisonment not more than five years (previously three years) or to both.

The notable amendment to the mining law by Act 900 is on the penalties for foreigners engaged in ASM and their Ghanaian accomplices. The original law did not have a separate subsection under Section 99 for illegal ASM by foreigners and their Ghanaian accomplices. Considering the onrush of foreigners to engage in galamsey, subsections 3, 4, and 5 of Section 99 of this Act addressed this serious omission. First, a foreigner engaged in ASM, if convicted, will be liable to a minimum fine of thirty thousand penalty units or to a penalty not more than three hundred thousand penalty units or a term of imprisonment not more than twenty years, or both (subsection 3). Second, if a Ghanaian is found guilty of aiding and abetting a foreigner to engage in ASM, they will be liable to a minimum fine of two thousand penalty units or to a penalty not more than twenty thousand penalty units or a term of imprisonment not more than five years, or both (subsection 4). In both cases, the equipment used to commit the offence and the proceeds obtained from it shall be seized and kept in the custody of the police (subsection 5). The confiscated equipment and proceeds will be forfeited to the state on the orders of the court that convicted the offender (subsection 6).

In 2019, the Minerals and Mining (Amendment) Act, 2019 (Act 995), was passed to further amended the principal law, Act 703. The amendments contained in this law focused mainly on redressing the problem of galamsey by extending the law to cover some issues omitted in the principal enactment and the subsequent amendment of it by Act 900. One of the major amendments is the insertion of a new section, Section 96A, on the "Provision of mining support services." It bars foreigners and non-Ghanaian companies from providing support services to small-scale mining. The other major amendment was on Section 99, an amendment that seeks to deal with the problem of galamsey. It imposed harsher penalties on foreigners and their Ghanaian accomplices engaged in illegal ASM. Subsections 3, for example, increased the penalty points for foreigners and their Ghanaian accomplices convicted for illegal mining offences: a foreigner who undertakes small-scale mining or aids someone to do so, shall be liable to: (1) a minimum fine of not less than one hundred thousand (previously thirty thousand) penalty units and not more than three hundred and fifty thousand penalty units; (2) and a term of imprisonment not less than twenty years, and not more twenty-five years (previously twenty years); and (3) or both the fine and imprisonment.

Similarly, the penalties for Ghanaians who abet foreigners to engage in ASM have been made severe: they will be liable to a minimum fine of not less than thirty thousand (up from twenty thousand) penalty units and not more than hundred thousand penalty units; and a term of imprisonment of fifteen years and not more than twenty-five years. Two amendments to the principal mining and minerals law (Act 703), within a short period of four years (in 2015 and 2019)—and focusing on imposing harsher penalties for offences related to illegal small-scale mining—illustrate a Ghanaian state that is, on paper, committed to fighting the galamsey menace.

Another key area of regulation in which galamsey emerged and flourished is the institutional context. The key quality of a state is its institutional architecture and how it effectuates its capacity to function as a state (Republic of Ghana, 2006, pp. 10–11); for example, its capacity to design good policies and implement them effectively. Besides the institutions already mentioned above—that is the 1992 Constitution of Ghana and The President, Head of the Executive arm of government—there is a gamut of institutions governing the mining sector. There are the institutions such as the Parliament of Ghana, the Ghana Police Service, and the Judicial Service of Ghana, that have general responsibilities of making, adjudicating, and enforcing the laws of Ghana, including those related to mining.

As demonstrated by Textbox 2.2, there are also state agencies and departments charged directly with the responsibilities of regulating mining. Ghana's main mining policy, the Minerals, and Mining Policy of Ghana lists and describes these institutions and the various roles they play to achieve its objectives (Republic of Ghana, 2014, p. 53). One of these institutions is the Minerals Commission purposely established by a military government, the Provisional National Defence Council (PNDC), in the 1980s, under a military law, PNDCL 154. It continued to exist after the transition to constitutional government in 1993 and was given legal backing by the Minerals Commission Act, 1993 (Act 450), passed by the Parliament of Ghana (Ayelazuno and Mawuko 2021). As spelt out by this Act, the Commission is responsible for formulating regulations in the mining sector; amending and modifying existing legislation; developing guidelines and standards for monitoring the environmental aspects of mining; making recommendations on minerals policy; advising government on minerals and mining matters; reviewing and promoting minerals development; linking the government and all the actors in the mining and minerals industry. The Minerals Commission is an institution under the Ministry of Lands and Natural Resources (MLNR). The MLNR is responsible for providing the overall policy oversight for the natural resources sector and ensuring "the efficient management of the nation's mineral resources and promoting their judicious exploration, exploitation and processing with minimal harm to the environment, for optimum benefit to society" (Republic of Ghana, 2014, p. 53).

The other key institution listed in the Minerals and Mining Policy of Ghana that is directly responsible for regulating the mining and minerals industry is the Environmental Protection Agency. The central role of this institution in the regulation of ASM is clearly stated in the above-mentioned policy: "The Agency sets guidelines for the compliance of environmentally permissible mining activities. The Agency maintains close liaison with the Minerals Commission to ensure that the latter's promotional, regulatory, and superintending roles over mining operations are consistent with the country's environmental requirements" (Republic of Ghana, 2014, p. 54). To be added to the institutions with direct responsibility in the regulation of ASM in Ghana are the Water Resources Commission, the Forestry Commission, Lands Commission, Office of the Administrator of Stool Lands; Metropolitan, Municipal, and District Assemblies (MMDAs), and the Geological Survey Department (Republic of Ghana, 2014, p. 54–55).

Textbox 2.2 Relevant Government Agencies and Departments Responsible for Mining and Minerals

- *Minerals Commission*—formulating regulations in the sector; amending and modifying existing legislation; developing guidelines and standards for monitoring the environmental aspects of mining; making recommendations on minerals policy; advising government on mineral matters; reviewing and promoting minerals development; linking the government and all the actors in the industry.
- *Ministry of Mines and Energy*—in charge of all issues in the minerals sector including the granting of mineral exploration and mining licenses and leases.
- *Geological Survey Department*—conducting geological studies and documenting all its findings.
- *Mines Department*—responsible for safety and health issues as well as resolving other technical issues in the mines.
- *Ghana Chamber of Mines*—private association of operating mines which promotes mining interest, exchanges information with government on mining, helps in reviewing mining legislation, negotiates miner's compensation and benefits with Miners Union.

- *Lands Commission*—maintain legal records of exploration licenses and mining leases, examines new license applicants, and initiate policies relating to stool and state lands.
- *Land Valuation Board*—evaluate property to be affected by mining and provide rates for compensation.
- *Environmental Protection Agency*—ensures environmentally sound resource
- exploitation through the promotion of research to improve the environment and ensure sustainable development of resources.
- *Forestry Commission*—responsible for the management of the country's forest and works with MC to ensure a balance resource exploitation and forest conservation.
- *Water Resources Commission*—responsible for the management of all water resources and work with MC to ensure balanced resource exploitation.

Source Aryeetey et al. (2004:8).

Public Policies on Mining in Ghana

Besides the above-mentioned mining rules, laws, and regulation of Ghana—often written in legal style, both in language and structure—the Ghanaian state has designed other forms of public policy which are not written in legal style. In ordinary parlance, these are what are usually identified with the term "policy." The Minerals and Mining Policy of Ghana mentioned above is a typical example of this notion of policy, and so are the Artisanal and Small-Scale Mining (ASM) Framework (ASM, 2015), Multilateral Mining Integrated Project (MMIP) Appraisal and Implementation Document (PAID) (MLNR, 2017), and the Small-scale and Community Mining Operational Manual (Minerals Commission 2021). Other policies with statements and actions of the state in relation to mining are the National Environmental Policy, the National Land Policy, and the National Water Policy (MLNR, 2017, p. 12). Space limitation will not allow an extensive review of these policies here, so what follows is a brief reflection of the Ghanaian state's definition of what the problem of mining is and what it seeks to do to address it; or what the public interest in mining is, and how to promote it.

The overarching mining policy in Ghana is the Minerals and Mining Policy of Ghana, designed in 2014. Underpinning the policy is the huge contribution of the mining sector, especially gold mining, to the economic growth of Ghana. As stated in the policy, the ASM is viewed by the Ghanaian state as a key component of this sector, because it makes "significant contributions to the country's foreign exchange earnings" and "offer[s] opportunities to support rural livelihoods, develop entrepreneurship and provide a source of industrial raw materials" (Republic of Ghana 2014, p. 12; Minerals Commission, 2021). Yet ASM is not done in a sustainable manner, as such, the state seeks to assist small-scale miners to operate in a technically, economically, and environmentally sustainable manner. To do this, the Ghanaian state will take the following interventions: improve access to finance for small-scale miners to upscale their activities; generate detailed geological information in designated areas for demarcation to artisanal and small-scale miners; simplify the procedures for them to apply for mining licences; develop participatory approaches to demarcating land for small-scale miners in which the mining communities participate in the process; promote the use of appropriate, affordable, and safe technology by providing information, extension services, and demonstration of these technologies; and to promote the interest of small-scale miners by "forming district mining committees and supporting the small-scale mining associations to help manage the sub-sector at the local level" (Republic of Ghana, 2014, pp. 17, 42–43).

The Artisanal and Small-Scale Mining (ASM) Framework states clearly the Ghanaian state's understanding of the important role ASM plays in the economy of the country: "Government recognizes that small-scale mining operations undertaken by Ghanaians offer opportunities to support rural livelihoods, develop entrepreneurship and provide a source of industrial raw materials" (Minerals Commission, 2015, p. 6). Because of this, the government of Ghana will do some of the following "to enhance the growth and opportunities in the small-scale mining sector": it will develop "measures to improve access to finance for small-scale miners"; simplify the procedures for applying for a licence to do ASM, a privilege reserved for only Ghanaians; "designate further areas to be reserved for small-scale mining activity based on technical and financial viability of the areas for small-scale mining activities"; "encourage the use of appropriate, affordable and safe technology"; "provide advice and support to small-scale miners on forming representative associations"; and "encourage mining companies to collaborate and give support to small-scale miners where it can be established that this will be in the mutual interests of the parties" (Minerals Commission, 2015, pp. 6–8). Furthermore, the government of Ghana will take measures "to mitigate the negative impacts of small-scale mining" by "disseminating information to raise awareness of health, safety and environmental risks, and will periodically revise and disseminate occupational health and safety guidelines for small-scale mining" (Minerals Commission, 2015, pp. 6–8).

The commitment of the Ghanaian state to streamline the ASM sector and integrate it into the broader economy is illustrated with more clarity and detail in the Multilateral Mining Integrated Project (MMIP), a policy document of the Ministry of Lands and Natural Resources (MLNR) which has oversight responsibility for ASM (Ayelazuno and Mawuko-Yevugah, 2021, p. 454). The MMIP enumerates several contributions the ASM sector makes to the Ghanaian economy, highlights the challenges of the sector, some of which it blames on the state itself, and details several steps the state is taking to address these challenges. The main development goal of the MMIP is "to improve the management of artisanal small-scale mining in Ghana to ensure that its contribution to socioeconomic development is felt within the mining communities through sustainable mining practices, minimizing its negative impact on the environment" (MLNR, 2017, p. 17). To accomplish this main goal, the MMIP sets out to accomplish the following measurable objectives: to create "district mining offices of the Minerals Commission to facilitate licensing and monitoring of small-scale mining activities"; to provide financial assistance to small-scale mining cooperatives; demarcate mineable areas specifically for small-scale mining; and help to form small-scale mining associations and District Mining Committees (MLNR, 2017, p. 10).

Another important policy document is the Small-Scale and Community Mining Operational Manual (Minerals Commission, 2021), perhaps, the latest policy document on ASM. In his Foreword to the document, the Minister of Lands and Natural Resources (MLNR), Mr. Samuel Abu Jinapor, began with an epigraph that reflects the Ghanaian state's understanding of the problems that have plagued the industry and the solution to them. The epigraph is Albert Einstein's oft-quoted words: "Insanity is doing the same thing over and over again and expecting different results." The Minister, who exercises the awesome powers of the President of Ghana over natural resources, argues that the ASM sector has been plagued by the galamsey menace and the strategies adopted to address the problem have failed. The Operational Manual states the change in approach to fighting the galamsey menace. Its purpose is "to clarify what acceptable standards are for and streamline small-scale mining of, especially gold which is the country's main mineral and which the sub-sector focuses, along with its affiliate Community Mining Scheme in Ghana" (Minerals Commission, 2021, p. 1).

The central plank of this new approach is the community mining scheme that, according to the Minister, the Operational Manual is supposed to bring "form and structure," the purpose of which is to "prevent a relapse of the activity into galamsey, thereby eliminating the negative aspects of the small-scale mining subsector of Ghana" (Minerals Commission, 2021, p. 1). As with the policy documents discussed above, the Operational Manual gives a background of the ASM industry in Ghana, highlighting particularly its important contribution to the Ghanaian economy, its evolution over the years, the negative environmental and social effects of it, and the unsuccessful measures that have been taken to address the latter. It then draws on the mining laws and other regulations documented above to provide legal anchorage to the community mining scheme and the concrete guidelines the Operational Manual provides for the scheme to work effectively.

In conclusion, this chapter has documented the laws, regulations, and policies governing the ASGM sector of Ghana. It demonstrates that the informality and criminality that characterize the sector, particularly the CMM discussed above, occur not due to the lack of a governance system, but in spite of the existence of it. This, for all intents and purposes, is puzzling, and poses a theoretical question: why does this happen? The next chapter reviews the theories offered to explain the puzzle—what we have all along referred to as the state-centric theories—and then builds on them to provide an alternative theory: state capture.

REFERENCES

Aubynn, T. (2017). *Regulatory structures and challenges to developmental extractives. Some practical observations from Ghana.* United Nations University World Institute for Development Economics Research. WIDER Working Paper 2017/179.

Ayelazuno J. A., and Mawuko-Yevugah, L. (2019). Large-scale mining and ecological imperialism in Africa: the politics of mining and conservation of the ecology in Ghana. *Journal of Political Ecology*, 26(1), 243–262.

Ayelazuno, J. A., and Mawuko-Yevugah, L. (2021). Between the Africa Mining Vision and the neo-patrimonial state: The agency gap in Ghana's regulation of artisanal and small-scale gold mining, *South African Journal of International Affairs*, 28(4), 555–582.

Hilson, G.M. (2017). Shootings and burning excavators: Some rapid reflections on the Government of Ghana's handling of the informal 'galamsey' mining 'menace'. *Resources Policy*, (54), 109–116. https://doi.org/10.1016/j.resourpol.2017.09.009.

Minerals Commission. (2015). *Artisanal and small-scale mining (ASM) framework*. Accra Minerals Commission. https://www.mofep.gov.gh/economic%20reports/artisanal-andsmall-scale-mining-asm-framework/2016-04-29 (Accessed 19 April 2021).

Minerals Commission. (2021). *Small-scale and community mining operational manual*. Accra: Minerals Commission. https://www.mincom.gov.gh/wp-content/uploads/2021/11/Small-Scale-and-Community-Mining-Operational-Manual-Sep.-2021-1.pdf (Accessed 6 December 2022).

Ministry of Lands and Natural Resources (MLNR). Project appraisal and implementation document (PAID) for the multilateral mining integrated project (MMIP) 2017, Accra. Available: https://delvedatabase.org/resources/project-appraisal-implementation-document-for-the-multilateral-mining-integrated-project-mmip-june-2017 (Accessed 22nd September 2022).

Ngaanuma, V. (2021). The constitutionality of nominal trusteeship in the regalian mineral ownership regime in Ghana. *Journal of Energy and Natural Resources Law*, 39(1), 83–104.

Republic of Ghana. (2006). *Minerals and Mining Act 703*. Accra: Ghana Publishing Corporation.

Republic of Ghana. (2014). *Minerals and mining policy of Ghana: Ensuring mining contributes to sustainable development*. Accra: Minerals Commission.

Tsikata, F. (1997). The vicissitudes of mineral policy in Ghana. *Resources Policy*, 23(1/2), 9–14.

CHAPTER 3

State-Centric Theories of the Galamsey Menace

Abstract This chapter reviews the main theoretical approaches used to explain the paradox of illegal ASM or galamsey discussed in the previous chapter. It focuses on three closely related state-centric theories found in the extant literature on illegal ASM in Ghana: (in)formalization, corruption, and neopatrimonialism. These theories are rooted in the broader context of informality and illegality of ASM and its negative environmental and socioeconomic harms—issues that are common across many minerals-rich countries in Africa, Asia, Oceania, and Latin America. Therefore, the *problematique* and discussion of this chapter may be germane to the ASM sectors of countries in other regions. While we do not claim that these are the only relevant state-centric theories, they are the most prominent in explaining the intractable problem of illegal ASM or galamsey in Ghana. The chapter sets the theoretical foundation for the next, in which we advance the understanding of the intractable problem of galamsey in Ghana and beyond by introducing an alternative theory: state capture theory.

Keywords Ghana · Gold · Galamsey · State-centric theories · Informality · Corruption · Neo-patrimonialism · Competitive clientelism

© The Author(s), under exclusive license to Springer Nature Switzerland AG 2025
J. A. Ayelazuno and M. A. Aziabah, *State Capture in the Militarized Fight Against Illegal Small-Scale Goldmining in Ghana*,
https://doi.org/10.1007/978-3-031-82673-3_3

In this chapter, we return to the paradox of galamsey mentioned above: a highly regulated, but chaotic, ASGM sector, of which the environmental destruction of capitalist medium-scale mining (CMM) is a signal example of this paradox. There is more than one theory proffered to explain this puzzling incapability: why an otherwise relatively capable Ghanaian state is incapable of governing its ASM industry in general, and the ASGM in particular. Focusing on the state, there are three closely related strands of theories which may be delineated from the extant literature on this subject: (in)formalization, corruption, and neopatrimonialism. The empirical context that these theories emanated—the informality and negative environmental and socioeconomic effects of the ASM industry—cut across many minerals-rich countries in Africa, Asia, Oceania, and Latin America (see Verbrugge 2015; IGF 2017; World Bank 2019; Zabyelina and van Uhm 2020; Verbrugge and Geneen 2020; Benites 2023; Rodríguez-Novoa and Holley 2023; World Bank 2023). Though focusing on Ghana, the *problematique* and discussion of this chapter may be germane to the ASM sectors of countries in these regions. In the rest of the chapter, we survey the state-centric oeuvre of work to establish the theoretical foundation for our alternative theory of the ungovernable ASGM sector of Ghana and beyond: state capture.

(In)formalization Perspective

The informalization perspective is based on a fundamental character-istic of the ASM industry across most developing countries: most of its operators and operations are in the informal sector of the economy (Hentschel et al., 2003, p. 9; IGF 2017; World Bank, 2019, 2023). This suggests a dichotomous conception of activities of the economy: formal and informal economic activities. In the seminal work of Keith Hart on the informal survival activities of the Frafra migrants in Nima, Accra (in the 1960s), this dichotomous notion was notable in the distinction Hart drew between "formal" and "informal income opportunities"; a distinction "based essentially on that between wage-earning and self-employment" respectively (Hart, 1973, p. 68). The examples Hart used to depict this distinction demonstrate that informal income opportunities are mostly in the unrecorded and unregulated sector of the economy, in terms of the official accounting of economic activities in the country; and outside the regulatory oversight of the state. Whereas the formal income activities are recorded and within the regulatory oversight of the state, the informal ones fall outside the regulatory framework of the state, including licencing, registration, taxation, and labour laws (Ayelazuno and Mawuko-Yevugah, 2021, p. 564). Other key characteristics of the informal income opportunities are: economic activities undertaken by the poor and unemployed who have no opportunity of earning a living in the formal sector of the economy; the economic activities undertaken are menial and low-earning; some of these economic activities may be criminal, others are not; and there is no watertight separation between the informal and formal sectors of the economy, because some of them interface with each other (Hart, 1973, p. 69). All these characteristics seem to manifest in the ASM industry of most developing countries, particularly Ghana—the main focus of this book.

Despite the interface between economic activities in the formal and informal sector of the economy, there is the dualist perspective of the informalization of ASGM in which the informal component "operates 'in the margins' of the global economy and functions as an 'informal safety net' for the rural poor" (Verbrugge and Geenen, 2020, p. 3; Hilson, 2013; Geenen and Verbrugge, 2020). However, there is the counteracting structuralist perspective of informalization that sees "the informal and formal economies as connected, the latter at times exploiting the former" (Hilson and Maconachie, 2017, p. 447). Research in gold mining has established clearly that the ASGM industry and the large-scale mining sector—widely viewed as the formal sector—are interconnected in the real world of the operations of these industries (Verbrugge and Geenen 2020; Geenen and Verbrugge, 2020; Gyan and Behrends, 2024). There cannot be a neat separation between the formal large-scale mining sector and ASGM sector because, there is a growing number of instances that large-scale mining "companies are involved in 'ASGM-like' activities, or because of functional linkages that connect ASGM to mining companies" (Geenen and Verbrugge, 2020, p. 86; see also Gyan and Behrends, 2024).

There is also the legalist perspective of (in)formalization, the "legalist deterrent-centred" school, that posits that the solution to the problem is the enactment of appropriate laws or fixing the lapses in the existing ones to effectively regulate the ASM sector (Hilson, 2013; Transparency International, 2022). This perspective is also associated with De Soto's view on property rights of the poor, which is based on his argument that their properties have no formal recognition, such as registration and titling of the land they own. He advocated for formalization of the property rights of the poor over their assets so that they can trade them freely in the market (Kumah, 2022, p. 706). There is a sense in which the legal and regulatory system of mining in Ghana, its evolution over the years—characterized by amendment of enactments and new laws and regulations—seem to fit closely with the legalist approach to addressing the informality challenge of the ASM industry in the country. Yet the problem continues not only to endure but is exacerbated—despite the plethora of mining laws enacted to formalize the ASM industry, calling the legalist perspective into question.

Despite the contested meaning and distinction between what constitutes an informal or formal sector of the economy, only a few people will reject the conventional wisdom that ASGM in most parts of the world, especially in Sub-Saharan Africa, is characterized by informality, or even criminality. This has spawned various formalization policies and programmes to address the problem (Hilson and Maconochie, 2017). However, well-crafted and impressive laws, regulations, and institutions (see Textbox 2.1 and Textbox 2.2 in Chapter Two) are not enough in themselves to guarantee formalization of the ASM sector. Formulation is not just limited to the design of the requisite legal, regulatory, and policy frameworks to regulate ASGM. What also matters to formalization is the capacity of a state to successfully implement and enforce the laws and regulations throug the relevant authorities (McQuilken and Hilson, 2016, p. 10; Ayelazuno and Mawuko-Yevugah, 2021; Hilson and McQuilken, 2014).

With a low formalization capacity alongside with the urgent livelihood imperative driving ASM in rural areas, it may be misleading to generalize all informal ASM as criminal, or even illegal. Because some businesses or livelihood activities are simply not regulated by the state because it lacks the capacity to do so; and not because these livelihood activities are specifically prohibited by law. Yet too often, informal businesses and livelihood activities are associated with negative stereotypes such as "evasion of the rule of law, underpayment or non-payment of taxes, and as work 'underground' or 'in the shadows'" (Perry et al., 2007, pp. 21). But such negative stereotypes may be unwarranted, as the reality may be different; which is that the state, for various reasons, lacks the capacity to regulate some of the livelihood activities of its citizen. In that case, those unregulated activities may be viewed more accurately as informal, but not illegal or criminal. In Ghana, informal livelihood activities and businesses are seen at almost every corner, indicating that they are not illegal, let alone criminal. However, their wide presence does not mean that some informal activities are not criminal or illegal. However, as correctly observed by Ayelazuno and Mawuko-Yevugah (2021), this distinction should be drawn based on the specific business or income-generating activities because, some informal activities may border on serious criminal activities, such as organized crimes, tax evasion, and smuggling. Based on the distinction drawn in this book between capitalist medium-scale (CMM) galamsey and traditional artisanal mining (TAM) galamsey (Chapter 1), the former is, relatively, criminal while the latter is an informal livelihood activity.

(In)formalization seems to be the dominant state-centric theory of the enduring galamsey menace in Ghana. Research has, for example, revealed that majority of ASM operators in Ghana, estimated to be in the range between 60 and 80 per cent, operate informally, without the security of a licence (McQuilken and Hilson, 2016, p. 13). The influential factor of this situation, adherents of the (in)formalization perspective will argue, is the lack of in-depth understanding by Ghanaian policymakers and multilateral and bilateral development institutions (aid-givers) of the real nature of the ASGM industry and its operators. Without a good understanding of the problem, these policymakers lack the requisite knowledge to design effective policies of formalization. The informality of the ASGM sector of Ghana and the emergence of the galamsey menace is, therefore, the "creation" of the Ghanaian government and development aid-givers such as the World Bank (Hilson, 2013). Articulating this view, Hilson and Hilson argue that the underlying cause for the failure of the Ghanaian state to formalize the ASGM industry is the "significant discrepancy between what the Government of Ghana believes it is formalizing— namely, a sector populated by rogue, opportunistic entrepreneurs—and the largely poverty-driven ASM industry that actually exists." (Hilson and Hilson, 2015; Minerals Commission, 2022).

Because of this knowledge gap, the formalization policy frameworks designed by the Ghanaian government are not meant to serve the Ghanaian subaltern classes, who, as we argued above, are engaged in traditional artisanal mining (TAM) as an alternative and time-tested means of livelihood. The main objectives of these policies and regulations— regardless what they say on paper—are in tension with the needs of "poverty-driven ASM" (Hilson and Hilson, 2015). The registration and licencing procedures illustrate this point. The mining law requires ASM operators to register with the Minerals Commission (MinCom), which will then grant them licences to operate in specific areas designated for small-scale mining operations. However, the subaltern classes are unable to follow the bureaucratic and cumbersome procedures involved in the registration process (Kumah, 2022).

This is how cumbersome the procedures are: first, there are fourteen processes involved, including, for example, the filling of multiple forms; the payment of various fees, both legal and illegal, which can total to as much as USD1000; multiple agencies are involved in the approval of an application; the Minister of Lands and Natural Resources must sign each application; and these processes must be repeated after three or five years to renew a licence (World Bank, 2019, p. 19; Kumah, 2022, p. 5). In addition, "applicants also end up paying an assortment of bribes and making several informal payments to various landowners, which can amount to tens of thousands of cedis" (Hilson, 2013, p. 60). On paper, the licencing of ASM is decentralized to the designated MinCom district offices. But the district assemblies have no power to issue mining licences. This is done in Accra by the Minister of Lands and Natural Resources after he/she is satisfied that all procedures have been followed. Besides the long time and procedures in processing the application, applicants also have to "chase" their applications in Accra (McQuilken and Hilson, 2016, p. 21). These cumbersome procedures and the frustration they are fraught make many people to opt to operate illegally. They are "one of the major disincentives for ASM operators to go through the processes of formalization" (Aubynn 2009, p. 66). They also create opportunities for bribery and corruption, further reinforcing the informality of the ASM sector.

As discussed, in its ostensible efforts to fight the galamsey menace, the Ghanaian state recently passed a raft of policies and laws that it thinks will address the legal and policy pitfalls in the ASGM sector. However, many pieces of these laws and policies—the advocates of the (in)formalization perspective will argue—illustrate the acute lack of understanding of the galamsey problem by the Ghanaian policymakers and their development aid-givers. The Community Mining Operational Manual, as discussed, provides the step-by-step guidelines for the community mining schemes (CMS). A cursory look at the guidelines for various aspects of the scheme reveals a long red tape of highly bureaucratic and cumbersome procedures; encompassing the demarcation of a community mining area, qualification for participation in CMS, checklist of amenities that must be provided at community mining sites, the administrative system of the CMS, and procedures for acquiring a mining licence (Minerals Commission, 2022, pp. 6–17). Essentially, the guidelines, regardless of the ostensible good intentions, exclude the subaltern classes or poverty-driven operators of the industry from engaging in legal/formal ASGM. They simply lack the financial and human resources to comply with them. Indeed, the urgency of the survival imperative driving TAM does not allow time and energy to go through these costly and cumbersome procedures.

Adherents of the (in)formalization perspective will also argue that the subaltern classes have been legislated out of legal and formal ASGM. For example, one of the qualifications for participating in the CMS is that a person must demonstrate the capacity to invest a minimum capital of Ghs100, 000 in the business (Minerals Commission, 2022, p. 7). This requirement literally shuts the door on the subaltern classes, because they cannot afford even a fraction of this amount. As a result, formal ASGM will be the preserve of the educated elites, the rich, and politically connected classes who have the resources and the right connections to obtain licences to operate formally and legally (Hilson and Hilson, 2015). In these circumstances, the subaltern classes are left with no alternative, but to engage in TAM without licence, an act the state considers illegal or even criminal.

But we should bear in mind that TAM predated both the colonial and postcolonial state that started the regulation of this livelihood strategy of the people (Ofosu-Mensah, 2010, 2021). TAM is also different from the CMM in terms of the challenges of formalization noted above because, as Chapter 1 has demonstrated, it is (semi-) mechanized and (semi) industrialized mining that cannot be viewed as ASM—by any stretch of interpretation. As we will demonstrate in Chapter 6, CMM is a criminal activity by the power elites who have captured the state and are operating with impunity.

CORRUPTION PERSPECTIVE

Corruption is something that most people seem to have an idea of what it is, yet an unanimously accepted definition is elusive in the academic literature (Doig and McIvor, 1999). It is not within the scope of this book to review the voluminous literature on the definition of corruption. A few conceptions of the phenomena will suffice, starting with the popular notion of corruption in Ghana. As scholars who have been embedded in the Ghanaian society for several decades, we know what most Ghanaians view corruption to be: it denotes a dishonest behaviour of Ghanaian politicians, public servants, or the educated elites who enrich themselves and their family members by stealing the resources of the state or taking bribes for the services they are paid to provide to the public. Transparency International (TI), a global movement that fights against corruption defines corruption "as the abuse of entrusted power for private gain" (Transparency International, 2024).

Breaking down the constituent elements of the concept, TI (2024) delineated the behaviours that constitute corruption, the groups of people involved in it, and where it happens. Corrupt behaviours include:

1. public servants demanding or taking money or favours in exchange for services;
2. politicians misusing public money or granting public jobs or contracts to their sponsors, friends, and families;
3. corporations bribing officials to get lucrative deals.

The people who may be engaged in acts of corruption, according to TI (2024), are wide ranging: politicians, government officials, public servants, businesswomen/men, and members of the public. Similarly, corruption happen in major facets of society: it happens in business, government, the courts, the media, and in civil society, "as well as across all sectors from health and education to infrastructure and sports."

Based on the perspective of TI (2024), corruption, particularly involving public servants and politicians, is not only an age-old problem that has characterized the body politic of Ghana since independence. More troubling, it is widespread, systemic, and resistant to reform. Scholars, commissions of inquiries, Ghana's Auditor General reports, the press, and reports of anti-corruption civil society organizations have documented evidence of corruption involving politicians and public servants in Ghana across the period, between the dawn of independence and present; that is, between the 1950s and 2024 (Armah, 1968; Werlin, 1972; Price, 2021; LeVine, 1975; Center for Democracy and Development ([CDD-Ghana], 2022); Hasty, 2005; Agyeman, 2016;

United Nations, 2022; Harsch, 2024). Perhaps, Ayi Kwei Armah's *The Beautyful Ones Are Not Yet Born* is where the endemic and destructive nature of corruption in the immediate postcolonial era in Ghana is described vividly with literary devices. Using both fictional and real characters, he illuminates what he referred to variously as the "filth," "corruption," "bribery," "decay," and the "rot" that have engulfed the body politic of Ghana in the immediate post-independence era and during Nkrumah's government. For Ayi Kwei Armah, the acts of corruption were so repugnant, systemic, and destructive to the extent that "corruption" as a concept or term does not capture the situation fully; thus, he used "rot," "decay," "rotten," and rottenness more than "corruption" and "corrupt" (Nkansah, 2021). As one observer of the corruption described by Armah noted gloomily, "[t]here is no repentance and there is always the preparedness to seize the earliest opportunity for more looting" (Armah 1968, p. 248). Similarly, The Anin Commission Report concluded, in part, that "The devout have vanished from the land. Corruption is endemic throughout the whole society" (Kraus, 1977, p. 1242).

This picture of corruption in the immediate post-independence era does not only capture the state of corruption in Ghana across the over sixty-five years of independence, but it has become gloomier: it is more endemic, systemic, and destructive (CDD-Ghana, 2022; Hasty, 2005; Agyeman, 2016; United Nations, 2022). Corruption is so pervasive in Ghana, a supreme court judge, Justice Jones Dotse, described it as a situation where the political, bureaucratic, and business elites conspire "to create, loot and share the resources of [Ghana] as if a brigade had been set up for such an enterprise" (Ayelazuno, 2019, p. 61).

The corruption perspective of galamsey is shaped by this long history of endemic and systemic political and grand corruption revolving on the post-independence Ghanaian state. Situated in this context, the adherents of this perspective will argue the laws and policies regulating AGSM are mostly not enforced and implemented because public servants responsible for doing that rather enrich themselves by collecting bribes. Galamsey, as a serious crime in Ghana, is committed in the glare of the state institutions responsible for enforcing the laws regulating it, such as the police and the other institutions listed in Text box 2.2 (Chapter two). As one of the proponents of the corruption perspective correctly argues, it is not because of the Ghanaian state's inability to enforce the laws that explain the impunity with which the crime of galamsey is committed. But rather the intentional ambivalence of government and law enforcement agencies (Teschner, 2012, p. 312).

Using the police as an example, Teschner argues that "[t]here is plenty of evidence that police corruption may be at the heart of law enforcement lenience." (Teschner, 2012, p. 312). Corroborating Teschner's argument, Crawford and the co-authors argue that the inundation of Ghana's ASGM sector by foreigners, mostly nationals of China—in blatant disregard of the law banning foreigners from engaging in the industry—is due to bribery and corruption (Crawford et al., 2017; Drechsler, 2020). Encapsulated in the phrase "Ghana—big man, big envelope, finish," bribery and corruption is so pervasive in the ASGM sector of Ghana it has created a certain disdainful perception among foreigners about the regulatory capacity of the state. The perception is that "big men"—state officials, politicians, and traditional authorities (the chiefs)—can be bribed with "big envelopes" of cash in order to facilitate business activities, both within and outside the law' (Crawford et al., 2017, p. 71). Drawing on their fieldwork on the Shaanxi Mining (Ghana) Limited (SMGHL) and its conflicts with members of the community it is located, they argue that "rent-seeking and corruption amongst state officials and traditional authorities has enabled the company to exploit the country's mineral resources and to operate at the margins of legality, circumventing and flouting laws and regulations with relative impunity." (Crawford et al., 2017, p. 71).

The corruption perspective of the galamsey problem, therefore, illustrates the ways in which career public servants and politicians use their offices and positions to accumulate wealth in CMM by circumventing the rules and regulations governing the ASM sector. They may accumulate wealth indirectly by collecting bribes or kickbacks from foreigners, to permit them to engage in mining, contrary to the laws banning foreigners from doing so. They may also accumulate wealth directly from CMM by owning mining concessions and providing heavy equipment for workers to mine gold illegally for them. Considering the historical, systemic, and endemic nature of corruption discussed, it is unsurprising that the ASGM sector reeks of it, because the lust and allure of gold "breeds greed and is a powerful aphrodisiac that lures people to do whatever it takes to get it, regardless of the calamitous consequences that this may engender" (Ayelazuno and Aziabah 2023, p. 1).

THE NEO-PATRIMONIAL STATE PERSPECTIVE

The neo-patrimonial perspective of the enduring existence of galamsey in Ghana is an approach that has been deployed by Political Scientists and New Institutional Economists to analyze the specific form of post-colonial state that emerged in most African countries. Not only is it as old as corruption, but the latter is one of the manifestations of a neo-patrimonial state. Even though corruption happens across the world, it is in neo-patrimonial states that it is the norm rather than the exception, and it is in this form of state that corruption can be systemic and widespread in scope, as described above in Ghana. Despite its Eurocentric background and the legitimate criticisms against it by influential African scholars (see for example, Mkandawire, 2015), the neo-patrimonial state and the concepts distilled from it have dominated Political Science and New Institutionalist Economics analysis of ineffective governance and institutions in relation to development challenges in Africa. This body of work argues that neo-patrimonial characteristics typify the postcolonial state that emerged in Ghana (and in most of Africa), producing empirical evidence to illustrate a distinctive dysfunctional, pathological, and ineffective form of an African state that is not just incapable of promoting the well-being of its citizens, but worse so, in Evans' (1995) view, is predatory of its own citizens (see Ekeh, 1975; Jackson and Rosberg, 1982; Allen, 1995; Bratton and van de Walle 1997a, b; Chabal and Daloz, 1999; Sandbrook, 2000; Van de Walle, 2003; Owusu, 2006a, b; Acemoglu and Robinson, 2012; Ayelazuno, 2019).

The neo-patrimonial perspective, thus, strikes at the heart of state theory: why is the state in minerals-rich developing countries incapable of governing the ASM sector to promote sustainable development? Implicit in this question are the following questions: just what is a state? And why are some states capable of promoting development and others cannot?

In answering these questions, a great deal of the Political Science literature on the neo-patrimonial state draws on Weber's notion of the state and the characteristics of its bureaucracy: a constituent element of the state. For Weber, "states are compulsory associations claiming control over territories and people within them" (Skocpol, 1985, p. 7). Constitutive of Weber's ideal state is its institutional architecture and the qualities of the bureaucracy that they possess; or the ways in which they are shaped by ration-legal rules, rather than personalistic or particularistic norms. The ideal state is made of administrative, legal, extractive institutions (Skocpol, 1985) which should work according to the tenets of a well-developed bureaucracy: "hierarchical, career-organized, competence-based, rules-and files-based" organizational structure (Drechsler, 2020, p. 219). Emphasizing the centrality of a well-developed bureaucracy to an effective state, Rueschemeyer and Evans argue that a "[b]ureaucratic organization is the most efficient form of organizing large-scale administrative activities. The existence of extensive, internally coherent bureaucratic machinery is the first prerequisite for effective state action" (Evans and Rueschemeyer, 1985, p. 50). Despite the weaknesses of Weber's ideal bureaucracy—red tape, slowness, and over-hierarchization—it captures the qualities of a modern state that can do the needed delicate balancing of staying "above and beyond particular interests—as well as responsive—to groups and citizens, but not at the cost of the commonweal" (Drechsler, 2020, p. 220).

Proponents of the neo-patrimonial state argue that the postcolonial state that emerged in most African countries were a pale imitation of a state with well-developed bureaucratic apparatuses. While the state may have all the appearance of institutions organized on the ideals of a well-developed bureaucracy, it operates more on (neo)patrimonial virtues. This means that its bureaucratic apparatuses or the institutions are commandeered by the political leader(s) in the service of their personal interests (Bratton and van de Walle, 1997, p. 62) (1997a, b). 62). The political leader(s) and public servants are supposed to exercise legal-rational authority, but most often, they exercise power as if they are patriarchal family heads, who take decisions over and allocate resources to subordinate members of the family in any form or manner of their own choosing.

To a greater or lesser extent, a neo-patrimonial state may be characterized, for example, by partiality in the application of rules and preferential treatment of some citizens; the blurring of the distinction between public office/property and personal ones; and state-citizens relationship is characterized by patron-client relationship (Rothstein and Varraich, 2017, p. 89). These lead to a paradox of formal institutions in Ghana; namely, whereas they exist, and may even be seen to be working, informal institutions exist side-by-side with them (Johnson, 1999). These are the parallel rules based on personalistic networks—known in Ghanaian parlance as "whom you know" or "who knows you"—and rules based on bribery and corruption, which govern the behaviour of public servants and their relationship with the public, or vice versa. In Ghana, it is common knowledge—including among the political elites and middle classes—that these informal institutions work, and one may argue, they do so more effectively and efficiently than the formal ones (Chabal and Daloz, 1999).

Considering the nature of the neo-patrimonial state—particularly its personalistic tendencies—it is predestined to be burdened with various perverted practices, conceptualized in the literature variously as corruption, patronage, big men leadership, clientelism, nepotism, and prebendalism. Conceptually, these practices can be nuanced and distinguished from each other. However, they all reflect a specific form of a state that, in appearance, functions on impersonal rules; but for all intents and purposes, serves the personal interest of political leaders and top public servants. As a result, institutions of state are dysfunctional, in terms of designing and implementing policies for the public good; enforcing laws and regulations impartially; and promoting equitable access to public service by all citizens irrespective of class, ethnicity, gender, and race.

These perverted practices and the dysfunctionality they engender in a state have been documented on the postcolonial Ghanaian state in a voluminous body of literature (Price, 1974; Sandbrook and Oelbaum, 1997; Sandbrook, 2000; Booth et al., 2005; Killick, 2005). The endemic and systemic corruption in Ghana discussed above is spawned by the neo-patrimonial nature of the postcolonial Ghanaian state. Most members of the Ghanaian political class and top public servants—the big men and women—have a personalistic understanding of holding public office. For example, they believe that "resources of the political system are his[/her] personal property; loyalty to him[/her] rather than to bureaucratic norms or procedures determines official position, and there is little if any distinction between a private and a public sector" (Driscoll, 2020, pp. 521–22).

Thus, public policies, as those designed to govern the ASGM industry, are hardly about promoting the public good. They may rather serve to open opportunities for the big men/women to amass wealth; especially those involving the implementation of development projects and the procurement of goods and services. As observed by Berman, "[f]or the dominant class in Ghanaian society, just as in the precolonial era, political office and power remained the principal road to the accumulation of wealth rather than entry into commercial agriculture or business activity, which became, instead, the rewards of power rather than its source" (Berman 2003, p. 32).

Even though these neo-patrimonial practices are present across many sectors and public services in Ghana, they are arguably most blatant and disturbing in the ASGM sector. Focusing on its capacity to regulate this sector, Ayelazuno and Mawuko-Yevugah (2021, p. 567) argued that Ghana's "ASM sector is associated with various forms of neo-patrimonial practices, which are widespread, palpable, and enduring." Based on scholarly and grey literature, they documented some of these practices, which by their nature are overlapping, encompassing well-founded allegations of the power elites, including politicians and public servants, directly operating CMM galamsey; deliberate inaction by relevant state organs and officials to enforce mining laws; the invasion of the ASGM sector by foreigners, facilitated by powerful government officials and chiefs who protect them from the enforcement of the mining laws for financial and other rewards; and closely related to this, is the bribery and corruption of state officials who then collude with the power elites to facilitate CMM galamsey. The result of all these neo-patrimonial practices is a Ghanaian ASM sector that is burdened with bribery, corruption, nepotism and criminality; all of which pivot on the complicity of the political class, bureaucratic elites, and other powerful and politically well connected people (Ayelazuno and Mawuko-Yevugah 2021, p. 567).

A case in point is the blatant disobedience of the law banning foreigners from participating in ASM in Ghana. In total contempt for this law, foreigners, especially, Chinese, have participated in the ASM sector as if the law does not exist (Hilson et al. 2014; Crawford et al., 2017; Crawford and Botchwey, 2017). With the complicity of fractions of the Ghanaian state, Chinese capitalists have travelled to Ghana and are engaged in galamsey; and have done so in the full glare of state agencies responsible for enforcing the mining laws, including (but not limited to) the police and immigration officers, and local government authorities. The numbers of Chinese involvement—in tens of thousands—and their open operations in broad daylight betokens a "culture of impunity" in which "small-scale mining was being undertaken collaboratively by Chinese miners and Ghanaians in a manner that was "out of control," with little or no respect for the law, and with little application of the law by the relevant authorities" (Crawford et al. 2015, p. 53).

Ghana is celebrated as a model of electoral democracy in Africa, but paradoxically, democracy is one of the main drivers of neo-patrimonial practices in its ASMG sector. The political context for this claim is the winner-takes-all electoral system adopted in Ghana, which has led to a zero-sum game, in which the winner takes all, and the loser loses everything. This has made the Ghanaian four-yearly elections extremely competitive, with some contesters winning or losing by only a few thousand votes and fractions of percentage points in both presidential and parliamentary elections (Ayelazuno and Mawuko-Yevugah, 2021). In this context, most politicians and political leaders of Ghana often have "extremely strong incentives to focus on short-term distributive politics rather than longer-term economic accumulation" (Kelsall, 2012, p. 680); something that is inextricably linked to their fixation with winning the next election to ensure their political survival. Underpinning their quest for political office is not the implementation of long-term development policies such as the enforcement of the laws governing the ASM sector, but rather development projects which will serve their short-term, personal goals (Abdulai and Hickey, 2016): for example, strategies and plans for winning the next elections to stay in power.

Situated in this political context, the four-yearly Ghanaian presidential and parliamentary elections breed and deepen patronage and clientelist practices in the ASGM sector (Bebbington et al., 2018). The leaders of both the National Democratic Congress (NDC) and New Patriotic Party (NPP)—the two dominant parties that have won and rotated power and governments in the last three decades—have politicized the intractable problem of galamsey to promote their narrow political interests of winning votes and staying in power or to come to power. On this claim, Ayelazuno and Mawuko-Yevugah (2021) have argued that the enforcement of ASM laws and the combating of galamsey have been thoroughly politicized in Ghana, with the political elites concerned to instrumentalize them for short-term political gains: to gain electoral advantage over their opponents, rather than building a sustainable and pro-poor ASM sector. But this way of politicizing galamsey makes the political class to adopt hypocritical and self-serving, albeit ambivalent, attitudes towards solving the problem of illegal ASM. In need of votes from the operators of galamsey, the politicians, while in opposition, will promise to streamline and support their operations by easing the institutional bottlenecks to make it easier for them to operate legally. But while in power, both the NDC and NPP have failed to fulfil their promises. Indeed, rather the contrary: they have mounted military crackdowns on galamsey operators, actions that are informed by political calculus (Ayelazuno and Mawuko-Yevugah, 2021).

In fact, these military crackdowns are usually characterized by the very neo-patrimonial practices that have led to the entrenchment of illegal/ informal ASM in Ghana in the first place. Besides the collusion and complicity of state agencies and officials in illegal ASM, unscrupulous practices such as corruption, bribery, and nepotism are perpetrated by high-ranking politicians and public servants during these military crackdowns. The security personnel deployed in these exercises, as well as influential private citizens have also been accused of engaging in these unscrupulous acts. It means that not only are these neo-patrimonial practices part of the causal factors of illegal/informal ASM in Ghana, but are also the reasons why militarized enforcement are inescapable headed for failure. As amply documented by Johnson (2019), the Ghanaian state's selective use of strongarm tactics to enforce ASM laws is based on the material or political interests it wants to protect in a specific place and at a particular time. For example, electoral advantage and protection of multinational mining companies (MNCs) are two competing interests that shape the use of such violent enforcement methods. In communities where illegal mining is in conflict/competition with MNCs, the state is ruthless in the use of violent enforcement because of the revenues the state collects from MNCs and the positive international image it wants to project of itself; namely, that it complies with global norms of governance. But at places where the above conflict/competition does not exist, the state is laxed in enforcing the law because the party in power wants to gain electoral advantage by courting the support of illegal ASM operators (Johnson, 2019, p. 9). Depending on the interests the state wants to protect, it deploys violence selectively "to enforce its authority swiftly and brutally in some contexts but remains relatively indifferent to informal extraction in others" (Johnson, 2019, p. 2).

Galamsey, thus, seems to be an avenue to promise and share patronage for electoral advantage, rather than a problem to be solved in the longer term and for the public good. Conceptualized as "competitive clientelism" (Abdulai and Hickey, 2016; Whitfield, 2018; Appiah and Abdulai, 2017; Abdulai, 2017), galamsey is part of the mechanics of winning elections in Ghana by using it to establish and service a vast patron-client support networks that the politicians of NDC and NPP have created (Paller, 2019). In this sense, the promises the NDC and NPP leaders make about addressing the challenges of licencing and to facilitate the seamless operations of small-scale miners are part of the means of servicing these support networks; as such, are part of the patronage that the NDC and NPP politicians distribute to prospective voters to win their votes (Paller, 2019; Driscoll, 2023). The corollary of this is the short term and sometimes, kneejerk approaches to addressing the problem—as military crackdowns—informed all the time by the calculation of the maximum electoral or material benefits that may accrue from one approach or the other (Aubynn, 2009; Abdulai, 2017; Bebbington et al., 2018). The NDC and NPP leaders are concerned more about getting the votes of ASM operators and their dependents than enforcing the mining laws and combating galamsey.

This chapter has appropriated the work of various scholars on the Ghanaian state's unsuccessful regulation of its ASM sector to present three perspectives of what this book conceptualized as state-centric theories of the problem under study here: the emergence and persistence of the criminal and destructive ASM industry known in Ghana as galamsey. These scholars have tried to explain why, an otherwise relatively capable Ghanaian state, both autocratic and democratic, are incapable of governing its ASM sector. The three perspectives state-centric theory of understanding/explaining the problem—(in)formality, corruption, and neopatrimonialism—are by no means viewed as the only theories in this field of study. However, we see them as the dominant theories that have helped to shed light on this intractable problem. Yet we think that the unsuccessful militarized fight against galamsey between 2017 and 2024 point to a deeper hollowing out of the Ghanaian state that these theories seem to have missed. The state capture theory, we argue, advances these theories to better capture this deeper hollowing of the Ghanaian state; a task we turn to in the next chapter.

References

Abdulai, A. G., & Hickey, S. (2016). The politics of development under competitive clientelism: Insights from Ghana's education sector. *African Affairs, 115*(458), 44–72.

Abdulai, A. G. (2017). Competitive clientelism and the political economy of mining in Ghana. ESID Working Paper No. 78. Manchester, UK: The University of Manchester. www.effective-states.org

Acemoglu, D., and Robinson, J. (2012). Institutions, political economy and growth. *Nobel Prize 2012 Presentations*.

Agyeman, E. (2016). *Fighting Corruption in the Public Sector of Ghana: The Role of Assets Declaration*, Institute of Economic Affairs (IEA Ghana). Ghana. https://coilink.org/20.500.12592/srb2zf (Accessed 29 August 2024). COI: 20.500.12592/srb2zf.

Allen, C. (1995). Understanding African politics. *Review of African Political Economy*, 22(65), 301–320.

Appiah, D., and Abdulai, A. G. (2017). Competitive clientelism and the politics of core public sector reform in Ghana. Global Development Institute Working Paper Series esid-082-17, GDI, The University of Manchester.

Armah, A. K. (1968). *The beautiful ones are not yet born*. Heinemann.

Aubynn, A. (2009). Sustainable solution or a marriage of inconvenience? The coexistence of large-scale mining and artisanal and small-scale mining on the Abosso Goldfields concession in Western Ghana. *Resources Policy*, 34(1–2), 64–70.

Ayelazuno, J. A. (2019). Electoral democracy and the attenuation of subaltern resistance in Ghana: Why democracy is increasingly becoming a poisoned chalice in Africa. *Nokoko*, 7, 47–78.

Ayelazuno, J. A., & Mawuko-Yevugah, L. (2021). Between the Africa Mining Vision and the neo-patrimonial state: The agency gap in Ghana's regulation of artisanal and small-scale gold mining. *South African Journal of International Affairs*, 28(4), 555–582.

Ayelazuno, J.A. and Aziabah, M.A. (2023). Making visible the galamsey scandals in Ghana: digital media as new technologies of democratic accountability." The Extractive Industries and Society 16 (101366), 1–9.

Bebbington, A., Abdulai, A. G., Humphreys Bebbington, D., Hinfelaar, M., and Sanborn, C. (2018). *Governing Extractive Industries: Politics, Histories, Ideas.* Oxford University Press.

Berman, B. J. (2003). Capitalism incomplete: State, culture and the politics of industrialization. In W. J. Tettey, K. P. Puplampu, & B. J. Berman (Eds.), *Critical perspectives on politics and socio-economic development in Ghana* (pp. 21–44). Brill.

Booth, D., Crook, R., Gyimah-Boadi, E., Killick, T., and Luckham, R. (2005). What are the drivers of change in Ghana? CDD/ODI Policy Brief 1: 11–10. https://cdn.odi.org/media/documents/1961.pdf (Accessed 15 December 2022).

Bratton, M. and van de Walle, N. (1997). *Democratic experiments in Africa: Regime transitions in comparative perspective*. Cambridge University Press.

Bratton, M., and Van de Walle, N. (1997). *Political Regimes and Regime Transitions in Africa, 1910–1994*. Inter-University Consortium for Political and Social Research.

Bryceson, D. F. (2000). Of criminals and clients: African culture and Afro-pessimism in a globalized world. *Canadian Journal of African Studies, 34*(2), 417–442.

Center for Democracy and Development (CDD-Ghana). (2022). The Ghana Governance and Corruption Survey Evidence from Households, Enterprises and Public Officials. World Bank https://documents1.worldbank.org/cur ated/en/749401468253174124/pdf/494770WP0GH0GA10Box341953B0 1PUBLIC1.pdf (Accessed 11 December 2022).

Chabal, P., and Daloz, J.-P. (1999). *Africa Works: Disorder as Political Instrument*. Indiana University Press.

Crawford, G., Agyeyomah, C., Botchwey, G., and Mba, A. (2015). The impact of Chinese involvement in small-scale gold mining in Ghana. IGC. https://www.theigc.org/sites/default/files/2016/08/Crawford-et-al-2015-Final-Report-1.pdf(Accessed 30 December 2022)

Crawford, G., & Botchwey, G. (2017). Conflict, collusion and corruption in small-scale gold mining: Chinese miners and the state in Ghana. *Commonwealth & Comparative Politics, 55*(4), 444–470.

Crawford, G., Agyeyomah, C., & Mba, A. (2017). Ghana – Big man, big envelope, finish: Chinese corporate exploitation in small-scale mining. In B. Engels & K. Dietz (Eds.), *Contested extractivism, society and the state: Struggles over mining and land* (pp. 69–99). Palgrave Macmillan UK.

Daron Acemoglu and James A. Robinson (2012). *Why nations fail: The origins of power, prosperity, and poverty*. Crown Business.

Drechsler, W. (2020). Good bureaucracy: Max Weber and public administration today. *Max Weber Studies, 20*(2), 219–224.

Driscoll, B. (2020). Democratization, party systems, and the endogenous roots of Ghanaian clientelism. *Democratization, 27*(1), 119–136.

Driscoll, B. (2023). *Power, Patronage, and the Local State in Ghana* (Vol. 97). Ohio University Press.

Ekeh, P. (1975). Colonialism and the Two Publics in Africa: A Theoretical Statement. *Comparative Studies in Society and History, 17*(1), 91–112.

Evans P. (1995). *Embedded autonomy: States and industrial transformation*. Princeton University Press.

Evans, P. B., Rueschemeyer, D., & Skocpol, T. (Eds.). (1985). Bringing the state back in. Cambridge University Press.

Geenen, S., & Verbrugge, B. (2020). Theorizing the global gold production system. In B. Verbrugge & S. Geenen (Eds.), *Global gold production touching ground: Expansion, informalization, and technological innovation* (pp. 17–52). Palgrave Macmillan.

Gyan, A., & Behrends, A. (2024). Governing the Ungovernable? Conceptualising embeddedness in Ghana's gold mining sector. *The Extractive Industries and Society, 19*, 101484.

Harsch, E. (2024). *Corruption, class, and politics in Ghana*. Ohio University Press.

Hart, K. (1973). Informal income opportunities and urban employment in Ghana. *The journal of modern African studies*, *11*(1), 61–89.

Hasty, J. (2005). The pleasures of corruption: desire and discipline in Ghanaian political culture. *Cultural Anthropology*, *20*(2), 271–301.

Hentschel, T., Hruschka, F., and Priester, M. (2003). Artisanal and small-scale mining: Challenges and opportunities. International Institute for Environment and Development and WBCSD. https://www.iied.org/sites/default/files/pdfs/migrate/9268IIED.pdf (Accessed 9 December 2022).

Hilson, G. (2013). "Creating" Rural Informality: The Case of Artisanal Gold Mining in Sub-Saharan Africa. *SAIS Review 33*(1), 51–64.

Hilson, G. and McQuilken, J. (2014). Four decades of support for artisanal and small-scale mining in sub-Saharan Africa: a critical review. *The Extractive Industries and Society*, *1*(1), 104–118.

Hilson, G., and Hilson, A. (2015). Entrepreneurship, poverty and sustainability: Critical reflections on the formalisation of small-scale mining in Ghana (Working Paper E-33112-GHA-1). International Growth Centre. https://www.theigc.org/wp-content/uploads/2015/04/Hilson-Hilson-2015-Working-Paper.pdf (Accessed 10 December 2022).

Hilson, G., & Maconachie, R. (2017). Formalising artisanal and small-scale mining: insights, contestations and clarifications. *Area*, *49*(4), 443–451.

Hilson, G., Hilson, A., & Adu-Darko, E. (2014). Chinese participation in Ghana's informal gold mining economy: Drivers, implications and clarifications. *Journal of Rural Studies*, *34*, 292–303.

Intergovernmental Forum on Mining, Minerals, Metals and Sustainable Development (IGF). (2017). Global Trends in Artisanal and Small-Scale Mining (ASM): A review of key numbers and issues. Winnipeg: IISD. https://www.iisd.org/system/files/publications/igf-asm-global-trends.pdf(Accessed 22 December 2022).

Jackson, R. H., & Rosberg, C. G. (1982). Why Africa's weak states persist: The empirical and the juridical in statehood. *World politics*, *35*(1), 1–24.

Johnson, M. F. (2019). Who governs here? Informal resource extraction, state enforcement, and conflict in Ghana. *Global Environmental Change*, *58*(101959), 1–11.

Kelsall, T. (2012). Neo-patrimonialism, rent-seeking and development: Going with the grain?. *New political economy*, *17*(5), 677–682.

Killick, T. (2005). The politics of Ghana's budgetary system. CDD/ODI Policy Brief 2: 1–6. https://cdn.odi.org/media/documents/1963.pdf (Accessed 15 December 2022).

Kumah, R. (2022). Artisanal and small-scale mining formalization challenges in Ghana: Explaining grassroots perspectives. *Resources Policy*, *79*, 102978.

Le Vine, V. (1975). Corruption in Ghana. *Transition*, (47), 48–61.

McQuilken, J., and Hilson, G. (2016). Artisanal and small-scale gold mining in Ghana. In: *Evidence to Inform an 'Action Dialogue'. IIED, London.*

Mkandawire, T. (2015). Neopatrimonialism and the political economy of economic performance in Africa: Critical reflections. *World Politics*, *67*(3), 563–612.

Nkansah, S. K. (2021). Corpus assisted approach to Armah's the Beautyful Ones Are Not Yet Born. *KENTE-Cape Coast Journal of Literature and the Arts*, *2*(1), 27–40.

Ofosu-Mensah, A. (2021). Transformation of Artisanal Small -Scale Mining (ASM) in Ghana: From Pre-Colonial to the Modern Era. *The Journal of African Policy Studies*, *27*(1), 57–94.

Owusu, F. (2006a). On public organizations in Ghana: what differentiates good performers from poor performers?. *African Development Review*, *18*(3), 471–485.

Owusu, M. (2006b). *Uses and abuses of political power: A case study of continuity and change in the politics of Ghana.* Ghana University Press.

Ofosu-Mensah. E. (2010). Traditional gold mining in Adanse. *Nordic Journal of African Studies*, *19*(2), 124–147.

Paller, J. W. (2019). Dignified public expression: A new logic of political accountability. *Comparative Politics*, *52*(1), 85–116.

Perry, G. E., Maloney, W. F., Arias, O. S., Fajnzylber, P., Mason, A. D., and Saavedra-Chanduvi, J. (2007). *Informality: Exit and Exclusion.* Washington, DC: The World Bank.

Price, R. (1974). Politics and culture in contemporary Ghana: The big-man small-boy syndrome. *Journal of African Studies*, *1*(2), 173.

Price, R. M. (2021). *Society and bureaucracy in contemporary Ghana.* University of California Press.

Rodríguez-Novoa, F., & Holley, E. (2023). Coexistence between large-scale mining (LSM) and artisanal and small-scale mining (ASM) in Perú and Colombia. *Resources Policy*, *80*, 103162.

Rothstein, B., & Varraich, A. (2017). *Making sense of corruption.* Cambridge University Press.

Sandbrook, R. (2000). *Closing the circle: Democratisation and development in Africa.* Zeds Books Ltd.

Sandbrook, R., & Oelbaum, J. (1997). Reforming dysfunctional institutions through democratisation? Reflections on Ghana. *The Journal of Modern African Studies*, *35*(4), 603–646.

Skocpol, T. (1985). Bringing the state back in: Strategies of analysis in current research. In: Evans, P., Rueschemeyer, D., Skocpol, T. (Eds.), *Bringing the State Back in.* Cambridge University Press, Cambridge, pp. 3–43.

Teschner, B. A. (2012). Small-scale mining in Ghana: The government and the galamsey. *Resources Policy*, *37*(3), 308–314.

The Minerals Commission. (2022, October 3). Re-alleged operations of Akonta Mining Ltd in Tano Nimri Forest Reserve [Press release]. https://www.min com.gov.gh/wp-content/uploads/2022/10/Alleged-Operations-of-Akonta-Mining-Ltd.pdf (Accessed 5 January 2023).

Transparency International [IT]. (2024). What is corruption. https://www.tra nsparency.org/en/what-is-corruption (Accessed 18 August 2024).

Transparency International. (2022). What is corruption? https://www.transpare ncy.org/en/what-is-corruption (Accessed 11 December 2022).

United Nations. (2022). *Corruption in Ghana—People's experiences and views.* Vienna: United Nations Office on Drugs and Crime (UNODC) https://www.unodc.org/documents/corruption/Publications/2022/GHANA_-_Corruption_survey_report_-_20.07.2022.pdf (Accessed 11 December 2022).

Van de Walle, N. (2003). Presidentialism and clientelism in Africa's emerging party systems. *The Journal of Modern African Studies*, *41*(2), 297–321.

Verbrugge, B. (2015). The economic logic of persistent informality: artisanal and small-scale mining in the southern Philippines. *Development and Change*, *46*(5), 1023–1046.

Verbrugge, B., and Geenen, S. (Eds.). (2020). *Global gold production touching ground: Expansion, informalization, and technological innovation.* Springer Nature.

Werlin, H. H. (1972). The roots of corruption–The Ghanaian enquiry. *The Journal of Modern African Studies*, *10*(2), 247–266.

Whitfield, L. (2018). *Economies after colonialism: Ghana and the struggle for power.* Cambridge University Press.

World Bank (2019). *2019 State of the artisanal and small-scale mining sector* World Bank.

World Bank. (2023). *2023 State of the artisanal and small-scale mining sector.* World Bank.

Zabyelina, Y., & van Uhm, D. (2020). The new Eldorado: Organized crime, informal mining, and the global scarcity of metals and minerals. In Y. Zabyelina & D. van Uhm (Eds.), *Illegal mining: Organized crime, corruption, and ecocide in a resource-scarce world* (pp. 3–30). Springer International Publishing. https://doi.org/10.1007/978-3-030-46327-4_1

State Capture and Illegal Artisanal and Small-Scale Gold Mining (ASGM)

Abstract This chapter is the theoretical core of the book. We deploy state capture theory to advance the state-centric theories used to explain illegal artisanal and small-scale gold mining (ASGM) in Ghana and beyond. The central question we address—both theoretical and political in nature—is, why has galamsey, particularly illegal capitalist medium-scale mining (CMM galamsey), persisted and even flourished despite repeated efforts by the Ghanaian state to stop it? More specifically, why has CMM galamsey exacerbated between 2017 and 2024 despite the Ghanaian President's vow to eradicate it, even at the cost of his presidency? We argue that state capture can address these questions fully and more persuasively. Yet to the best of our knowledge, state capture has rarely been deployed to explain the governance failures in the natural resources governance sector of Ghana. Acts or omissions bordering on state capture are often treated merely as a form of political or grand corruption. In this chapter, however, we posit that state capture depicts a deeper, systemic institutional paralysis than the abuse of office by unscrupulous public servants or politicians, or a group of them. In a captured state, even its most powerful and coercive organs—such as the military and the police—are ineffective when confronted by the influence and power of the elite classes, organizations, and individuals. What defines a captured state is not where corruption or criminal influence occurs—whether in the design of policy/regulation or the implementation of them. It is rather the extent to which the capacity of the state has been hollowed out that distinguishes state capture from other perversions of the state. The capacity of a captured state is deeply hallowed it is no longer a provider of public service and goods. Its institutions and their functions are often repurposed from serving public good to serving the power elites, both within and outside the state. To understand the depth of the paralysis of the Ghanaian state in the fight against CMM galamsey—to such an extent that even the presidency and the military have failed—state capture theory offers a critical analytical lens. State capture theory is better equipped with the analytical tools to probe and expose the deeper hollowing of the state and the entrenched governance failures in the Ghanaian ASGM sector. The chapter draws on the state-of-the-art literature and the empirical case of South Africa to provide the analytical tools to analyze state capture in the failed militarized fight against CMM galamsey in Ghana.

Keywords Ghana · South Africa · State capture · Power-elites · Shadow state · Kleptocracy · Regulatory capture · Repurposing the state

State capture is the theory we propose to advance the state-centric theories on illegal artisanal and small-scale gold mining (ASGM) in Ghana and beyond. The question that this theory addresses—at once theoretical and political—is, why has galamsey, particularly illegal capitalist medium-scale mining (CMM galamsey), persisted and flourished despite efforts by the Ghanaian state to stop it? More specifically, why has CMM galamsey exacerbated between 2017 and 2024 despite the Ghanaian President/Head-of-State's vow to eradicate it at the cost of his presidency? We argue that state capture holds promise to address these questions fully and more persuasively.

In Ghana, state capture has recently (circa, 2023 and 2024) entered the political discourses of the country; perhaps, publicized widely by the Member of Parliament (MP) for North Tongu, Hon. Samuel Okudzeto Ablakwa. In his exposés on political corruption, particularly the sale of public land and properties, he deploys the discursive power of state capture to demonstrate the direct enabling of these alleged corruption scandals by top Ghanaian government officials, as well as whom the alleged beneficiaries are. Mostly, they are the same high government officials and their cronies. But in the academic literature, to date—and to the best of our knowledge—state capture has not been deployed to explain the poor quality of governance and the aggravation of political corruption in Ghana. In the specific case of natural resource governance, and the intractable problem of the worsening galamsey menace, we are not aware of any work that deploys the insights of state capture to understand and address this problem.

In this book, we hope to draw on the insights of state capture to shed greater light on why the Ghanaian state has failed to control, let alone eliminate CMM galamsey—especially between 2017 and 2024—including the deployment of military swoops to do so. State capture, in our view, is more illuminating of the CMM galamsey problem than the other state-centric theories discussed in the preceding chapter. This argument, one must hasten to add—and at the risk of sounding repetitive—should be situated in the context of the environmentally exacerbating CMM galamsey, despite the vow of the Ghanaian President to fight it at the cost of his presidency. In pursuit of the fulfilment of his vow, he deployed the most powerful coercive organ of the state, the Ghana Armed Forces (GAF), to do the fighting.

We argue that a deeper understanding and convincing explanation of this puzzle may be impossible if we rely on the lessons of the related and broad notions of corruption, neopatrimonialism, clientelism, patronage, and particularism (Rothstein and Varraich, 2017, p. 9). To be sure, all these—conceptually and empirically—throw light on the morbid symptoms of a deeply perverted form of a Ghanaian state and its poor quality of governance. But there is the need to drill down to the depth to which the capacity of this state has been so deeply atrophied by these perversions, to such an extent that the two most powerful organs of the Ghanaian state, the presidency and the military, have failed to win the war the former declared against galamsey, and deployed the latter to fight it. On this, state capture theory offers a critical analytical lens; because, and to reemphasize, it is better equipped with the analytical tools to probe and amplify the deeper hollowing of the state and the entrenched governance failures in the Ghanaian ASGM sector.

State Capture: What Is It?

State capture is relatively a young state theory (Rothstein and Varraich, 2017, p. 94), and like many social phenomena and their theories, they are always contested. But social science concepts usually (or should ideally) reflect the phenomena they seek to capture in the real world (Goertz, 2006). The common imagination of anything that is captured is the arrest and detention of that thing, thereby disabling it, regardless of how powerful it may be. The state is the most powerful entity in any national society, a leviathan in Thomas Hobbes' formulation. If this powerful creature is under the control of a group of people or a class—the powerful elites in society—it becomes malleable to their personal interests. This malleability can reach a degree that the state loses its awesome powers and great autonomy, and is, thus, literally captured; as when a soldier is captured by an enemy army. This means, rather than a leviathan, the state is weak and dysfunctional in relation to its captors, usually the powerful elites of society. It becomes something worse than a "lame leviathan" (Callaghy, 1987), in terms of the power and autonomy of the state to function in the interest of the public good. Being so disempowered and malleable to the interests, whims, and caprices of the power elites, the state becomes a leviathan caged in an iron cell. It is extremely incapacitated to exercise its powers over—and autonomy in relation to—its captors: the power elites in society.

The law enforcement and military metaphors used above, in our view, magnify the worst form of lethargy a captured state is characterized; because of the cumulative and deadening weight of various forms of morbidities: corruption, neopatrimonialism, clientelism, patronage, and particularism (Rothstein and Varraich 2017, p. 9). Kleptocracy, as will be discussed later, is perhaps the worst state of mobidity that draws closer to state capture, in the ways in which the vast network of kleptocratic actors within and outside the state, seize control of its apparatuses to serve their political and economic interests (Chayes, 2017). For this book, and with respect to the governance of the ASGM sector in Ghana, the cumulative effect of all these pathologies of the state has configured a captured form of the Ghanaian state, which is at its highest degree of dysfunctionality and the poorest level of quality of governance. It has been captured by the power mining-elites, within and outside the state, and is incapacitated to govern the ASGM sector in the public interest, as envisaged by the African Mining Vision.

The treatises on state capture often present it as a different form of political or grand corruption. As schematically illustrated by Rothstein and Varraich (2017) with their umbrella concept of corruption, state capture is one of the variants of corruption that revolves on the malfeasances, malpractices, unscrupulous acts, and abuses of public office by topmost government officials to enrich themselves and their cronies. For the foregoing authors, corruption is the concept that encompasses all other related concepts like clientelism, patronage, state capture, and patrimonialism. All these have serious negative effects on quality of governance and service delivery to citizens, because "the rules of the democratic system are systematically biased so as not to favour any general or public interest but instead various private interests" (Rothstein and Varraich, 2017, p. 15).

This notion of state capture as a form of corruption is also espoused by Hellman et al. (2000), a paper which has attained the status of pioneering work on state capture (see also, Hellman et al., 2003; Hellman and Kaufmann, 2018). In this work, they set out to unbundle "state capture" from other forms of corruptions such as procurement and administrative corruption (Hellman et al. 2000). They conceptualize and theorize state capture by situating it in the political and economic context of the post-communist Eastern European and the former Soviet Union countries. Their definition of state capture, alongside the distinction they draw between it and other forms of corruption, are based on the relationship between firms/private actors and the state, as well as the distributions of rents between the former and the latter. In their oft-cited definition of state capture, they argue it connotes the "shaping or the formation of the basic rules of the game (i.e. laws, rules, decrees and regulations) through illicit and non-transparent private payments to public official" (Hellman et al., 2000, p. 2). In contrast, administrative corruption is "the attempts by individuals and firms to alter the implementation of laws, policies and regulations to their benefit through the provisions of illicit private gains to public officials" (Hellman and Kaufmann, 2018, p. 2).

Situated in the above-mentioned context, Hellman et al. (2003, p. 752) observed that "after only a decade of transition, the fear of the leviathan state has been replaced by a new concern about powerful oligarchs who manipulate politicians and shape institutions to advance and protect their own empires at the expense of the social interest." They measure state capture based on the interaction between the state (mainly politicians occupying political office) and the firms (the captors), checking for the leverage of the latter over the politicians and public officials responsible for forming rules and regulations governing the economy.

State capture crystallizes, in their view, when firms use various forms of leverage to get the state "to intervene in the economy and distribute regulatory and legal advantages to them" (Hellman et al., 2003, p. 755). The leverage of firms may be based on "size, ownership ties to the state, control over labor, and the economic impact on their local communities which affects the well-being of potential voters and consequently electoral outcomes" (Hellman et al., 2003, pp. 755–56). It may also be based on "illicit and non-transparent private payments to public officials, leading to a collusion between them and these public officials. A collusion in which the politician uses political power to provide rents to firms in return for private economic gains, which further his political or economic objectives" (Hellman et al., 2003, p. 756).

Formulated and propounded this way, Hellman and his co-authors sought to draw a distinction between state capture and administrative/procurement corruption. The latter ones are aimed at influencing the implementation of policy, in which market players such as firms pay bribes to government officials to skew the implementation of policies to their advantage; or they pay kickbacks to influence the award of contracts in their favour. In the case of state capture, the emphasis is on the forming or formulation of rules, regulations, and policies. This means influencing the design of institutions—the contents of legislation, rules, laws, decrees, or regulations—to align them closely with the servicing of the interests of the influencer-firms, rather than the interests of the public.

Making a similar distinction, Rothstein and Varraich (2017, p. 15) note that state capture is corruption that "takes place on the input side of the political system, unlike other types of corruption that occur at the output side. That means, from the start, the rules, regulations, laws, and policies are made in favour of the captors; and for that matter, corruption, rent-seeking, nepotism, clientelism, and any form of quid pro quo exchanges are not critical to the power elites' goal of getting the state to do their bidding." In this sense, state capture, as observed by Dávid-Barrett (2023, p. 225), involves changes of laws and institutions; and because of this, "it shapes the rules of the game under which the whole society must operate, with a much wider and longer-lasting impact than forms of corruption that simply distort one-off transactions." In addition, state capture often involves "deliberate decisions by firms, but most other forms of corruption may be extortion" (Hellman et al., 2003, p. 769), as the firms and other private actors are compelled to pay bribes or kickbacks to facilitate their businesses or get the services they need from public officials.

State Capture Is Different from Regulatory Capture

A closely related, albeit different, theory to state capture is "regulatory capture." Indeed, the seminal work of Hellman and their co-authors on state capture was based on it (Hellman and Kaufmann, 2018, p. 20). But regulatory capture concerns mainly with the regulatory function of the state: the intervention of the state in the economy to regulate the activities of industries and service providers (Dal Bó, 2006; Novak, 2013). So, regulatory capture focuses on regulatory institution/s of the state and their inability to act because of the powerful influence on them by the regulated organizations. In this way, the latter then operate freely with little or no regulation. In the oft-cited formulation of the Chicago School's Economist, George Stigler, "as a rule, regulation is acquired by the industry and is designed and operated primarily for its benefit" (Novak, 2013, p. 26). Rather than being regulated by the state, Stigler suggests that the industry to be regulated rather manipulates the regulatory organs to serve its interest.

From Political Science perspective, Samuel Huntington is reputed as the pioneer of this theory, a reputation based on his analysis of the regulatory work of the Interstate Commerce Commission (ICC) of the USA (Huntington, 1952). He deploys the nutrition metaphor of "marasmus" in the title of his article to capture the decline and loss of vitality of the ICC as a regualatory body. The marasmus, which represents the state of stunting, wasting, or malnourishment—all related to hunger or malnutrition—represents the ways in which the regulatory capacity of the ICC has atrophied drastically because of the influence of powerful special interest groups. In the reading of Novak (2013, p. 27), Huntington deployed this metaphor to capture the "infectious influence of pervasive railroad interest in almost every aspect of ICC policymaking."

So powerfully influenced, Huntington argues that the ICC has lost the key prerequisite of a regulatory body, which is autonomy. This is the quality that invests the ICC, or any other regulatory body, with objectivity and impartiality. Having lost its autonomy through the overwhelming influence of the regulated organizations, the state regulator becomes powerless and useless. This, according to Huntington, was what happened to the ICC, so he advocated for it to be scrapped.

However, despite the similarity between state capture and regulatory capture, the former is broader in scope; and the capturing is not limited to the regulatory functions of the state. It encompasses other core functions of the state, and the modalities of capture are also far-reaching in scope and depth (Dávid-Barrett, 2023, p. 227).

State Capture and the Disabling of State Capacity

The capacity of the state to function effectively as such—for example, to perform its administrative, coercive, taxation, service delivery, and regulatory functions—should determine whether a state is captured by one class or the other to serve its interests. When so captured, the state is seriously incapacitated to function—for example, keeping law and order—in the public interests. This, in our view, brings out the light and shade of state capture as something distinct from corruption. State capture has to do with systemic institutional paralysis, a deeper perversion of the state than the unscrupulous behaviour of public servants or politicians, or a group of them, who abuse their offices to serve their personal interests. In a captured state, even the highest state/public officials and organs of state, charged with the responsibilities of leadership—including the responsibility to check corruption and other abuses of public offices— are all incapacitated to act when confronted with these abuses.. Indeed, if a state is captured, even its most powerful and coercive organs as the military and the police are incapacitated to act when confronted with criminal acts of the influential and powerful elite classes, organizations, or individuals.

But the distinction between state capture and other forms of corruption seems not to place emphasis on the differential impact the influence of power elites has on the incapacitation of the state to act in the public good; rather than serving the selfish interests of the power elites. If this is the distinguishing factor, then whichever end of the spectrum—between policymaking and implementation—that the corrupting influence takes place will not be the determining factor in state capture. The common denominator in state capture, we think, is the disabling of the state to function and serve the public good, regardless of where the corruption or corrupting influence happens in the spectrum between policy/regulation formation and implementation.

But as already discussed, it appears the main distinction between state capture and other forms of corruption is often based on the policymaking end of the spectrum. Essentially, if the public officials are influenced to design the rules of the game to serve the interests of the influencers-class/-individual, it is state capture. But if they are influenced to manipulate the implementation of the rules and regulations to serve the interests of the influencers-class/-individual, then it is a different form of corruption: for example, administrative or procurement corruption. Emphasizing on this, Hellman and Kaufmann (2018, p. 2) in their submission to the State Capture Commission (SCC) of South Africa argued that it is "not the size of the bribe nor the level in the political system where the bribery occurs, but rather whether the corruption is directed to distort the intended implementation of laws or to shape the formation of the laws themselves."

It is on this distinction that the intervention of Dávid-Barrett (2023) is timely and serves to advance the theory of state capture. Rather than limiting state capture to the conventional domain of analysis discussed, Dávid-Barrett pushed the boundaries to include two more domains: the "implementation of policy" and "accountability ecosystem" (emphasis original). Conceptualized as "a three-pronged approach" to state capture, the policy implementation prong of state capture has been defined as the control of policy implementation by the influencers-class/-individuals "largely through appointments or budgetary allocations to state-owned enterprises, the civil service, and quasi-independent regulatory bodies; this equates to agency capture" (Dávid-Barrett, 2023, p. 228). On accountability ecosystem state capture, it is about the control by the influencers-class/-individual of "formal checks and balances such as the judiciary and the supreme audit institution, as well as the broader civil society space including the media" (Dávid-Barrett, 2023, p. 228).

The additional domains and mechanisms of state capture provided by Dávid-Barrett (2023) point to different areas of the function of the state that are disabled or incapacitated when a state is captured. This makes the incapacitation of some organs of state or the state in general by the corrupting influence of the power elites the most important factor in state capture. In this sense, regardless of which end of the spectrum of policymaking and implementation that it happens, or of which level in the hierarchy of the organization of government it happens, or who the influencers-class/-individual are, state capture reflects the debilitating effect of the influence or control on the capacity and functionality of the state in specific spheres of its functions: administrative, service provision, extractive, regulatory and coercive functions. Functions, which in the ideal state, should serve the public good, not the narrow, selfish interest of the power elites.

As correctly noted, the concept and mechanisms of state capture "allows us to pinpoint how institutions are sometimes systematically and intentionally weakened, in order to facilitate kleptocracy" (Dávid-Barrett, 2023, p. 231). And we should hasten to add, to facilitate all the other perversions of the state—nepotism, neopatrimonialism, clientelism, cronyism, and prebendalism—which incapacitate the state to function in the interests of the public. But among these perversions, kleptocracy is the closest facsimile of state capture.

Kleptocracy, like state capture, demonstrates the worse form of the pathology of the state in which its apparatuses are commandeered by a network of political and other elite classes to serve their economic and political interests; and doing so with political protection from those in control of the reins of state. A state under a kleptocratic regime "is controlled and run for the benefit of an individual, or a small group, who use their power to transfer a large fraction of society's resources to themselves" (Acemoglu et al., 2004, p. 163). In this sense, analyses of kleptocracy often focus on "how state institutions are set up to allow elites and their families to systematically loot, while protecting these elites politically" (Cooley and Sharman, 2018, p. 39). As the study of Sara Chayes in Honduras and elsewhere illustrates, in states under kleptocratic regime, corruption is baked into the functioning of the institutions of such states, and forms "the operating system of sophisticated networks that link together public and private sectors and out-and-out criminals—including killers—and whose main objective is maximizing returns for network members" (Chayes, 2017, pp. 3–4). In this connotation, kleptocracy, unlike state capture, does not need influencers-class/-individuals to incapacitate the functioning of the state as the provider of public good. But by its nature and purpose, the state is, nevertheless, disabled by kleptocracy; because the state is used by the kleptocrats to serve their own interests and the vast network of complicitous actors they have established both within and transnationally, "to assist in camouflaging their financial flows and polishing their reputations" (Cooley and Sharman, 2018, p. 40).

For state capture, we argue that the emphasis should be placed on the deeper extent of the incapacitation of the state to function in the interest of the public good; either because of the illegal and criminal influence by private actors on the state or its control from within by kleptocratic political elites. In both instances, the cumulative effect is the extreme lethargy of the state to function in relation to serving the public good—especially, to promote the well-being of the subaltern classes. Fine-grained empirical analysis of state capture, for example, in South Africa, illustrates this incapacity as the main measurement of the phenomenon.

LESSONS OF STATE CAPTURE FROM SOUTH AFRICA

At this juncture, we turn to South Africa for lessons on state capture. In Sub-Saharan Africa, it is South Africa under President Jacob Zuma that state capture has been reinterpreted and deployed to analyze the distinct form of state—the shadow state—witnessed in this era. A brief background to this will establish the context of state capture under President Zuma.

The Gupta family's (Atul, Ajay and Rajesh Gupta) relationship with senior government officials and President Zuma himself and his family bear all the hallmarks of state capture and kleptocracy discussed above (see Myburgh, 2017; Shai, 2017). The evidence supporting this claim is overwhelming and well-documented by various authoritative sources. For example, the Zondo Commission or State Capture Commission (SCC) reports of how a high court determined there was prima facie evidence to show the relationship between President Zuma and the Gupta family evolved into state capture, "underpinned by the Gupta family having power to influence the appointment of Cabinet Ministers and directors in boards of State-Owned Enterprises (SOEs), and leveraging these relationships to get preferential treatment in state contracts, access to state-provided business finance and the award of business licences" (February and Mirzoyev, 2024, p. 17; see also Myburgh, 2017).

But the powerful influence of the Gupta family over the South African state is not reflected only in the appointment of cabinet ministers. It is also refracted through the impunity with which they breached the security protocol of South Africa in pursuit of their profligate lifestyles, which is evocative of the flamboyancy of the network of actors in a kleptocratic regime. They illegally landed a civilian plane carrying 200 wedding guests at a military airbase in Waterkloof, in April 2013. The passengers in the plane were guests and relatives of the Gupta brothers, coming from India to South Africa to attend an extravagant wedding of their niece (February and Mirzoyev, 2024, p. 11; Harding, 2015). This was a blatant breach of a sensitive security facility, but nobody was punished because, it is alleged that President Zuma authorized it. Even though he denied this, the events that followed seem to lend credence to the allegation. For example, his chief of protocol and two air force officials who were charged for offences connected to the security breach were set scot-free because the charges were quietly dropped. Indeed, the president's chief of protocol was rewarded with an ambassadorial appointment to the Netherlands (February and Mirzoyev, 2024, p. 11; see also Harding, 2015).

The Shadow State in the State Capture of South Africa

State capture in South Africa has spawned a voluminous body of work, both scholarly and grey, analyzing the phenomenon, with many good lessons distilled for understanding and analysing state capture elsewhere: for example, in Ghana. As the engagement with this oeuvre will illustrate, state capture is different from corruption as we know it because of one distinct property: the incapacitation of the state to function as a formal state, with high quality of governance (that is the delivery of services to citizens and the promotion of public good). As observed by one authoritative source, "[w]hile political corruption is not new in post-apartheid South Africa, the ten-year Zuma administration marked a shift from political corruption in the form of kickbacks and contracts for relatives to a more structural pattern of systematic state capture pursued with impunity" (Bracking, 2018, p. 169). Drawing on the distinction between what Sarah Chayes argued as political corruption that has led to the criminalization of the state and a corresponding deterioration of security, Bracking (2018, p. 170) reminds us that "the case of South Africa is not one of state capture by a criminal network, but an 'insider political project' at work to repurpose state institutions to suit a constellation of rent-seeking networks."

In a research report on the South African case (Bhorat et al., 2017; Friedenstein, 2017), henceforth, referred to as *How South Africa is being stolen*—which was later turned to a book (Chipkin and Swilling, 2018)— Haroon Bhorat and their co-authors advanced the theory of state capture by operationalizing the key conceptual apparatuses that constitute the building blocks of this theory. And for our purpose here, the clarity and nuances that they brought to these concepts help to map out the contours of state capture in the ASGM sector of Ghana, as well as the key actors involved. They drew a clear distinction between corruption and state capture. State capture, according to *How South Africa is being stolen*, is different from systemic or endemic corruption of the type discussed above in Ghana. This is because, in the case of state capture, the unscrupulous acts—the malfeasance and malpractices—of political and public office-holders subvert the autonomy of the state to the extent that, it equates to literally handing it over into the hands of the powerful elite classes to use it the way they want. It is this high level of the disabling of the state that is conceptualized as "de facto silent coup" in *How South Africa is being stolen* (Bhorat et al. 2017: 3). Their report note that "[w]hile corruption is widespread at all levels and is undermining development, state capture is a far greater, systemic threat. It is akin to a silent coup and must, therefore, be understood as a political project that is given a cover of legitimacy by the vision of radical economic transformation" (Bhorat et al., 2017, p. 4). The foregoing authors then define state capture as "systemic and well-organized by people with established relations...The focus is not on small-scale looting, but on accessing and redirecting rents away from their intended targets into private hands. To succeed, this needs high-level political protection, including from law enforcement agencies, intense loyalty and a climate of fear; and competitors need to be eliminated" (Bhorat et al., 2017, p. 5). In this sense, the main purpose of the state—to promote the public good with its powers—is completely eviscerated.

This perverting of the state is conceptualized by *How South Africa is being stolen* as repurposing state institutions: "the organised process of reconfiguring the way in which a given state institution is structured, governed, managed and funded so that it serves a purpose different to its formal mandate" (Bhorat et al., 2017, p. 5). The repurposing of institutions, as Haroon Bhorat and their co-authors explain, is not meant only to accumulate wealth. It serves many purposes, key among them, is to consolidate "political power to ensure longer-term survival, the maintenance of a political coalition, and its validation by an ideology that masks private enrichment by reference to public benefit" (Bhorat et al., 2017, p. 5).

With the state repurposed, two forms of state exist side-by-side: the ideal "Weberian state" that functions based on legal-rational rules and the "shadow state" that is based on "well-organized clientelistic and patronage networks." This configures a parasitic relationship between the two, in which "the latter feeds off the former in ways that sap vitality from formal institutions and leave them empty shells incapable of executing their responsibilities" (Bhorat et al., 2017, p. 4). This means that, and as illustrated by the main theories of state capture discussed above, the capture does not only happen at the stage of the formulation of public policy, but can happen in the implementation of these policies with the emergence of the shadow state on one hand, and on the other, the dysfunctionality of the formal state.

The chief actors in the formation of a captured state and the beneficiaries of its dysfunctionality are the unscrupulous public and political officeholders of the constitutionally defined state and the "power elite." The definition of the "power elite" in South Africa by *How South Africa is being stolen* captures accurately a similar class and captors of the state in Ghana's ASGM sector. It is "a relatively well-structured network of actors located in government, state institutions, SOEs [state-owned enterprises], private businesses, security agencies, traditional leaders, family networks and the governing party" (Bhorat et al., 2017, p. 5). The cardinal characteristic of members of this class is their "direct (and even indirect) access (either consistently or intermittently) to the inner sanctum of power to influence decisions" (Bhorat et al. 2017: 5–6).

Essentially, the "power elite" is a class whose members are not just capitalists or firms seeking to facilitate the accumulation of super-profits by bribing public officials. Instead, it is a blend of powerful people in society, including public officials (especially the senior-most in the hierarchy of ranks) and in the private sector. But all members of the power elites share the same interest: to create a shadow state to serve their variegated interests. This class is, therefore, distinct from the lower classes—what we refer to as the subaltern classes—who are powerless politically because they do not have access to the powerful politicians and topmost public servants to influence decisions or get favours. Nor do they have material wealth, the source of power of some fractions of the power elite, namely the capitalist class. So, not only is there gaping inequality between the power elite and the subaltern classes in material wealth; but there is also, and perhaps, a bigger and gaping inequality between them in political power and influence.

The class division and dynamics at play in the theory of state capture are not the typical Marxist approach to class. In this case, the class relations and power are not based on relations of production between the capitalist class and the proletariat in the organization of (re)production. Rather, the class relations in this formulation draw closer to the social stratification school of class in sociology. That is the division of people into the elite class and the other classes below it, based on the status they occupy in the hierarchical stratification of society. A stratification based on the unequal distribution and possession of resources, privileges, power, and the domination over other classes (Scott, 2007).

In conclusion, this chapter serves as the theoretical core of the book, in which we engage critically with the literature on corruption, state capture, and other related perversions and pathologies of the state. While state capture is often treated as a form of corruption or subsumed under corruption—viewed as the umbrella concept and phenomenon—we argue that what distinguishes state capture is the great extent of the incapacitation of the state to serve the public interest and promote the well-being of all citizens, especially the subaltern classes. At issue in a captured state is not where corruption occurs, whether in policy/regulation design or in their implementation. What matters most is how deeply incapacitated the state is to render public services to promote the wellbeing of citizens. Because its core functions have been thoroughly repurposed, with state institutions becoming tools for advancing the servicing of the interests of the power elites, both within and outside government. The case of of South Africa under President Zuma exemplifies this. It illustrates quintessential state capture, which is centred on President Zuma and his family's ties to the Gupta family, as well as a sprawling network of actors within and outside government. The chapter draws on cutting-edge literature and the South African example to offer analytical tools to analyze state capture in the failed militarized fight against illegal and capitalist medium-scale mining (CMM galamsey) in Ghana.

REFERENCES

Acemoglu, D., Verdier, T., and Robinson, J. A. (2004). Kleptocracy and divide-and-rule: A model of personal rule. Journal of the European Economic Association, 2(2–3): 162–192.

Bhorat, H., Buthelezi, M., Chipkin, I., Duma, S., Mondi, L., Peter, C., ... and Friedenstein, H. (2017). Betrayal of the promise: how South Africa is being stolen. State Capacity Research Project, 1–72.

Bhorat, H., Buthelezi, M., Chipkin, I., Duma, S., Mondi, L., Peter, C., Qobo, M., Swilling, M., and Bracking, S. (2018). Corruption & state capture: What can citizens do? Daedalus, 147(3), 169–183. https://doi.org/10.1162/daed_a_00509

Callaghy, T. M. (1987). The state as lame Leviathan: The patrimonial administrative state in Africa. In Z. Ergas (Ed.), *The African state in transition* (pp. 87–116). Palgrave Macmillan.

Chayes, S. (2017). When corruption is the operating system: the case of Honduras. Washington, DC: Carnegie Endowment for International Peace.

Chipkin, I. and Swilling, M. (2018). Shadow state: The politics of state capture. Johannesburg: Wits University Press.

Cooley, A., Heathershaw, J., and Sharman, J. C. (2018). The rise of kleptocracy: Laundering cash, whitewashing reputations. *Journal of Democracy, 29*(1), 39–53.

Dal Bó, E. (2006). Regulatory capture: A review. *Oxford review of economic policy, 22*(2), 203–225.

Dávid-Barrett, E. (2023). State capture and development: a conceptual framework. *Journal of International Relations and Development, 26*(2), 224–244. https://doi.org/10.1057/s41268-023-00290-6

February, J., and Mirzoyev, S. (2024). Special report: Commissions, corruption and state capture: charting the way forward for South Africa. https://saiia.org.za/wpcontent/uploads/2024/05/SAIIA_SR_Com missionsCorruptionState.pdf (Accessed 24 August 2024).

Friedenstein, H. (2017). Betrayal of the promise: How South Africa is being stolen. State Capacity Research Project, 1–72. https://www.wits.ac.za/media/wits-university/news-and-events/images/documents/Betrayal-of-the-Promise-25052017.pdf (Accessed 19 December 2022).

Goertz, G. (2006). Social science concepts: A user's guide. Princeton University Press.

Harding, A. (2015). Guptagate: The scandal South Africa's Zuma can't shake. BBC News Service. https://www.bbc.com/news/world-africa-309 23275 (Accessed 24 August 2024).

Hellman J. S., Jones G., and Kaufmann D. (2003). Seize the state, seize the day: state capture and influence in transition economies. *Journal of Comparative Economics, 31*(4), 751–773.

Hellman, J. S., and Kaufmann, D. (2018). *State Capture in Transition.* Submission to the Judicial Commission of Inquiry into Allegations of State Capture, Corruption and Fraud in the Public Sector including Organs of State. https://resourcegovernance.org/sites/default/files/documents/state-capture-in-transition.pdf (Accessed 25 August 2024).

Hellman, J. S., Jones, G., and Kaufmann, D. (2000). Seize the State, Seize the Day. State Capture, Corruption, and Influence in Transition. *World Bank Policy Research Working Paper No. 2444.* Washington, DC: World Bank.

Huntington, S. P. (1952). The marasmus of the ICC: The commission, the railroads, and the public interest. *Yale LJ,* 61, 467.

Myburgh, P. L. (2017). *The Republic of Gupta: A story of state capture*. Penguin Random House.

Novak, W. J. (2013). A revisionist history of regulatory capture. In: Carpenter, D., and Moss, D. A. (Eds.). *Preventing Regulatory Capture: Special Interest Influence and How to Limit it*. Cambridge University Press, pp. 25–48.

Rothstein, B., and Varraich, A. (2017). *Making Sense of Corruption*. Cambridge: Cambridge University Press.

Scott, J. (2007). Power, domination and stratification: Towards a conceptual synthesis. *Sociologia*, 55: 25-39.

Shai, K. B. (2017). South African state capture: A symbiotic affair between business and state going bad (?). *Insight on Africa*, 9(1), 62–75.

CHAPTER 5

Militarized Fights Against Galamsey, 2017–2024

Abstract In this chapter, we argue that the militarized fights against galamsey predate the period under scrutiny here. However, we limit our analysis of state capture to the period between 2017 and 2024, a period during which three successive military interventions were organized to fight galamsey: Operation Vanguard, Operation Halt II, and Operation Halt Relaunched (hereafter, Operation Halt III). We argue that three main features make these failed militarized fights in this period distinct. First, these operations were launched to fulfil the personal vow of President Akufo-Addo, the Commander-in-Chief of the Ghana Armed Forces (GAF), to fight and stop galamsey, even if it cost him the presidency. This is the first time, in the last three decades of democratic government in Ghana, a sitting Ghanaian president has publicly tied his political future to the fight against galamsey. Through this bold declaration, the president elevated galamsey to a national crisis of catastrophic proportions that threatens the very existence of the ecosystem of Ghana. Second, the blanket ban on ASM by the government of Ghana: both legal and illegal ASM was banned for over a year. This signalled an uncompromising stance of the government on the issue, further underscoring the president's commitment to combat and eradicate galamsey. Third, unprecedented military operations: for the first time in Ghana's recent democratic history, three successive military operations were rolled out within eight years to fight galamsey. These factors are crucial to our analysis of state

J. A. Ayelazuno and M. A. Aziabah, *State Capture in the Militarized Fight Against Illegal Small-Scale Goldmining in Ghana*, https://doi.org/10.1007/978-3-031-82673-3_5

capture. For example, the president, who is the most powerful political officeholder, the highest politician through whom the state can be captured, was the one leading the war against galamsey. Also, the ban on ASM and the three successive military operations illustrated the president's determination to keep his vow. Yet, under his leadership the fight against galamsey failed. This failure is central to our argument, as it raises two poignant questions: Why did the militarized fight against galamsey fail? And why did the president order the suspension of the military operations when the galamsey menace had aggravated? No official reasons were given for the suspensions. (But What). But what is indisputable is the inconsistency between the reasons for launching the operations and the suspension. We see this as evidence of state capture, which is often marked by internal contradictions, engendered by the symbiotic relationship between the formal state and the shadow state—with the latter feeding off the former.

Keywords Ghana · Galamsey · President Akufo-Addo's vow · Militarised fight · Operation Vanguard · Operation Halt · Operation Halt II · Operation Halt III

The militarized fights against galamsey predates the period under scrutiny here. In September 2006, the Kufuor-led New Patriotic Party (NPP) government authorized a nationwide "sweep" of illegal artisanal mining communities under a military operation code-named Fight Against Illegal Mining (Ayelazuno and Mawuko-Yevugah, 2019, p. 246). Another notable example is Operation Flush Out in 2013. Following media reports of Chinese involvement in galamsey, the NDC government, led by President John Mahama, formed a high-level Inter-Ministerial Task Force in May of that year to combat illegal small-scale mining. A police-cum-military task force was constituted to undertake the operational aspect of the combat, code-named *Operation Flush Out*. Operation flush out, as its name indicates, was supposed "to flush out Ghanaians and foreigners engaged in illegal mining in the country" (Hilson et al., 2014; Asamoah and Osei-Kojo, 2016, p. 6).

Operation Flush Out led to the arrest, detention, and deportation of thousands of foreigners, as well as the seizure of equipment used in illegal mining. Despite these arrests and deportations, Operation Flush Out was generally a failure. Corruption and the lack of political will to act, the very reasons why galamsey exists in Ghana, infected the task force. Hyped as a task force against illegal mining, there were neither prosecution of either the arrested Ghanaians nor the foreigners. The licenses of the Ghanaian ASM operators who colluded with the Chinese were not revoked. The image of the taskforce itself was tarnished with allegations of bribery and corruption against its members (Crawford and Botchwey, 2017, 2018; Crawford et al., 2016).

Even though failed militarized fights against galamsey are not new, we limit our analysis of state capture to the period between 2017 and 2024, during which three successive military operations were mobilized to fight galamsey: Operation Vanguard, Operation Halt II, and Operation Halt Relaunched (hereafter, Operation Halt III) (Aziabah and Ayelazuno, 2024). We identify three main features that set apart these failed militarized fights in this period. First, and as already discussed, these operations were mobilized to fulfil the vow of President Akufo-Addo, the Commander-in-Chief of the Ghana Armed Forces (GAF), to fight to end galamsey, if even that will cost him the presidency. This is the first time—in the last three decades of democratic government in Ghana—a sitting Ghanaian president has publicly tied his political future to the fight against galamsey.

In making this vow publicly at a two-day workshop on galamsey organized for traditional leaders in July 2017, President Akufo-Addo said: "I have said it in the Cabinet, and perhaps this is the first time I am making this public, that I am prepared to put my Presidency on the line on this matter [the galamsey menace]" (Graphic Online, 2017a, 2017b). When he gave the State of the Nation Address (SONA) to Parliament in 2018, a year after Operation Vanguard was rolled out, the president touted his strong commitment to fighting galamsey:

Mr. Speaker, problems associated with our environment and the galamsey phenomenon have taken up a lot of the time and energy of this government...The fight against galamsey is being spearheaded by a high-powered Inter-Ministerial Committee, led by the globally acclaimed Ghanaian scientist, Prof. Kwabena Frimpong Boateng, Minister for Science, Technology, Environment, and Innovation, supported by the indefatigable Minister for Lands and Natural Resources, John Peter Amewu. This Committee is waging a valiant struggle to bring the galamsey phenomenon under control...We cannot look on, as our very existence as a country is put in jeopardy and our water bodies, forests and land mass are destroyed. (Ghanaweb, 2018)

Embedded in this quote is the president's discursive strategy to pitch the galamsey problem as a national crisis of cataclysmic proportions, as something that threatens the very existence of the ecosystem of Ghana. In line with this, the president referred to galamsey as a "menace"; and to his militarized approach to dealing with it as the "fight against illegal mining," the "war against galamsey" and "the fight against galamsey" (Ayelazuno and Mawuko-Yevugah, 2019, p. 570).

The second distinct feature of the period under study is the blanket ban on ASM by the government of Ghana: a ban was put on both legal and illegal ASM for over a year. In March 2017, the government placed a six-month ban on all ASGM activities in the country. The ban on ASGM was extended several times and lasted approximately two years and was subsequently lifted on 17th December 2018; but only for the miners who have been vetted and approved by the IMCIM. It also suspended the issuance of new licenses for small-scale mining for a year (Hilson, 2017; Ayelazuno and Mawuko-Yevugah, 2019; Bansah, 2019). Both actions were in pursuit of the fulfilment of the president's vow.

The third distinct property of this period is the three successive military operations organized to fight galamsey. This is the first time that the government of Ghana has mobilized three successive military operations within a eight years period to fight galamsey. This has never happened in the last three decades of the efforts of the democratic state of Ghana to regulate its ASGM industry.

The three distinct feature are significant in the analysis of state capture, because the most powerful political officeholder, through whom the state can be captured, was the one leading the war against galamsey. Also, the ban on ASM and the three successive military operations are illustrative of the president's determination to keep his vow. Yet, the fight against galamsey has failed under his leadership. We see this contradiction as characteristic of state capture, because by its nature, it is permeated with internal contradictions, engendered by the symbiotic relationship between the real state and the shadow state, with the latter feeding off on the former. In the sections that follow, we present empirical material on these three failed militarized fights against galamsey in Ghana—Operation Vanguard, Operation Halt II and Operation Halt III—to illustrate state capture in the country's ASGM industry.

OPERATION VANGUARD

This is the first military intervention organized to combat galamsey when President Akufo-Addo took over the reins of the state in January 2017 (Aziabah and Ayelazuno, 2024). Before proceeding further, a bit of context in which Operation Vanguard was mobilized is needed here. Despite his spearheading of the fight against galamsey, President Akufo-Addo may be said to have done this under pressure by civil society groups who were concerned about the environmental damage of galamsey. It all began with Citi FM, an Accra-based radio station, which took to twitter to mobilize public support against galamsey and to pressurize the Ghanaian government to act quickly to stop the menace. With the twitter handle #StopGalamsey, the campaign garnered momentum and quickly attracted the "support of other local media outlets and produced a lengthy petition that included signatures from key ministerial figures—past and present— which Citi FM personnel presented to Parliament on 7th April 2017" (Hilson, 2017, p. 110).

The signatories of Citi FM's petition included people from powerful media organizations such as high-ranking officials at the Graphic Communications Group Limited, the Ghana Independent Broadcasters Association, the Ghanaian Times, the Ghana Journalists Association, the Ghana Broadcasting Corporation, and the Christian Council of Ghana (Hilson, 2017, p. 110). The media campaign led to the emergence of an elite class alliance between the political class, media owners, and the middle class; united by the ostensible goal of fighting galamsey because of the environmental menace it has caused, particularly the pollution of river bodies (Aziabah and Ayelazuno, 2024). The alliance led to the formation of the Media Coalition Against Galamsey (MCAG), with Mr. Kenneth Ashigbey, who was then the Managing Director of Graphic Communications Group Ltd, as the Convenor of the Steering Committee. The MCAG main objectives were to "carry out public education on the ills of illegal mining activities; carry out advocacy with stakeholders to ensure the eradication of galamsey and to promote sustainable mining" (Sojková, 2022: 378).

The media campaign also played a major role in lumping together the subaltern classes, doing informal ASM for survival, with the power elite classes engaged in destructive mechanized medium-scale mining to accumulate wealth—illegal, albeit, capitalist medium-scale mining (CMM). It then represented both survivalist and money-making galamsey as equally responsible for causing environmental menace in Ghana. Indeed, the Ghanaian mass media were the leading organs of the above-mentioned class alliance that spearheaded the misrecognition, misrepresentation, and stigmatization of all ASM operators as an environmental menace and all other negative stereotypes (Ofori and Ofori, 2018, p. 365). The #StopGalamsey campaign, as one influential study has argued, framed the discourses that pressurized the government to authorize Operation Vanguard (Sojková, 2022). Both the subalterns and the power elite classes were framed negatively as an environmental menace and engaging in destructive criminal activities.

The Launching of Operation Vanguard

In keeping with his vow to fight galamsey at the cost of his presidency, the president ordered the establishment of a joint task force (JTF) of military and police personnel, code-named *Operation Vanguard*, to undertake the fight. The four hundred (400) men of Operation Vanguard underwent a short pre-deployment training (Edu-Afful, 2022; Hilson and Maconachie, 2020; Graphic Online, 2017a, 2017b), including a four-hour training on Voluntary Principles on Security and Human Rights (VPSHR). This was aimed at equipping the personnel with skills for engagement in civilian areas, to reduce the risks of human rights abuses during the operation (The Fund for Peace [FFP], 2018). True to its military nature and the weight of the state behind it, the personnel assembled at the Headquarters of the Ghana Armed Forces (GAF), Burma Camp, Accra, on 31 July 2017 for the launch of the operation. The political and security leaders of the state institutions directly and indirectly involved in the operation were present in the launch: Minister of Defense, Minister of the Interior, Minister of Lands and Natural Resources, Minister of Science and Technology, Minister of Communication, Minister of Water Resources and Sanitation, the Inspector General of Police (IGP) and the Chief of Defense Staff (CDS) (Hilson and Maconachie, 2020; Graphic Online, 2017a, 2017b).

After the launch, the security men were deployed to mining areas, mainly in the Eastern, Central, Ashanti and Western Regions, to begin its work of fighting galamsey. The deployment was organized in military style, commanded by an army officer of the rank of Colonel. Three Forward Operating Bases (FOBs) were created in the regions "identified as hotspots of illegal mining, namely, Ashanti, Eastern and Western regions" (Edu-Afful, 2022, p. 47). Another FOB was created later at Kyekyewere, in the Central Region. Illustrative of the military nature of the operation and the importance the state attaches to it, the then Chief of Defence Staff (CDS), Lieutenant General Obed Boamah Akwa, led a high-powered delegation of state security personnel to visit the new FOB on 26th April 2018. The purpose of the visit was to apprise themselves of the activities of Operation Vanguard in the Central Region. The delegation comprised of the then Director General in-charge of Police Intelligence, COP Christian Tetteh Yohuno, who represented the Inspector General of Police (IGP); the Chief of Defence Staff of the Ghana Armed Forces (CDS) and some senior police and military officers. The CDS "warned illegal miners (galamseyers) to put a stop to their activities or risk being dealt with severely by the law" (Daily Guide Network, 2018). The composition of the delegations seems to suggest that the fight against galamsey was the highest priority of the coercive apparatuses of the Ghanaian state.

The president, members of his government responsible for supervising Operation Vanguard, and the commanders of *Operation Vanguard* have touted its success. For example, its personnel arrested several hundreds of illegal miners, some of whom were prosecuted. They have also confiscated hundreds of heavy equipment used for galamsey (Ayelazuno and Mawuko-Yevugah, 2019, p. 247; Aziabah and Ayelazuno, 2024). Operation Vanguard is also credited with the improvement of the turbidity of water bodies; for example, the Densu River is reported to have witnessed significant improvement (Eduful et al., 2020).

However, Operation Vanguard has been accused of egregious human rights abuses, such as shooting and maiming people (Hilson, 2017; Ayelazuno and Mawuko-Yevugah, 2019; Bansah et al., 2022; Aziabah and Ayelazuno, 2024), as well as burning confiscated mining equipment, an act felicitously described as the "showy destruction of excavators at the mining sites" (Bansah et al., 2022: 4). Interestingly, these human rights abuses have been advocated by top government officials such as the Attorney General and Minister for Justice (Bansah et al., 2022, p. 4). Indeed, the president lent his support for these abuses. So, he could make the following argument;

> I say with all the emphasis at my command, that no rights can accrue to or flow from the criminal venture of galamsey. The equipment, which is being used for an illegal or criminal purpose, cannot confer on the owner

or any other person any rights whatsoever. I know there are some who believe that the ongoing exercise of ridding our water bodies and forest zones of harmful equipment and machinery is unlawful and, in some cases, harsh. I strongly disagree, and I would advise those who take a contrary view to go to court to vindicate their position, if they so wish.... (Bansah et al., 2022, p. 4)

The First Deputy Speaker of Ghana's parliament, Mr Joseph Osei-Owusu, took the president's disregard for human rights in the fight against galamsey to a whole different—and one must hasten to add—appalling level. Frustrated that the measures outlined by the president are not working, he advocated something more drastic to fight the galamsey menace: "Shoot to kill." According to one Ghanaian leading news organization, he said in parliament that "nobody had the right to mine illegally in the country..." that "the approach used in preventing illegal mining was not yielding the needed results..." and that "if he had his way, he would legislate for security agencies to shoot and kill people engaged in the destruction of the environment." This, according to him, "would deter others from engaging in illegal mining and destroying the environment" (Graphic Online, 2018). In the same news report, this outlandish proposal seemed to have been endorsed by no less a prominent Ghanaian political leader than Mr. Osei Kyei-Mensah-Bonsu, the Majority Leader of parliament. Mr. Kyei-Mensah-Bonsu is reported to have argued that the constitution of Ghana allowed the use of force to prevent the commission of crime, and that such an exercise of force might lead to death. According to him, "illegal miners had destroyed water bodies, while illegal sand winning and harmful activities had destroyed the forest cover" (Graphic Online, 2018). He seems to be suggesting that these are some of the serious crimes the constitution justifies the exercise of force (that may lead to death) to prevent or control them.

It is especially puzzling that leaders of the Ghana democratic state—many of them respected lawyers—have justified and even advocated the abuse of human rights, including killing, in the militarized fight against galamsey. What could explain this puzzling support for egregious human rights abuses by leaders of the democratic state of Ghana, even the president of the country? At first glance, it may seem the president's unwavering commitment to fulfil his vow to end galamsey at all costs may be the reason. But the reality is likely more complex.

While the troubling democratic and moral implications of these leaders' attitudes lie outside the scope this book, their views are important as evidence of state capture. This is not because their views illustrate they are part of the inner sanctum of the power of the Ghanaian state the mining-power elites have influenced. Nor are they the direct beneficiaries of the influence, monetarily or politically. Rather, it is because their attitudes highlight the puzzling failure of the Ghanaian state to win the war against galamsey, despite the advocacy and commitment by its most powerful fractions to fight it; including the disregard for human rights and the virtues of democracy. This approach resembles a de facto declaration of state of emergency in the fight against galamsey. Yet, as we have argued all along, it turned out to be a dismal failure. State capture is the most convincing explanation of this puzzling failure.

It was a dismal failure, because, as it turned out, Operation Vanguard was abruptly ended by the president and his government. On 11th May 2021, four months after the president had started his second term of office, his Minister for Lands and Natural Resources, Mr. Samuel Abu Jinapor, announced that *Operation Vanguard* had been suspended. In the *Meet the Press* forum, organized by the Ministry of Information to inform citizens about what their government is doing on their behalf, the minister announced;

> Activities and operations of Operation Vanguard has (*sic*) been suspended for the time being. Operation Vanguard is no more in operation as we speak. We had a meeting... myself, the Minister for National Security, Minister for Interior, Defense and Information. The Committee that the President has put together to spearhead this effort, we came to a firm conclusion that the activities or operations of Vanguard are to cease. (Myjoyonline, 2021a; Ghanaweb, 2021a, 2021b)

This announcement was not because galamsey has been combated successfully. In fact, the operation was suspended at the time the environmental menace of galamsey was still alive and well. Indeed, CMM galamsey continued to flourish even as late as the time of writing the final draft of this book, in August 2024.

Thus, the decision to suspend the military operation adds a new layer to the puzzling failure of the militarized fight against galamsey. The point is the abrupt suspension of *Operation Vanguard* was in direct contradiction of the Ghanaian president's vow and determination to fight and end galamsey. In fact, the president had to call for a national consultative dialogue on small-scale mining because of the worsening galamsey menace. The dialogue was held in Accra between 14th and 15th April 2021—that is less than a month before the suspension of Operation Vanguard. The president who was present at the dialogue, gave an address in which he lamented the galamsey menace, just as he did before he ordered Operation Vanguard to fight it;

> We have had beautiful and majestic rivers and streams. Today, there is not much to celebrate about the Pra or the Birim, and there is not much to be excited about over our famed thick forests and the animals that inhabit them. Unacceptable mining and logging practices have laid them to waste. (Ghanaweb, 2021a, 2021b)

Why did the president order the suspension of Operation Vanguard less than a month after publicly lamenting about its devastating environmental effects? Sinceno official reason was given for the suspension, the reason remains unknown. What is, however, indisputable is the inconsistency between the suspension and the very reasons the president launched Operation Vanguard in the first place. We argue that this reflects one of the core internal contradictions of the captured state, shaped by the symbiotic relationship between the real state and the shadow state, with the latter feeding off the former.

OPERATION HALT

Unlike *Operation Vanguard*, there was no systematic pattern of events leading to the establishment of *Operation Halt*, and details are lacking on how it was formed and deployed. Also, it is not clear when Operation Halt I (or the first Operation Halt) was formed and when it ended and was succeeded by Operation Halt II or Operation Halt II relaunched. In fact, it is not clear which *Operation Halt* succeeded *Operation Vanguard*, or whether there was a time in point that both existed side-by-side, and if so, the division of labor between them. Based on a policy brief of the Danish Institute for International Studies, the first Operation Halt (Operation Halt I) was established under the Forestry Commission to deal with the illegal exploitation of timber in forest reserves, especially in Brong-Ahafo and Western Regions (Albrecht et al., 2021).

Operation Halt I may have emerged from the National Consultative Dialogue on Small-Scale Mining held from 14 to 15th April 2021 at the Accra International Conference Center (Aziabah and Ayelazuno, 2024). The two-day consultative dialogue produced several resolutions, which were outlined in a communique issued, which read in part;

> The Dialogue emphatically charged government to take steps to put in place systems that would rigidly apply the law, noting particularly the sanctions/penalties imposed by Act 995, to all those who infringe the law, irrespective of political colour or socio-economic status or class; indeed, the better placed in society and who ought to know better should have the most punitive of the penalties applied to them. (MLNR, 2021)

The first news report on a military operation against galamsey, which we argue, *was Operation Halt I*, was reported two weeks after the conclusion of this two-day consultative dialogue. It was a news release by the Ministry of Information, signed by the Minister, Mr. Kojo Oppong Nkrumah, which stated in part;

> In furtherance of the resolution of the final communiqué of the Stakeholder Dialogue on Small Scale Mining on April 14 to April 15, and to ensure that mining within water bodies is immediately stopped; the President of the Republic, Nana Addo Dankwa Akufo-Addo has authorized the Ghana Armed Forces to commence an operation to remove all persons and logistics involved in mining from Ghana's water bodies. (Ghanaweb, 2021a, 2021b)

Giving further details on this operation, without calling it Operation Halt, the news release stated that 200 officers of the army were assigned for the operation, and it had already commenced on 28th April 2021 on The River Pra in the Central Region.

The activities of *Operation Halt I* elicited mixed public reactions because the operation only focused on demobilization/decommissioning of all mining-related equipment (such as excavators, changfan machines, crushers, and so on) found within a 100-meter radius of river bodies. Whereas a section of the Ghanaian public found the destruction of mining-related equipment on or near water bodies a deterrent exercise, many believed the task force was fighting illegality through illegal means. For instance, on 16th May 2021, operatives of *Operation Halt I* raided some mining sites at Larbikrom, Dompem, and Pamen, all in the Atiwa

District of the Eastern Region of Ghana during which over 20 excavators and other mining equipment were set ablaze (Citi Newsroom, 2021). Interestingly, some of the destroyed equipment belonged to a company named Xtra Gold Mining Limited, a company with connections to the National Women's Organizer of the president's political party (the NPP), Madam Kate Gyamfuah, a national executive officer of the party (Myjoyonline, 2021b). This case will be discussed further in the next chapter; but to adumbrate, it illustrates some of the internal contradictions of the captured state and the key factor shaping it, namely, the symbiotic, albeit, contradictory relationship between the real state and the shadow state.

This operation was referred to as *Operation Halt II* by Graphic Online in its news report on the briefing by the Minister of Defence, Mr. Dominic Nitiwul on 30 April 2021. According to the reporter, Kweku Zurek, the Minister announced that unlike previous operations, "all equipment that will be seized under a new effort to end galamsey will be destroyed on-site" (Graphic Online, 2021). The Defence Minister said the president ordered the operation, which was carried out on River Pra. It led to the seizure and destruction of nine excavators, 127 chang-fans, and one fuel pump used for illegal mining in the River Pra. In addition, two nationals of China were arrested for illegally mining in a forest reserve and were handed over to the National Security agents for further investigation and criminal procedures.

Based on the above news report on the anti-galamsey operation on the River Pra on 28th April 2021, we refer to it here as *Operation Halt II*, which was mounted approximately two weeks before the announcement of the suspension of Operation Vanguard. Going by the date of the announcement of the suspension (11th May 2021), *Operation Halt II* started when *Operation Vanguard* was still in existence. Indeed, when the Minister of Lands and Natural Resources made the announcement about the suspension of Operation Vanguard, he also stated that there was an ongoing military operation code-named *Operation Hall II*, deployed to ensure that no mining was done within 100 meters radius around water bodies and in the forest reserves;

> 'Operation Halt II' would run alongside other measures being implemented by the Ministry, such as the declaration of river bodies as red zones for mining, the suspension of reconnaissance and prospecting activities in forest reserves except in exceptional cases, and the ban on the manufacture, sale and use of "changfans". Others are the procurement of speed boats to

patrol the rivers, the recruitment of river guards to support the protection of the rivers, the introduction of mercury-free gold Katchas, the establishment of 83 Small Scale Mining Committees in all mining districts in the country, the revamping of Community Mining Schemes, and the introduction of the National Alternative Employment and Livelihood Programme which now engages about 80,000 people in alternative livelihood projects. (Graphic Online, 2022; MyJoyOnline, 2021; Ghanaweb, 2021a, 2021b)

Operation Halt II was deployed in phases. The second phase of Operation Halt II, according to a news report of Daily Guide Network, was announced by Kojo Oppong Nkrumah, the Minister for Information, in a statement dated 7th May 2021. He said "the new phase of the operation focuses on the tributaries of the Pra river which have also been significantly affected by the activities of illegal miners" (Daily Guide Network, 2018). This phase of the operation was undertaken by 400 soldiers of all ranks. The Minister advised members of the public to "stay away from mining in water bodies to avoid any action by the forces" (Daily Guide Network 2018). The Minister of Defence, Mr Dominic Nitiwul, in his press briefing on 11th May 2021 announced the end of this phase. He touted its successes: twenty-eight excavators, 267 changfans with platforms, 18 water pumping machines and a milling machine were confiscated and destroyed along the 100-metre stretch of the Pra River and its tributaries between Twifo Praso and Daboase. The Minister announced that "[t]he third phase of the operation will be launched in other parts of the country soon" (Graphic Online, 2021).

The third phase, according to a Graphic Online news report, focused on River Ayensu and Birim in the Eastern Region (3News.com, 2021). Giving details of the success of this phase of the operation, MyJoyOnline.com reports that "a total of 49 excavators, 228 Changfans and 87 water pumping machines among other mining equipment were destroyed" (MyJoyOnline.com, 2021a, 2021b). The fourth phase of Operation Halt II focused on illegal mining on the River Ankobra and its tributaries. A statement issued by Kojo Oppong Nkrumah, the Minister for Information on 27th May 2021, announced the commencement of the operation. He said "[t]he operation is being undertaken by four hundred and one men of all ranks" (3News.com, 2021; Graphic Online, 2021).

As with Operation Vanguard, top government officials justified the human rights abuses by the personnel of Operation Halt II, so the Minister of Defence could say;

> The law already outlaws mining within the river bodies and 100 metres to each of the flanks of the river, if you do any activity there it is an illegal activity. The President has directed that we clean up the river bodies and like I said, we are not taking any equipment home, we are not seizing any equipment, no equipment will be returned home. It's not like before where you will seize equipment, they will all be destroyed on-site, it is as simple as that. So, there is nothing like we are taking excavators, nothing will come home, everything will be destroyed at sight. (Graphic Online, 2021)

It is important to underscore that no part of Ghana's Minerals and Mining (Amendment) Act 2019 (Act 995) mandates state authorities to destroy or burn seized mining equipment. Instead, the law requires that such equipment be confiscated and transferred to local government units where it can be put to productive use.

Military swoops/crackdowns on illegal ASM have historically failed in Ghana and elsewhere. At best, they succeed temporarily to drive illegal ASM operators underground, only for them to return later—and often more determined than before. As discussed previously, government official talking tough in the face of the failures of the military crackdowns reflects the contradictions of the captured state. The officials of the formal Ghanaian state continue to project power, authority, and control. But the reality is that the militarized fights against galamsey have failed, because the shadow state is stronger, and is continuously working to protect the mining-power elites to engage in CMM galamsey—despite these military crackdowns. This explains the bizarre and contradictory actions of the state: it demobilized a military operation that has been in action for over four years, and then formed new ones to deal with the same problem. These are some of the morbid symptoms of the captured Ghanaian state, co-existing with a shadow state, which is sustained by a vast network of kleptocratic actors of CMM galamsey.

Operation Halt III

On 13th October 2022, the Minister of Lands and Natural Resources announced the relaunch of Operation Halt II (herafter Operation Halt III) when he took his turn at the Meet the Press event of the government. The Minister said the relaunch took place on 11th October 2022 after a review of the earlier operation because of "the resurgence of galamsey activities across the country" (Graphic Online 2022). Giving further details on the operation, the Minister claimed that "the new Operation Halt II was well thought-through and was ready to take care of the current resurgence of the galamsey menace, with funding secured to ensure its sustainability" (Graphic Online 2022).

Despite his claim that Operation Halt III was well thought-through, the Minister gave the military personnel extra-legal discretion on how mining equipment seized during the operation should be handled: they should use their discretion whether to decommission or seize the equipment, and assured them that no one will interfere with this discretion—not even he, the Minister. This aspect of the operation is far from being thought-through, because it breaches the mining law on the handling of these equipment. The Minerals and Mining (Amendment) Act, 2019 and the government's own new law on this issue—the "Minerals and Mining (Mineral Operations—Tracking of Earth Moving and Mining Equipment) Regulations, 2020 (LI 2404)"—provide explicit rules regulating the seizure of pieces of equipment used in illegal mining and the procedures of handling them. As already noted, these laws do not give such wide discretionary powers that the Minister gave to the military personnel deployed to fight galamsey (Bansah et al. 2022: 4). As argued above, these flagrant violations of the laws in a democratic state, with the support of elected representatives of citizens, demonstrate the inherent contradictions and the morbid symptoms of the captured state.

A month after the personnel of Operation Halt III were deployed, the army released a report detailing its achievements. In October alone, the operation led to the seizure of 30 excavators and the destruction of four others, while another four were immobilized on site. The operation also "destroyed 103 Changfan machines, nine (9) water pumping machines, five (5) generator sets, two (2) fuel storage tanks and other improvized mining equipment and structures and seized an additional six (6) motorbikes and one (1) motor king tricycle" (Citi Newsroom, 2022). The list of actions taken by the military not only highlights the violation of mining laws, but also underscores the troubling lack of transparency in how the military used the discretionary powers it was given to handle the mining equipment seized during the operation.

The destruction of some pieces of equipment, while seizing others, raises a fundamental question: what informed the decision to destroy, decommission, or seize? The answer is not clear, but the issue lends evidence to the contradictory co-existence of the formal, albeit, weak Ghanaian state and the shadow state. This situation is embedded with internal contradiction, because the formal state must be seen to exercise all the qualities it is supposed to have; but the shadow state that feeds off it, and sucks its vitality in the process, continues to show its power and endurance in the flourishing of CMM galamsey, despite the repeated military crackdowns.

As of the September 2024 that we type these words, we do not know whether Operation Halt III is still active or discontinued. To the best of our knowledge, it was the last in a series of military operation launched by the government to fulfill the vow of the president to end galamsey. However, recent comments by leading politicians of the president's political party demonstrate that all military operations have been disbanded. Specifically, the Western Regional Minister, Mr. Kwabena Okyere Darko-Mensah, and the NPP parliamentary candidate for the Amenfi East Constituency, Mr. Ernest Frimpong, are the politicians under reference here. In June 2024, the two politicians and other officials of their party had a meeting with illegal ASM operators (galamsey operators) in the Western Region. A video of the meeting showed the parliamentary candidate, Mr Ernest Frimpong, saying that all anti-galamsey task forces had been disbanded by the government, hence no soldier has the authority to stop anyone from mining. He even went as far as to incite operators of galamsey against the military; saying "if anyone comes around and says because if he is a soldier, leave the site and dismantle your machines, don't be moved by the uniform he is wearing, if he beats you, equally beat him. Fight him, I will come to your defense" (Starrfm.com.gh, 2024; Pulse.com.gh, 2024). According to the Parliamentary Candidate, nobody has authority to arrest galamsey operators; and anyone who comes to arrest them is doing so illegally and should be arrested.

Unsurprisingly, the parliamentary candidate received massive applause from the galamsey operators attending the meeting. Yet the Western Regional Minister, who was present in this meeting, did not rebut the claim of the parliamentary candidate. As the Chairman of the Regional Security Council (REGSEC) and the highest appointee of the president—who vowed to fight galamsey at the cost of his presidency—his loud silence is significant for two reasons. First, it lends credence to the claim by his party's parliamentary candidate's that all military operations against galamsey had been disbanded. Second, he tacitly endorsed the incitement of galamsey operators against personnel of the Ghana Armed Forces (GAF). Both implications undermine national security and embolden galamsey operators, specifically those engaged in CMM galamsey, to continue their criminal destruction of the ecosystem.

To date, neither the minister nor the parliamentary candidate has been rebuked publicly by the president of Ghana or any senior official from the presidency. The parliamentary candidate was arrested and later released on bail. We are not aware of any further action/s to prosecute him or any disciplinary actions against him by the authorities of his political party. This follows follows a familiar pattern. Politicians facing criminal investigation related to the militarized fight against galamsey are often set free. As the next chapter will illustrate, such police actions against Mr. Horace Ekow Ewusi and Charles Bissue, both top politicians of President Akufo-Addo's political party, the NPP, have not resulted in any punitive measures, either criminal or political. Indeed, both Ewusi and Bissue have been elevated to parliamentary candidates of the NPP for the 2024 Ghana elections.

With the lens of state capture, all these are morbid symptoms of the access and influence of the inner sanctums of state power by a vast network of kleptocratic actors of CMM galamsey in Ghana. With this kleptocratic access and influence, the power elites of CMM galamsey, both within and outside the captured state, have repurposed even the most powerful and coercive apparatuses of the Ghanaian state—such as the police and the military—to work to protect their criminal mining activities rather than fighting them. This illustrates the parasitic relationship between the shadow state and the formal state, in which the former feeds off the latter, sucking it dry of its vitality; and leaving it like an orange that has been sucked dry.

These morbid symptoms of state capture are also visible in the GAF's response to the incitement of galamsey operators by the NPP parliamentary candidate against soldiers. In a press release dated 10th June 2024, Brigadier General E Aggrey-Quashie, the Director General of Public Relations of GAF, wrote: "The Ghana Armed Forces (GAF) has taken note of viral videos on social media calling for attacks on soldiers and other security personnel. We strongly, wish to caution the public against such utterances." Furthermore, he reminded the public that "such calls are not only unlawful but also pose a significant threat to the security and stability of our nation." He then registered the GAF's condemnation of any form of incitement or encouragement of violence against its soldiers (3News.com, 2024). This response by GAF appeared timid evasive. Despite the direct and clear incitement against its personnel, GAF is here engaged in a balancing act: trying to defend its personnel, while avoiding confrontation the powerful political elites. For this reason, the press release, though a reaction to the behaviour of the above-mentioned politicians—who are closer to the president and his political party—was vague about whom the GAF was reacting to; because the press release avoided mentioning directly the politicians who incited the galamsey operators against the soldiers.

This chapter has provided a bird's-eye view of the successive, albeit unsuccessful, military crackdowns—with different codenames—organized by the President and Commander-in-Chief of the Ghana Armed Forces to prosecute his vow to fight and end galamsey at all cost. All these military operations have been disbanded, but galamsey and its environmental menace have aggravated. To all intents and purposes, CMM galamsey is alive and well in Ghana. As discussed earlier, the failure of the president and his government to fight the galamsey menace was recently brought to the attention of the public by the Ghana Water Company Ltd (GWCL). The company announced that because of the high pollution levels of major rivers in Ghana by CMM galamsey, it was facing acute shortage of fresh water for treatment and distribution to the public.

This has re-ignited public outrage at the galamsey menace and the government for its failure to solve the problem. As we conclude this book (in the last quarter of 2024), the history of the president's vow to fight and defeat galamsey—at all cost—has come full circle: the spectacle of the worsening state of the pollution of rivers has been illuminated in the media space, the public is outraged, and campaign against the galamsey menace in social media and by civil society organizations is re-ignited. But this time around, the president has resorted to loud silence. Besides a terse press statement issued by the Minister for Information which, as discussed earlier, indicated that the president has instructed the formation of a ministerial ad hoc committee to *evaluate* the government's approach to fighting galamsey, no word is uttered by the president. At least, as at

September 2024 when we were revising the final drafts of the chapters of this book, the president has not said anything about galamsey. In the next chapter, we document the deep state capture that has led to this spectacular failure of the militarized fight against illegal ASGM (galamsey) in Ghana—specifically capitalist medium-scale mining (CMM) galamsey.

References

3News.com (2021). *Operation Halt II enters 4th phase.* https://3news.com/featured/operation-halt-ii-enters-4th-phase/ (Accessed 15 October 2022)

3News.com (2024). *'Attacking soldiers is a grave offense punishable by law'—GAF responds to NPP PC inciting 'galamseyers' against military.* https://3news.com/news/attacking-soldiers-is-a-grave-offense-punishable-by-law-gaf-responds-to-npp-pc-inciting-galamseyers-against-military/ (Accessed 15 September 2024)

Albrecht, P., Aubyn, F., and Edu-Afful F. (2021). *Halt and Vanguard: Two military operations in Ghana and their consequences.* DIIS. https://www.diis.dk/en/research/halt-and-vanguard (Accessed 15 October 2022)

Asamoah, K., and Osei-Kojo, A. (2016). A contextual analysis of implementation challenges of small-scale mining laws in Ghana: A case study of Bekwai Municipality. *Sage Open,* 1–11. https://doi.org/10.1177/2158244016665885

Asare-Donkoh, Franklin—GBC Ghana Online (2023, April 25). *Akufo-Addo's claim of fighting galamsey was the biggest scam—NDC.* https://www.gbcghanaonline.com/news/politics/akufo-addos-claim-of-fighting-galamsey-was-the-biggest-scam-ndc/2023/ (25 September 2024)

Ayelazuno, J. A., and Aziabah, M. A. (2023). Making visible the galamsey scandals in Ghana: Digital media as new technologies of democratic accountability. *The Extractive Industries and Society, 16,* 101366. https://doi.org/10.1016/j.exis.2023.101366

Ayelazuno, J. A., and Mawuko-Yevugah, L. (2019). Large-scale mining and ecological imperialism in Africa: The politics of mining and conservation of the ecology in Ghana. *Journal of Political Ecology, 26,* 243–262.

Aziabah, M. A., and Ayelazuno, J. A. (2024). The failure of the militarised fight against 'Galamsey' in Ghana: A critical overview of the class and political dynamics. *Journal of Planning and Land Management, 3*(2), 31–51.

Bansah, K. J. (2019). From diurnal to nocturnal: Surviving in a chaotic artisanal and small-scale mining sector. *Resources Policy, 64,* 101475. https://doi.org/10.1016/j.resourpol.2019.101475

Bansah, K. J., Acquah, P. J., and Assan, E. (2022). Guns and fires: The use of military force to eradicate informal mining. *The Extractive Industries and Society*, *11*, 101139.

Citi Newsroom (2020). *'Galamsey' fight: All 'stolen' excavators will be found soon—Frimpong-Boateng.* Citi Newsroom. https://citinewsroom.com/2020/02/galamsey-fight-all-stolen-excavators-will-be-found-soon-frimpong-boa teng/ (Accessed 15 August 2022)

Citi Newsroom (2021). *Xtra-Gold Mining Ltd. angry over burning of its equipment by anti-galamsey taskforce.* Citi Newsroom. https://citinewsroom.com/2021/05/xtra-gold-mining-ltd-angry-over-burning-of-its-equipment-by-anti-galamsey-taskforce/ (Accessed 15 August 2022)

Citi Newsroom (2022). *Operation Halt II seizes 30 excavators, arrests 8 suspected illegal miners.* https://citinewsroom.com/2022/11/operation-halt-ii-seizes-30-excavators-arrests-8-suspected-illegal-miners/ (Accessed 24 December 2022)

Crawford, G., and Botchwey, G. (2017). Conflict, collusion and corruption in small-scale gold mining: Chinese miners and the state in Ghana. *Commonwealth & Comparative Politics*, *55*(4), 444–470.

Crawford, G., and Botchwey, G. (2018). Militarisation and criminalisation of artisanal and smallscale gold mining: The state and the so-called "galamsey' menace' in Ghana. *Review of African Political Economy*, *451*(56), 321–334.

Crawford, G., Agyeyomah, C., Botchwey, G., and Mba, A. (2016). *The impact of Chinese involvement in small-scale gold mining in Ghana.* Policy Brief 33110, International Growth Centre, LSE and Oxford University. https://www.theigc.org/wp-content/uploads/2016/08/Crawford-et-al-2015-Final-Report-1.pdf (Accessed 30 December 2022).

Daily Guide Network (2018, April 27). *CDS warns galamsey operators.* https://dailyguidenetwork.com/cds-warns-operation-vanguard-person nel-against-protecting-galamseyers/ (Accessed 17 August 2022).

Edu-Afful, F. (2022). The anatomy of Ghanaian domestic military operations: Exploring operations vanguard and calm life. *Contemporary Journal of African Studies*, *9*(1), 39–52. https://doi.org/10.4314/contjas.v9i1.4

Eduful, M., Alsharif, K., Eduful, A., Acheampong, M., Eduful, J., and Mazumder, L. (2020). The illegal artisanal and small-scale mining (galamsey) 'menace' in Ghana: Is military-style approach the answer? *Resources Policy*, *68*, 101732. https://doi.org/10.1016/j.resourpol.2020.101732

Ghanaweb. (2018). FULL SPEECH: President Nana Akufo-Addo's 2018 SONA, 8 February 2018. https://www.ghanaweb.com/GhanaHomePage/NewsArchive/FULL-SPEECH-President-Nana-Akufo-Addo-s-2018-SONA-624767 (Accessed 22 December 2022)

Ghanaweb. (2021a). *Galamsey: Operation Vanguard no more—Jinapor.* https://www.ghanaweb.com/GhanaHomePage/NewsArchive/Galamsey-Operation-Vanguard-no-more-Jinapor-1258675 (Accessed 23 December 2022).

Ghanaweb. (2021b). FULL TEXT: President Akufo-Addo's address at National Consultative Dialogue on small scale mining. https://www.ghanaweb.com/GhanaHomePage/NewsArchive/FULL-TEXT-President-Akufo-Addo-s-address-at-National-Consultative-Dialogue-on-small-scale-mining-1235215 (Accessed 15 August 2022)

Graphic Online (2017a). *'Operation Vanguard' launched to wipe out galamsey.* https://www.graphic.com.gh/news/general-news/operation-vanguard-launched-to-wipe-out-galamsey.html (Accessed 1 August 2022).

Graphic Online (2017b, July 11). *I will put my Presidency on line to stop galamsey—President.* https://www.graphic.com.gh/news/general-news/i-will-put-my-presidency-on-line-to-stop-galamsey-president (Accessed 17 March 2018).

Graphic Online (2018). *Parliament debates 'shoot-to-kill' order against galamseyers.* https://www.graphic.com.gh/news/general-news/parliament-debates-shoot-to-kill-order-against-galamseyers.html (Accessed 1 August 2022)

Graphic Online (2021). *All galamsey equipment will be destroyed on-site—Minister.* https://www.graphic.com.gh/news/general-news/all-galamsey-equipment-will-be-destroyed-on-site-minister.html (Accessed 15 August 2022).

Graphic Online (2022). *Operation Halt II relaunched: As chiefs, MMDCEs empowered.* https://www.graphic.com.gh/news/general-news/operation-halt-ii-relaunched-as-chiefs-mmdces-empowered.html (Accessed 14 October 2022).

Hilson, G. M. (2017). Shootings and burning excavators: Some rapid reflections on the Government of Ghana's handling of the informal 'galamsey' mining 'menace'. *Resources Policy, 54,* 109–116. https://doi.org/10.1016/j.resourpol.2017.09.009

Hilson, G., and Maconachie, R. (2020). For the environment: An assessment of recent military intervention in informal gold mining communities in Ghana. *Land Use Policy, 96,* 1–11.

Hilson G., Hilson A., and Adu-Darko, E. (2014). Chinese participation in Ghana's informal gold mining economy: Drivers, implications and clarifications. *Journal of Rural Studies, 34,* 292–303.

Ministry of Lands and Natural Resources [MLNR] (2021). National Consultative Dialogue on small-scale mining. https://mlnr.gov.gh/wp-content/uploads/2022/06/Communique-01_NATIONAL-CONSULTATIVE-DIALOGUE-ON-SMALL-SCALE-MINING-copy.pdf (Accessed 15 August 2022)

MyJoyOnline (2021a). *Activities of Operation Vanguard suspended by government.* https://www.myjoyonline.com/activities-of-operation-vanguard-suspended-by-government/ (Accessed 23 December 2022)

Myjoyonline. (2021b). *Xtra Gold Mining Limited not mining illegally—Kate Gyamfuah's Secretary defends.* https://www.myjoyonline.com/xtra-gold-mining-limited-not-mining-illegally-kate-gyamfuahs-secretary-defends/#google_vignette (Accessed 23 December 2022)

Ofori, D. R., & Ofori, J. J. (2018). Digging for gold or justice? Misrecognition and marginalization of "illegal" smallscale miners in Ghana. *Social Justice Research, 31*(4), 355–373.

Pulse.com.gh (2024). *NPP Amenfi East Parliamentary Candidate urges illegal miners to beat soldiers—Video.* https://www.pulse.com.gh/news/politics/npp-amenfi-east-parliamentary-candidate-urges-illegal-miners-to-beat-soldiers-video/xmexhet (Accessed 14 September 2024)

Sojková, I. (2022). Framing illegal artisanal and small-scale gold mining in the Ghanaian media during the# StopGalamsey campaign. *The Journal of Modern African Studies, 60*(3), 371–396.

Starrfm (2024). *VIDEO: Beat up soldiers attempting to stop you from mining—Amenfi East NPP PC to illegal miners.* https://starrfm.com.gh/video-beat-up-soldiers-attempting-to-stop-you-from-mining-amenfi-east-npp-pc-to-illegal-miners/ (Accessed 21 September 2024)

The Fund for Peace [FFP] (2018, February 28). *Operation vanguard pre-deployment training: Increasing awareness of voluntary principles on security and human rights in the Ghana public security sector.* https://fundforpeace.org/2018/02/28/operation-vanguard-pre-deployment-training/ (Accessed 22 December 2022).

CHAPTER 6

State Capture in the Militarized Fights Against Galamsey, 2017–2024

Abstract This chapter draws on the insights of state capture theory to analyze the militarized fight against galamsey, launched as part of President Akufo-Addo's vow to fight and end its environmental menace, even at the cost of his presidency. He made this pledge in 2017, during his first year in office, and referring to the stakes of the 2020 Ghanaian presidential election. Even though he won the 2020 presidential elections, at the time of finalizing the writing of this book (September 2024), his vow remained unfulfilled. Indeed, illegal capitalist medium-scale mining (CMM), which we conceptualize as CMM galamsey had flourished and continued to flourish despite the series of militarized fights mounted against galamsey in general. This contradiction presents an intellectual and political puzzle, which we contend can be explained with the insights of state capture. We argue the Ghanaian state under the government of President Akufo-Addo has been captured by the mining-power elites, both within and outside government, through a sprawling network of kleptocratic actors. These actors have configured a shadow state that feeds off the formal state. As a result the military fights against galamsey between 2017 and 2024 were bound to fail. Drawing on empirical evidence, we show that the militarized operations against galamsey selectively enforced the ASM laws, targeting only the powerless and the "unconnected" subaltern class, while protecting the powerful and the politically well connected. The militarized fights were shaped by class

© The Author(s), under exclusive license to Springer Nature Switzerland AG 2025
J. A. Ayelazuno and M. A. Aziabah, *State Capture in the Militarized Fight Against Illegal Small-Scale Goldmining in Ghana*, https://doi.org/10.1007/978-3-031-82673-3_6

alliance and political power. The powerful and politically well-connected class have captured the state, repurposing its institutions to protect their interests. As such, galamsey is not an enemy that can be fought with military might, weaponry, and operational strategies. By deploying such strategies, one misses the complex interplay of forces and acts of state capture that have created, nurtured, and deepened CMM galamsey before the military operations were launched to fight it. The military's focus on the arrest of miners and seizing of mining equipment in the field, signals barking up the wrong tree: they have not correctly identified the enemy they are fighting, let alone fight it. Yet this enemy, the shadow state, is amorphous and difficult to identify and fight. The key conclusion of this chapter—and the book as a whole,—is that the president's tough rhetoric and military crackdowns on galamsey were façades, masking the shadow state.

Keywords Ghana · Galamsey · State capture · Failed militarized fights · Political scandals · Missing excavators · Missing drones · Aggravation of rivers-pollution · Pillaging of forest reserves

This chapter draws on state capture theory to analyze the militarized fight against galamsey, in pursuit of President Akufo-Addo's vow to fight and end its environmental menace, even at the cost of his presidency. This was a vow made in the first year of his first term, referring to the stakes of the 2020 Ghanaian presidential election. This means, he was prepared to be voted out of power by the operators of galamsey because of his fight against their operations. He won the 2020 presidential elections—and at the time of writing the final draft of this book (September 2024)—he was left with just three months to the end of his second term (and last term), making a total of eight years as president. Yet the evidence mentioned in the preceding chapters and documented in more detail in this chapter, show that he has failed to fulfil his vow, despite the deployment of the Ghana Armed Forces (GAF) and other security services to fight galamsey.

Indeed, illegal capitalist medium-scale mining (CMM), which we conceptualized as CMM galamsey—industrialized and semi-industrialized, mechanized and semi-mechanized—has flourished and continue to flourish despite the militarized fights the president launched against galamsey. The unprecedented environmental destruction that

CMM galamsey has inflicted on Ghanaians has aggravated and the destruction continues, eight years into the vow of the president to fight and defeat galamsey at all cost. This presents us an intellectual and political puzzle, which we have argued throughout this book, can be explained with state capture theory.

In the rest of this chapter, we present evidence to support this argument: the Ghanaian state under the government of President Akufo-Addo has been captured by the mining-power elites, both within and outside government, through a vast network of kleptocratic actors who have configured a shadow state that feeds off the formal state. As a result, the militarized fight against galamsey between 2017 and 2024 failed, the evidence of which we turn to below. The upshot of the analysis in this chapter, and the book in general, is that the president's vow to fight galamsey at the cost of his presidency was a façade, using his tough rhetorics to hide the shadow state.

The Power Elites, CMM Galamsey, and the Biases of Military Operations

It is an open secret in Ghana that powerful politicians and people with close connection to them—the power elite—are engaged in CMM galamsey. The king of Asante, the Asantehene, Otumfuo Osei Tutu II, is one of the most eminent Ghanaians to pronounce on this open secret, doing this in the presence of the top government officials who were leading the military fights against galamsey. During his opening address at one of the government's public fora to find solution to the galamsey menace—dubbed "Dialogue" between the government and stakeholders in the small-scale mining sector—the king said 30% of people in the forum, which included government officials, knew the people engaged in galamsey. In fact, some of them were participating in galamsey themselves (Graphic Online, 2021a, 2021b). The king, whose kingdom is one of the parts of Ghana endowed with gold and one of the "hotspots" of galamsey in Ghana, was making this bold and serious allegation against the power elite, including politicians, on solid ground. Considering his eminence and his high stakes in the fight against galamsey, one would imagine he made these charges based on solid evidence at his disposal. Indeed, he disclosed that he would have said many "tough things," but he was prevailed upon by two Ministers of the government to stick to his prepared speech (Frimpong—Graphic Online, 2021b). The "tough things" the king mentioned are things that will embarrass the power elite, including officials of government.

The Asante king has unceasingly made this claim at other public fora that he had the opportunity to voice his views on the galamsey menace. Such an opportunity availed itself when one of the leading news media companies, The Multimedia Group, visited the Manhyia Palace in Kumasi to give him a copy of their groundbreaking documentary on galamsey, *Destruction for Gold*. The king did not mince words when he talked about the involvement of politicians and other powerful people in galamsey. "Galamsey operations are very complex," he said, "with a lot of people involved. We will never succeed in the fight if we approach it lackadaisically. There are some collaborators in corridors of power as well as some politicians and some businessmen involved. They own excavators used in these operations. A lot of them" (Myjoy.online.com 2022). The king also posed rhetorical questions, which point to state capture: "Doesn't the gold produced from galamsey pass through our airport before being sent abroad? Don't we have equipment that detects them? Why all this noise about galamsey? Are we saying we don't know those behind galamsey?" (Myjoyonline.com 2022).

Scholarly research and government sources lend weight to the charges the Asantehene made against politicians and other members of the power elite. Based on empirical research, this body of work has documented evidence on the complicity of some Ghanaian politicians and public officials in the illegal mining undertaken by Chinese nationals through, for instance, protecting and assisting these foreigners to get fake immigration documents to enter the country to engage in galamsey (Ocquaye, 2023; Hilson et al., 2014; Hausermann and Ferring, 2018). There is also evidence that suggests that some politicians (district chief executives, members of parliament, and political party leaders) and traditional authorities are directly involved in illegal ASM operations (Eduful et al., 2020: 10). As discussed further below, the political and economic interests of members of the power elite class in galamsey—of which politicians and senior public servants are a big component—are the main cause of the inundation of galamsey by Chinese nationals.

Against this background, one is on solid ground arguing that *Operation Vanguard*, for example, was "a selective enforcement of ASM laws, shaped by class alliance and political power. The powerful and the politically well-connected were protected to carry on with galamsey, while the subaltern classes, mining for survival, were subjected to the strict and violent enforcement methods [of this Operation]" (Ayelazuno and

Mawuko-Yevugah, 2021, p. 571). The war against galamsey was, therefore, against the powerless and the "unconnected" to the higher echelons of state power. Despite the macho posturing of the president and his appointees—that these military operations were an all-out war against galamsey—the evidence points to biases in the operations and swoops, in favour of the mining-power elite who have captured the state and are in control of the powerful shadow state.

Far from being an all-out war against galamsey, the illegal mines and mining by people connected to politicians occupying high political offices were protected from the above-mentioned military operations. Drawing on the analogy of the fishing practices in some advanced countries known as "catch and release," Eduful and their co-authors likened the discriminatory approach of Operation Vanguard to this fishing practice. When personnel of *Operation Vanguard* arrest illegal miners or seize the mining equipment of galamsey operators connected to the centers of power in the state, pressure "from above" is put on them to release them: so, they "catch and release" them. Indeed, in some cases, the mining sites of these powerful operators of galamsey are "no-go" areas, and personnel of these military operations cannot patrol these areas, let alone confiscate their mining equipment (Eduful et al., 2020, p. 10).

The former Chief Executive Officer of the Forestry Commission (FC), the late Mr. Kwadwo Owusu Afriyie, an appointee of the government, confirmed on national TV—PM Express on Joynews—that people in higher authority were thwarting the fight against galamsey, by using their powers to promote "catch and release." He claimed that people arrested for illegal mining in forest reserves have been released and are back to the forest reserves to continue their illegal mining. Using a case of the arrest of some people, both civilians and soldiers, for engaging in galamsey in the Apapraman forest reserve in the Ashanti region, he said phone calls are usually made to some people in higher authority, who then order the release of the culprits (The Ghana Report, 2019a). A forestry officer told a researcher a similar story about Chinese nationals who extended their illegal mining activities to a forest reserve adjacent to a mining concession they had permit to mine in. Upon getting the tip-off, the forestry officer went with the police and arrested some of the Chinese nationals and detained them. In less than three hours after the arrest, he received a call from a big man in Accra who ordered him to release them. He complied and released them (Hausermann and Ferring, 2018).

What has become popularly known in Ghana as the *missing exca-vator saga* is, perhaps, one of the rare cases that the power elite, specifically senior political appointees of state, are heard discussing a framework to use the missing excavators to do mining. They need to do this because their party needed money—to wit in twi, "party hia sika." About 500 excavators were confiscated during Operation Vanguard and parked at the premises of various Metropolitan, Municipal and District Assemblies (MMDAs)—the local government agencies of the state. Surprisingly, in January 2020, the Minister of Environment, Science and Technology and Innovation, and Chairman of the inter-Ministerial Committee on illegal mining (IMCIM), Professor Kwabena Frimpong-Boateng, announced that "hundreds of the confiscated excavators have gone missing" (Ayelazuno and Mawuko-Yevugah, 2021, p. 571).

The minister wrote a letter to the police and reported the theft; in which he provided further and better particulars about the crime: he stated that Mr. Ekow Ewusi—who was then the Vice Regional Chairman of the incumbent president's party, the NPP—was "contracted to cart excavators and other vehicles and pieces of equipment seized by Operation Vanguard to designated areas for safekeeping." However, the Minister "received information that he sent an unknown number of the equipment to unauthorized locations, including one in Tema." He stated further in the letter that Mr. Ewusi's action was confirmed by the care-taker of the Tema depot where some of the excavators were parked. According to the Minister, Mr. Ewusi had sold an unknown number of pieces of equipment, including excavators (Citi Newsroom, 2020). Based on this complaint, the police arrested Mr. Ewusi and five others: Fred-erick Ewusi, Joel Asamoah, Adam Haruna, Frank Gyan, and John Arhin (Pulse.com.gh 2020).

As illustrated by Fig. 6.1, the Minister wrote another letter on 5th February 2020, giving further information to the police about the theft. He asked the police to investigate Mr. Seth Mantey, a journalist, and Mr. John Ofori-Atta, then the National Security Coordinator for the Central Region. The Minister claimed that Mr. Mantey confessed to him that he allowed his bank account to be used to receive and distribute money from the sale of excavators stolen by Mr. Ewusi. The money was cashed and given to Mr. John Ofori-Atta, who shared it with Mr. Ekow Ewusi (The Ghana Report, 2020; Pulse.com.gh, 2020; African Eye Report, 2020).

Again, in March 2021, the former chairman of IMCIM, Prof Frimpong-Boateng, submitted a confidential report to the Chief of Staff at the presidency, alleging the culpability of high government officials in

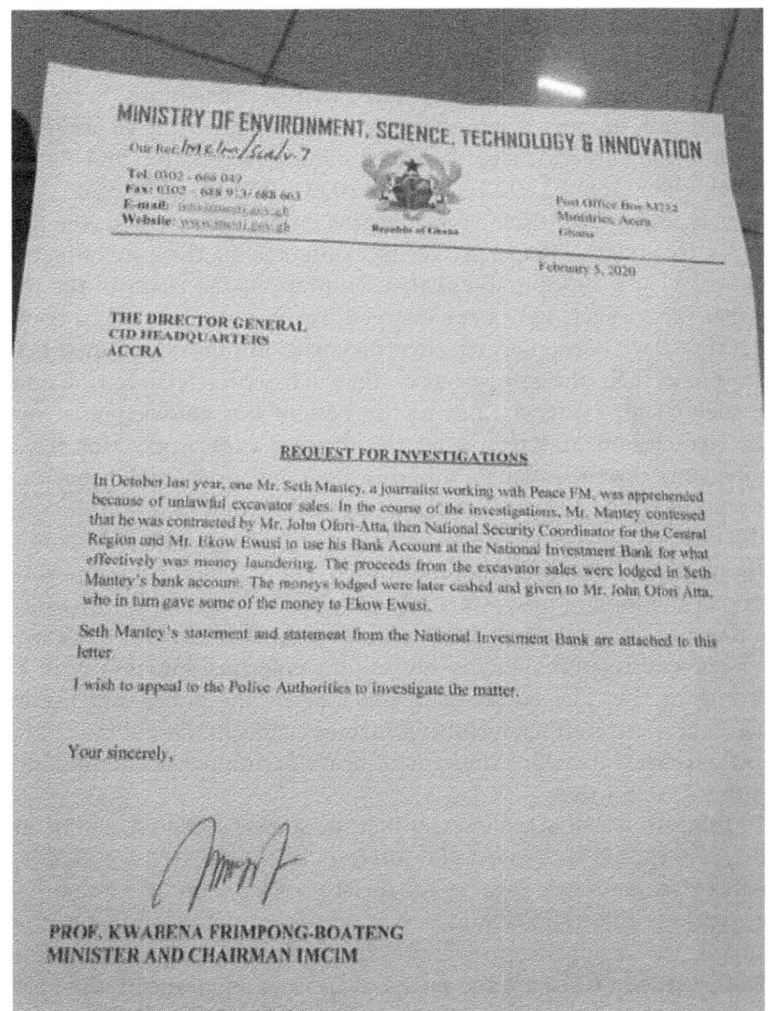

Fig. 6.1 Prof Frimpong Boateng's letter of complaint to the police (*Source* The Ghana Report, 2020)

galamsey and requesting that action be taken by the president against them. However, no action was taken until the report was leaked in October 2023. This elicited a hurriedly instituted police investigation at the instance of the presidency (Ayelazuno and Aziabah, 2023; Graphic Online, 2023a, 2023b, 2023c, 2023d). However, a legal opinion from Ghana's Attorney General's office stated that the allegations "were bare" and could not support a criminal case against 12 of the 15 individuals cited for criminality in respect of illegal mining (Ayelazuno and Aziabah, 2023; Graphic Online, 2023a, 2023b, 2023c, 2023d).

To date, more than three years after the crime was reported, the police have yet to update Ghanaians on the outcome of their investigations. However, what is indisputable is that, contrary to the claim of the president that the suspects have been charged, there is no evidence to confirm this. If they have been charged, then they have not been arraigned before court, more than three years after they have been charged. In addition, there is no evidence, and to the best of our knowledge, that the police have found and recovered the missing excavators. Nor has the complainant, Prof Kwabena Frimpong-Boateng, updated Ghanaians on the outcome of the police investigations into his complaint and the search for the missing excavators. All these belie the existence of a modicum of a functioning state that keeps law and order. The state has been repurposed to protect the mining interests of the power elite in galamsey. In a formal state that has not experienced this repurposing, these serious cases would have been investigated meticulously and the culprits found and dealt with according to law. The handling of this case by the police and the loud silence over it are another surprising turn of events in the militarized fight against galamsey; namely, hundreds of heavy earthmoving equipment got missing without a trace.

Yet this is to be expected in cases that the state is captured, and its institutions repurposed to protect the interests of the power elite. The state becomes dysfunctional, despite its surface appearance of a functioning state—such as the military and police personnel deployed in Operation Vanguard, the confiscation of hundreds of excavators, and the arrest of suspects accused of stealing the seized excavators. Underneath this surface appearance of a state is the stronger shadow state that strongly influences the formal state to serve the interests of the powerful elite class. From very reliable sources and the media reportage so far, it seems this is what happened with the missing excavators. Credibility is lent to these sources by the silence of government officials who promised to get the culprits and deal with them according to law and to recover the stolen equipment. To date, this has not been done, and these officials have remained silent. One such source is a member of *Operation Vanguard*, the leader of the special monitoring, evaluation, evacuation and investigation operations, Mr. Nana Boadi. He granted interviews to the media, in which he said 315 excavators were confiscated as of 31st January 2020. However, only 127 excavators were left. He then said that "some of the machines have gone back to the mining site" (Ghanaweb, 2020). In another interview with a different media house, he said "they [excavators] are with the miners. We can find them anywhere they are mining and we have started retrieving them" (Myjoyonline.com, 2020).[1]

This claim is consistent with the allegation made by an MP of the governing party, the Assin Central MP, Kennedy Agyapong, against Prof Frimpong-Boateng the complainant of the missing-excavators case. According to the MP, the complainant conspired with Mr. Ekow Ewusi, the suspect, to release some of the equipment to his own son, Mr. Jojo Frimpong-Boateng, to do illegal mining. He asked rhetorically, "How can you seize people's excavators for illegal mining and turn around to give it to your son for his mining activities?" He also accused Prof Frimpong-Boateng and the suspect of renting some of the confiscated equipment and pocketing the money. Prof Frimpong-Boateng has denied these allegations and told journalists that "he [his son] is not involved in anything and the world will get to know soon" (Citi Newsroom, 2022).

Another piece of evidence of state capture is an audio recording of two people, believed to be the Minister, Prof Frimpong-Boateng (complainant) and Ekow Ewusi (suspect) that went viral on social media. This audio recording has become associated with the saying in Twi language, "*party hia sika*" (to wit, "the party [NPP] needs money"). The two people are heard discussing a plan to deploy the confiscated excavators to do mining, because the party needs money. From state capture perspective, what is instructive in the conversation is a voice believed to be the Minister endorsing this plan: "…Did you tell me that you are done forming the team? We talked about the framework…we all know that the party needs money…I told you that Chairman Wontumi has some concession so go there and inspect the place…but after the meeting, you told me that you are done with everything and your guys have started working…" (Pulse.com.gh, 2020). The Minister who made the complaint about missing excavators is discussing a plan to deploy the same excavators to do mining to get money for their party, because "*party hia sika.*"

[1] https://www.myjoyonline.com/weve-started-retrieving-missing-excavators-operation-vanguard-taskforce-member/.

However, the same voice became angry when a voice believed to be Ekow Ewusi (suspect) suggested that the Minister had granted a request by another NPP MP, Elvis Morris Donkor, the Member of Parliament for Abura, Asebu, Kwamankese (AAK) in the Central Region, for an excavator to use on some galamsey sites (The Pulse, 2020). To this, the voice believed to be the Minister's is heard yelling, "Ekow please go away…don't annoy me today. Please walk out…the way you are talking I don't like it…you can't come here to accuse me. You go, when I'm ready I'll call you…I'm doing something for tomorrow" (Pulse.com.gh, 2020). At the very least, the audio demonstrates a secret conversation between two politicians of the governing party about the missing excavators. In the absence of an official update on the status of the case, this audio provides us with the only available information about what happened to the confiscated excavators: they were released to the power elite to do galamsey.

To the best of our knowledge, neither the Minister nor Mr. Ekow Ewusi has denied that the voices on the audio are theirs. In addition, Mr. Ewusi who is the suspect in the stealing case has not been tried for the alleged crimes. Reminiscent of the kleptocratic dynamics of state capture, we are told by Prof Frimpong-Boateng that the Senior Minister, Yaw Osafo Marfo, tried to protect Mr. Ekow Ewusi's reputation. The Senior Minister is arguably the highest appointee in the government of President Akufo-Addo, perhaps the most powerful official after the Vice-President. Yet Prof Frimpong-Boateng made a serious allegation against him; that the Senior Minister vowed to protect the reputation of Mr. Ekow Ewusi. In furtherance of this, the Senior Minister, according to Prof Frimpong-Boateng, described him (Prof Frimpong-Boateng) as a bad person and asked people to gang up against him (Ayelazuno and Aziabah 2023: 6). Despite the seriousness of these allegations, which were widely publicized in the mass media, we are not aware of a denial or legal action by the Senior Minister to demonstrate that they are false. This is not the only case that the Senior Minister was involved in state capture in the militarized fight against galamsey. As the discussion below on another example of state capture—En Huang (Aisha Huang), the Chinese national who is notorious for engaging in CMM galamsey—will illustrate, the Senior Minister was seen in a viral video on social media, justifying the freeing of this foreigner who breached the mining laws of Ghana. Considering his higher position of power in the government of President Akufo-Addo, his actions are clear examples of the inner sanctums of power who have been influenced by the mining-power elites to repurpose the institutions of the formal Ghanaian state to protect their mining interests. They also illustrate the ways in which the shadow state, controlled by the mining-power elites, feeds off the formal Ghanaian state.

To be added to this is the apparent untouchability of Mr. Ekow Ewusi; namely, despite his major role in the missing excavators, he has not been held accountable. On the contrary, the leadership of his party who suspended him indefinitely as Vice Chairman of the Central Region, reduced the punishment to definite suspension, and subsequently lifted it by the end date (Citi Newsroom, 2022). That is not all. He was elected as the NPP's parliamentary candidate for the Cape Coast North Constituency in December 2023 (GNA, 2023). Considering that the case of the missing excavators was partly the reason for his suspension, the decision of the leadership of the party to lift the suspension of Mr. Ewusi, and to crown it all, nominate him as the parliamentary candidate of the party, are signal evidence of state capture by the power elite in the militarized fight against galamsey.

Why this claim? Four reasons: first, because of the *missing excavators saga* is arguably the most hideous political scandals in the militarized fight against galamsey in pursuit of the fulfilment of President Akufo-Addo's vow to fight and defeat illegal ASGM at all cost. As argued elsewhere, "the 'missing excavators' was the bombshell political scandal that hit the IMCIM and Operation Vanguard, with traditional mass media organizations and journalists, as well as citizens and civil society organizations, using digital media to publicise it widely" (Ayelazuno and Aziabah 2023: 6). Second, several tens of millions of US dollars—that could have been used to promote the human development of the subaltern classes—have been spent on these militarized fights. Third, this scandal is also, perhaps, the biggest indictment on the president and his government's commitment to fighting the galamsey menace. Fourth, the missing excavators's scandal marred *Operation Vanguard* to such a great extent it had to be disbanded abruptly and without any explanation to date.

Mr. Ekow Ewusi is one of the key political actors—to be more precise, kleptocratic political actor—at the centre of this scandal: the infamous missing excavators scandal. Yet he is left off the hook, both in the police investigation and the disciplining processes of the president's political party, the NPP. Paradoxically—but unsurprisingly, with the lens of state capture—he gets rewarded with elevation from a Regional Vice Chairman of the NPP to a parliamentary candidate of the party, with a good chance of becoming a member of the parliament of Ghana. And if he does, he will become a legislator, including legislating on mining in general, and ASGM specifically. Yet the leader of the NPP and the president of Ghana—who vowed to fight galamsey at the cost of losing his presidency and committed millions of dollars to this fight—is loudly silent. This bears striking similarity with state capture in South Africa under Jacob Zuma discussed in chapter four. In one of the cases of state capture, the charges of security breaches against the president's Chief of Protocol—charges related to the landing of a civilian plane at a military airbase by the Gupta family—were secretly dropped; and the inculpated appointee rewarded with an ambassadorial appointment to the Netherlands. Like state capture in South Africa under President Zuma, the powerful influence of the mining-power elites over the Ghanaian state officials is directed at the inner sanctums of the power of the state, an influence that has repurposed a gamut of state apparatuses, including the presidency, to promote their material and political interests in galamsey.

As we were about to submit this book manuscript to the publisher, another scandal bearing striking resemblance to the missing excavators was gaining traction in the media space. Drones procured at the cost of 3 million US dollars to boast the militarized fight against galamsey were reported missing, and the relevant state institutions responsible for their procurement, use, maintenance and security are evasive in their responses to enquiries about their whereabouts (The Fourth Estate, 2024). "For close to two years, from October 2022 to May 2024," the investigative story just cited reports, "The Fourth Estate persistently sought to find out the whereabouts of the drones from three ministries and the Office of the President but got no answers" (The Fourth Estate, 2024). Yet it is indisputable that drones were acquired in 2018 as part of the resources needed to prosecute the president's war against galamsey. Professor Frimpong-Boateng, the cabinet minister who was responsible for overseeing this war, made known that a total of 90 drones were ordered for this purpose (Frimpong-Boateng, n.d. p. 40).

Supposing the drones procured were 90 (not 200), this still leaves questions begging for answers, as the Fourth Estates investigative report correctly pointed to: where and when were the drones used, and to what effect? Where are these drones now, as the galamsey menace has aggravated? Going by the dynamics of state capture that characterized the missing excavators, one can predict the answers to these questions would not be forthcoming from the government of President Akufo-Addo.

Mining in Forest Reserves and River Bodies with Impunity

The investigative documentary by Erastus Asare Donkor of The Multimedia Group, titled *Destruction for Gold* (which is in three parts), illustrates the persistence of CMM galamsey and the horrific pollution of water bodies and destruction of the vegetative cover of Ghana (Donkor, 2022a; 2022b; 2022c).[2] This calls to question the success of the military operations touted by the Akufo-Addo government. Reminiscent of the biases of these operations in favour of the power elite, the documentary also captured powerful politicians and other influential people mining in forest reserves under the protection of heavily armed soldiers of GAF, with their names embossed on their uniforms. Part I of *Destruction for Gold* shows the soldiers aggression towards Asare Donkor and his team. The leader of the soldiers was also seen reporting to someone on phone, saying they are on the *"Halt duties"* and some policemen and media have come to their location. This means, the soldiers were part of the *Operation Halt* operatives, but rather than fighting galamsey, they were protecting the mines of some special people: the power elites. One must be an extraordinarily powerful state captor to be assigned armed soldiers of GAF to guard their mines, amid the militarized fight against galamsey.

Akonta Mining Limited is one of the mining companies that was captured by *Destruction for Gold mining* in the forest reserves. The company belongs to the Ashanti Regional Chairman of the NPP, Mr. Bernard Antwi Bosiako; popularly known as Chairman Wontumi. Chairman Wontumi may be one of the most powerful influential people in Ghana, because the Ashanti Region is popularly referred to as the "World Bank" of the NPP; not only because the electorates in this region are predominantly loyal supporters who vote massively for the NPP in elections. But also, because it is the region with a high registered number of voters who vote for the NPP in the whole country. And without these voters and their loyalty to NPP, the party may never win the presidential elections in Ghana (see Ayelazuno, 2011). If the Ashanti Regional Chairman of the NPP has a mining company, as Chairman Wontumi has,

---

[2] Destruction for Gold (Part 1): https://www.youtube.com/watch?v=8wE8ya-po_c; Part 2: https://www.youtube.com/watch?v=0NC7ALzpYEM; Part 3: https://www.youtube.com/watch?v=2roPsklYJew.

he will not only be a strong influence on mining policies, but their implementation; as such, he will be a potential powerful state captor. The rest of this section shows that, indeed, he is.

The Minister of Lands and Natural Resources released a press statement on the revelations in the documentary, confirming that the Ministry had heard about the allegations against Akonta Mining Limited. The press statement said the Ministry had taken note of a "publication about certain operations by Akonta Mining Limited in the Tano Nimiri Forest Reserve in the Amenfi West Municipality in the Western Region." It further stated that the company "has a mining lease to undertake mining operations in some parts of Samreboi, outside the Forest Reserve," but it has "no mineral right to undertake any mining operations in the Tano Nimiri Forest Reserve." The Minister then directed the Forestry Commission to "forthwith, ensure that the company does not carry out any operation in the Forest and to take the necessary action against any person found culpable in this matter" (Myjoyonline.com, 2022).

The Minerals Commission, the state institution that regulates mining in Ghana, also released a press statement supporting the Minister's statement. The Commission's statement made a startling revelation: Akonta Mining Limited has applied for a licence to mine in the Tano Nimiri Forest. And the application has gone through all the phases of approval and is at the very last stage: the approval by the Minister of Lands and Natural Resources. The press statement noted that the application dated 25th August 2022, "has not been determined by the Minister, who is mandated by law, to grant or refuse such applications" (The Minerals Commission, 2022; Pulse.com.gh, 2022).

In the words of the Minister of Lands and Natural Resources, the application has gone through an elaborate process from the Forestry Commission, through the Minerals Commission, to gazette; a process during which the company paid some fees to the state. It is left with just him, the Minister, to approve the mining lease for the company to mine legally in the Tano Nimiri Forest, but he had not yet determined that application—which means he had not yet given approval. He indicated that Akonta Mining Limited has written a petition to him with their side of the case, backing it with documents. As such, he has appealed to Ghanaians to exercise patience and wait for the various ongoing investigations to determine whether a crime has been committed or not by the mining company (Metro TV, 2023).

Based on the evidence in the documentary, *Destruction for Gold*, four prominent Ghanaians have reported the alleged case of illegal mining by Akonta Mining Limited to the police for further investigation (Graphic Online 2022a, 2022b, 2022c). The case has also attracted the attention of the Office of the Special Prosecutor (OSP), an anti-graft state agency, who is also investigating the allegations (Citi Newsroom, 2023). Occupy Ghana, a civil society organization, sent a petition to the Minister of Lands and Natural Resources, expressing its dissatisfaction with the action the Minister had taken on the alleged illegal mining of Akonta Mining Limited in the forest reserve. The organization argued that the above-mentioned directive of the Minister was not enough and requested him to do more. The organization, thus, demanded the minister do the following: refer the facts and evidence in his possession, that show that the said mining company is undertaking mining operations in breach of the Act, to the police and the Attorney General for further investigations and prosecution (Metro TV, 2023).

However, the Akonta Mining Limited case must be situated in the long history of galamsey and the failure of the Ghanaian state to control it, despite the environmental menace it causes. As the preceding sections have illustrated, research and other reliable sources have amply demonstrated that the power elite of Ghana—including powerful politicians—are involved in galamsey. More so, this power elite class has captured the state and it is incapacitated to fight the galamsey menace. The pattern of events of the Akonta Mining Limited's case does not depart from this long history of the involvement of the power elite in galamsey and the state capture that underpins it. The case is characterized by some curious contradictions. For example, the application by the company passed through all the above-mentioned approval phases at a time when the Minister of Lands and Natural Resources had directed that "there should be no further issuance of permits for mining in Forest reserves, except in exceptional circumstances" (MLNR, 2021). Indeed, Operation Halt II was mounted to enforce this directive. Furthermore, this application went through all these processes of approval at a time the Minister of Lands and Natural resources was leading the "Green Ghana Project"—a project touted as part of the Ghanaian president's "aggressive national afforestation/reforestation programme to restore the lost forest cover of Ghana and to contribute to the global effort to mitigate climate change" (MLNR, 2021).

From a state capture perspective, there is no reason to hope that the case of the alleged illegal mining of Akonta Mining Limited will be handled differently from the case of the missing excavators. To date, more than a year since the allegations of illegal mining in forest reserves were made against the company of the powerful Ashanti Regional Chairman of the NPP, there is no evidence that the owner of the company or the directors of the company have been arrested—let alone charged and arraigned before court. While the outcome of these technical criminal investigations is awaited, Erastus Asare Donkor's investigative documentary, *Destruction for Gold*, has documented, in real time, ample evidence of the company mining in the forest. And to date, the company has not taken any legal action against Erastus Asare Donkor and his employers for false publication and bringing its reputation into disrepute, thus lending credence to the allegations.

We must hasten to add that we may be overly optimistic to nurse the hope that there would ever be an outcome from the criminal investigations into the Akonta Mining case. Because the president of Ghana has already told the whole world—while these investigations are still ongoing—that Akonta Mining Ltd has not been involved in illegal mining. In his own words, "I want to assure you all that Akonta Mining is not engaged in any form of illegal mining anywhere in Ghana as we speak" (Citi Newsroom, 2023). The president who vowed to fight and defeat galamsey at all cost—including sacrificing his job of president—has publicly declared a company being investigated for doing galamsey as innocent. This is solid evidence of state capture; especially, considering the forum that he made this public declaration: the 28th National and 16th Biennial Congress of the National Union of Ghana Catholic Diocesan Priests Association in Koforidua. One would have thought this is a forum in which religious issues should occupy the mind of the president, who is a devout Christian himself. But he was in a hurry to clear the Regional Chairman of his party. This is a clear signal of the inner sanctum of power of state that the mining-power elites, as Mr. Bernard Antwi Bosiako, have accessed and influenced to promote their material and political interests.

STATE CAPTURE IN THE FORMULATION OF REGULATIONS: MINING IN FOREST RESERVES

The preceding discussion on allegations of mining in the forest levelled against Akonta Mining Ltd revealed that the company was almost about to get a mining lease/licence to mine in the forest reserve. The oxymoron—licence to mine in forest reserve—is an interesting one that cannot be missed in state capture analysis of the militarized fight against galamsey. It is even more interesting, considering that the government of Ghana has initiated a programme, The Green Ghana Day, which it aims to plant trees across the country to green it. Several millions of Ghana cedis, from both government and private sources, have been spent on this project. According to Mr. Abu Jinapor, the Minister of Lands and Natural Resources, besides funding sourced from the private sector— "corporate Ghana" in his words—the government of Ghana allocates funds to support the programme. It allocated Ghs2 million each in 2021 and 2022, Ghs2.5 million in 2023, and Ghs1.5 in 2024 (Asaase Radio, 2024).

Despite this contradiction—and redolent of state capture at the input end of the policy formation and implementation spectrum—the government passed the Environmental Protection (Mining in Forest Reserves) Regulation 2022 (L.I.2462). Specifically, it was passed in 2022, having been initiated by the Minister of the Ministry of Environment, Science, Innovation and Technology, "in the exercise of the powers conferred on [him] by Section 62(1) of the Environmental Protection Agency Act, 1994 (Act 490)" (Nature and Development Foundation, 2023, p. 7). Even though the purpose of the law, on the surface, seems well-intentioned, a deeper dive into its details reveals a shocking permissiveness in the pillaging of the forest reserves of Ghana by so-called licenced or legal mining activities. As the title of the law illustrates, its main purpose is "to address the environmental aspects of mining activities within forest reserves" (TaylorCrabbe and ClientEarth, 2024). But hidden in this innocuous purpose is something more sinister: it allows unlimited mining in forest reserves, contingent upon certain conditions (Nature and Development Foundation, 2023), major among them is the discretion of the president of Ghana: she/he may allow mining and prospecting in forest reserves if he/she deems it necessary in the national interest (The Fourth Estate, 2024).

Compared to existing Ghanaian policies governing forest reserves, the law is retrogressive in terms of the protection of forest reserves. For example, the National Land Policy bans mining in forest reserves; but the Environmental Guidelines and the Forest and Wildlife Policy permits a limited area of mining in forest reserves. In contrast, L.I 2462 "appears to permit mining in all forest reserves in Ghana, provided the procedures specified in the L.I are complied with" (TaylorCrabbe and ClientEarth, 2024, p. 2). Based on the institutional deficiencies and corruption in Ghana, one can predict that these procedures will be flouted with impunity. To make matters worse, and evocative of state capture, the law does not impose harsher punishment on offenders. As one legal opinion on the law noted, the penalties spelt out for breaching the law fall short of coming close to a deterrent to environmental criminals and vile mining capitalists:

> Its most severe penalty for a breach is a mere one-year imprisonment term and a fine of 250 penalty units (3000ghc). This feeble stance becomes even more evident compared to similar regulations like the Timber Resource Management and Legality Licensing Regulations, 2017, which prescribes a range from 250 to 1000 penalty units and a potential imprisonment term of up to two (2) years. (Nature and Development Foundation 2023, p. 13)

Little wonder that the Ghana Institute of Foresters (GIF), which was dismayed and enraged upon hearing about the enactment of the law, described it as an "outrageous Legislative Instrument that permits unlimited mining in our forest reserves" (GIF, 2023).

Because of its environmentally obnoxious nature, several environmental activists and civil society organizations (CSOs) raised alarm about it. They include Nature and Development Foundation; A Rocha Ghana; Occupy Ghana; Media Coalition against Galamsey; WACAM; Oxfam Ghana; Ghana Youth Environment Movement; Eco-conscious Citizens; Hen Mpoano; Ghana Environment Advocacy Group; Youth Alliance for Green Ghana; Concerned Citizens of Atewa Landscape; Centre for Agroforestry Business Development (CABuD); Domestic Lumber Trade Association (DOLTA); Ghana Institute of Foresters (GIF), and many more (see Nature and Development Foundation 2024). These CSOs advocated the immediate review of the law, because it was "fraught with 'sinful provisions' that made all forest reserves candidates for mining" (Graphic Online, 2023a, 2023b, 2023c, 2023d)

The enactment of the law, according to Mr. Mustapha Seidu, the Director of Nature and Development Foundation, has seen the rapid increase in the granting of mining leases in forest reserves: "eight more mining leases had been granted in forest reserves, while 14 more applications for leases in forest reserves were under consideration by the Minerals Commission" (Graphic Online, 2023a, 2023b, 2023c, 2023d). The records of the Minerals Commission indicate an upsurge in applications for mining concessions in forest reserves since June 2022, when the LI 2462 was presented to Parliament (The Fourth Estate, 2024). Figure 6.2 shows that some of these applications have been approved for companies to mine in forest reserves. As the class dynamics of the present-day ASGM sector of Ghana illustrate (Aziabah and Ayelazuno, 2024), these leases, to be sure, would have been granted to the power elites, not the subaltern classes. The latter, as already noted, do not have the financial capital and access to the inner sanctum of power of the state to influence the granting of mining leases to them in forest reserves. It is logical to conclude that the law was made to promote the interest of the mining-power elite, who influenced higher government officials and politicians to formulate and operationalize that law via legislation.

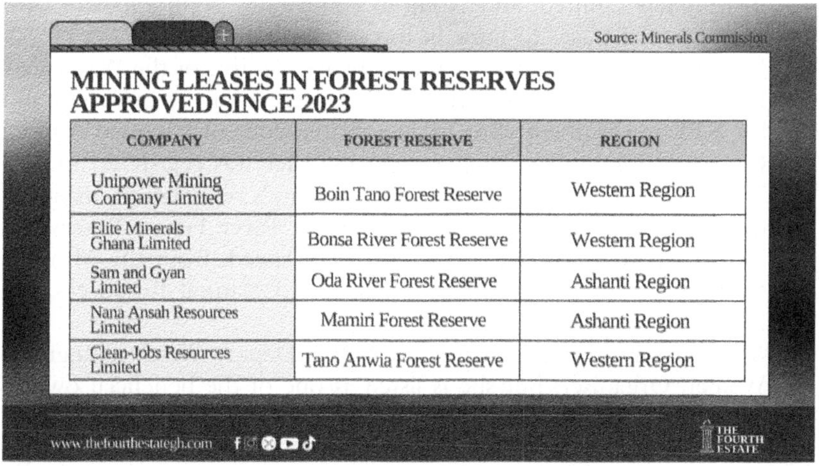

Source: Minerals Commission

MINING LEASES IN FOREST RESERVES APPROVED SINCE 2023

COMPANY	FOREST RESERVE	REGION
Unipower Mining Company Limited	Boin Tano Forest Reserve	Western Region
Elite Minerals Ghana Limited	Bonsa River Forest Reserve	Western Region
Sam and Gyan Limited	Oda River Forest Reserve	Ashanti Region
Nana Ansah Resources Limited	Mamiri Forest Reserve	Ashanti Region
Clean-Jobs Resources Limited	Tano Anwia Forest Reserve	Western Region

www.thefourthestategh.com f ⓒ ⊗ ▢ ♪

THE FOURTH ESTATE

Fig. 6.2 Mining leases approved for mining in forest reserves (*Source* The Fourth Estate, 2024)

True to this claim, Investigative journalists of *The Fourth Estate* have found that, since the passage of the law, "at least 25 companies had filed 32 applications to mine and prospect in 24 forest reserves as of August 13, 2024" and a "number of these companies [were] owned by politicians from the governing New Patriotic Party" (The Fourth Estate, 2024). According to this investigative journalism report, key among these power elites connected to the president and his party are:

1. Mr Sam Pyne, the Chief Executive of the Kumasi Metropolitan Assembly (KMA) and former Ashanti regional secretary of the NPP, who is a joint shareholder and beneficial owner of Sam and Gyan Limited, a mining company incorporated in 2017. This has been corroborated by the Minerals Commissions of Ghana as seen in Fig. 6.2. Sam and Gyan Limited has been granted a lease to mine in the Oda River Forest in the Ashanti Region.

2. Francis Owusu-Akyaw, the NPP's 2024 Parliamentary candidate for the Juaben Constituency in the Ashanti Region, a former member of the defunct IMCIM mentioned above. He is the contact person for about 15 mining companies, including Sam and Gyan Limited, Unipower Mining Company Limited, Hapic Mining Limited, and FJ Minerals Limited; and as Fig. 6.2 illustrates, some of them have been granted leases to mine in forest reserves.

3. Emmanuel Boakye is the District Chief Executive of the Wassa East District, in the Western Region, an appointee of the president and his NPP government. But he is a shareholder of Essaman Mining Company Limited, a mining company that was registered in July 2024. Within eight days after this company's registration, its application to mine in the 75-year-old Subri River Forest Reserve in his district was processed at a breakneck speed, from the Minerals Commission to the Ministry of Lands and Natural Resources, the last phase of approval.

4. Ms Angelina Bint Ntaama is the NPP's Deputy Western Regional Women Organiser, but she is listed as one of the beneficial owners of Essaman Mining Company Limited.

Little wonder that the government will rather defend the law—LI 2462—than review it, as demanded by environmental activists and CSOs.

So, the Minister of Lands and Natural Resources, Mr Samuel Abu Jinapor, who is responsible for the president's fight against galamsey and the implementation of the Green Ghana Day, defends the law. He argues that "the law was promulgated on sound reasoning" and as such, "the focus should be on the guidelines, protocols, and exercise of discretion in relation to the issuance of the forest entry permit" (Ghenvironment.com, 2023). But if probed with the evidence of the destruction of the environment by galamsey despite the existence of all the great laws and regulations, Mr. Abu Jinapor's optimism about the checks and balances of the law does not stand up to scrutiny. Citing the destruction of the Apamprama forest reserve in the Ashanti Region as an example, Erastus Asare Donkor reminded the Minister that entry permits were often abused, and that the regulatory bodies, after issuing the permits, do not check whether they were used for the purpose for which they were granted or not (Ghenvironment.com, 2023). Considering his role and defence of all the contradictions and controversies of the captured state, the Minister of Lands and Natural Resources, Mr Samuel Abu Jinapor, seems to be the face of the captured Ghanaian state in the militarized fight against galamsey.

But with the benefit of the insights of state capture, this highly controversial law, passed by the government of President Akufo-Addo—who vowed to fight the environmental menace of galamsey at all cost—demonstrates the powerful influence of the mining-power elite over the president and some of his cabinet ministers. In this case, the captured state has been repurposed to protect the interests of the mining-power elite, rather than protecting the forest reserves and the environment. Unlike most of the examples of state capture documented in this chapter, the influence of the power elite over state officials happened in the formulation/design of the law on mining in forest reserves. This is a form of state capture that is baked into the institutional architecture of the state to protect the interests of the mining-power elite in Ghana. And in that connection, it has engendered a profound disenabling of the formal state to act to protect the public good; namely, the protection of forest reserves that have been protected for decades until this law was made.

Capitalist Medium-Scale Mining (CMM) Galamsey in Plain Sight of the State

CMM galamsey—mechanized and semi-mechanized illegal ASGM under-taken to accumulate illicit wealth—involves the use of earthmoving equipment such as excavators, stone-crushers, and changfans (a China-made machine). These pieces of equipment are transported on vehicles from cities such as Accra, Tema, Takoradi, and Kumasi—where they were imported from abroad—into the rural areas to do CMM galamsey. From the importation of these equipment, through clearing them from the ports to their transportation and arrival at the mining sites in the rural areas, there are a gamut of state security agencies that could easily have stopped mechanized galamsey before it even began. There are state security agencies along the chain of the movement of these pieces of equipment such as the Ghana Ports and Habours Authority, Ghana Customs, and Ghana Police Service that could easily have stopped the movement of these equipment.

The Ghanaian state, determined to fight galamsey at all cost, is aware that a great number of the heavy earthmoving equipment imported into the country are used to do galamsey. Indeed, the state passed a law, the Minerals and Mining (Mineral Operations—Tracking of Earthmoving and Mining Equipment) Regulations, 2020 (L.I. 2404)[3]—that empowered the Minerals Commission to track earthmoving machines and equipment used to mine minerals in Ghana (Graphic Online, 2022a, 2022b, 2022c). The question then is why the state has not used its security agencies, mentioned above, to monitor and stop the importation and movement of these equipment to the rural areas to be used for galamsey.

With the benefit of the insights of state capture, the answer to the foregoing question is straightforward: all these state security agencies are part of the state apparatuses captured by the powerful operators of mech-anized and semi-mechanized galamsey. The frontline personnel of these security agencies may be paid some bribes by the power elite (the state captors), but their corrupt acts are not the main motor driving mech-anized galamsey. In terms of power hierarchy, these personnel are less

---

[3] See https://mlnr.gov.gh/index.php/lands-minister-commissions-centre-to-track-exp losive-vechicles-and-excavators/#:~:text=In%202020%2C%20Government%20promulg ated%20the,equipment%20used%20in%20mineral%20operations.

powerful than those public servants up the hierarchy of power: the political office holders and heads of these security agencies who have already been captured. The above-mentioned law suggests that the solution to mechanized galamsey lies in tracking heavy mining equipment digitally. Even without this law, the state could have stopped the movement of these equipment to rural areas for galamsey, as the chain of the movement of these pieces of equipment is visible and happens in the plain sight of state security agencies and other government institutions. The law merely adds to the overload of laws on the mining industry, but which have not prevented galamsey because of state capture.

Having made it to the rural areas and mining sites, these pieces of heavy earthmoving equipment are used to clear vegetative cover from huge tracts of land, and to dig and move mountains and mountains of soil. This mechanized mining happens in remote villages and in the forest, to be sure. But some even happen close to human settlements—in villages and towns. The pictures and video clips used in news reportage, commentaries, and documentaries on galamsey illustrate that mechanized mining and the environmental damage it causes cannot be hidden from the state and its numerous agencies at the local government level. These visual images show that the sheer magnitude of the vegetation that is cleared and the earth that is dug and moved are so conspicuous that they can easily be seen by the casual observer (see Donkor 2022a; 2022b; 2022c).[4] As noted by Teschner, "galamsey activities" are so ubiquitous in places that 'the casual observer may not believe that it could possibly be illegal', leading him to characterize galamsey as "alegal" in other words, "intentionally tolerated by law enforcement" (Crawford and Botchwey, 2017, p. 448). Only recently, in July 2024, contractors working on three of the four bypasses on the Accra—Kumasi Highway reported that illegal mining activities were affecting progress of their work. They complained that the illegal mining activities had "made the soil soggy, requiring more filling to compact the road, which has consequently delayed project timelines" (Ghanaweb, 2024). State agencies namely, the EPA and Minerals

---

[4] See, for example; https://www.pulse.com.gh/news/local/6-arrested-over-500-missing-excavators/pxzk01d; Mining & The Environment: Ghana's water bodies worse than pre-anti galamsey fight (17-1-22); https://www.youtube.com/watch?v=-occK7qQUBE; Over 30 fully-armed military protecting miners pillaging Manso Forest—JoyNews Prime (18–1-21) https://www.youtube.com/watch?v=mhEVWkopRBU; Destruction for gold part 1 https://www.youtube.com/watch?v=8wE8ya-po_c.

Commission, came out to distance themselves from allegations that they had granted permits for illegal mining to take place. In particular, the EPA official for the Asante Akim Central Municipal Assembly declared in an interview: "We received a letter from the Asante Akim Central Municipal Assembly that they wanted to undertake a dredging exercise to prevent flooding … So, whatever is taking place there aside from the dredging activity is illegal since no company or individual has been given the licence to mine there" (Graphic Online, 2024).

There is therefore a sense in which mechanized and semi-mechanized galamsey is happening in the plain sight of the Ghanaian state that claims to be fighting galamsey. Every galamsey site is in the jurisdiction of a local government authority: a district, municipal, or metropolitan assembly, each of which is headed by a chief executive appointed by and representing the president. All these local government administrative units are part of a bigger unit, a region, headed by a minister appointed by the president. The regional ministers supervise the district, municipal, and metropolitan assemblies, and their political heads. As a representative democracy, Ghana is divided into 275 constituencies, with each represented in parliament by an elected representative. Ghanaians living anywhere in Ghana have an MP who represents their interest in parliament. The National Security Council, headed by the president, is decentralized, with Regional Security Councils (REGSEC) and District Security Councils (DISEC) at the regional and districts/municipal/metropolitan levels. A cardinal responsibility of these security councils across all levels is to ensure peace and stability of the country by enforcing law and order.

Despite the presence of all these local level state institutions, mechanized and semi-mechanized galamsey happens in broad daylight and literally before their eyes. Yet the state claims it is fighting galamsey at all cost. This paradoxical situation is often referred to as the "lack of political will" to fight galamsey and "political interference" in the fight against galamsey. However, this understates the gravity of the dysfunctionality of the state in the face of galamsey; namely, a state captured by operators of mechanized galamsey, who are within and outside the state. The state is, thus, repurposed to protect the power elite. To suggest that the problem of galamsey is caused by the "lack of political will" and "political interference" makes light of a more serious problem.

The Onrush of Chinese Nationals to Galamsey

Despite a law banning foreigners from engaging in ASGM directly or providing mining services, foreigners—mostly nationals of China—are engaged in galamsey with the impunity described above. The influx of Chinese nationals into Ghana has transformed galamsey from artisanal mining to mechanized mining. They introduced new technology and machinery, replacing traditional methods of pickaxe, shovel and pan. The Chinese have introduced the widespread use of excavators, wash plants (trommel) and crushing machines (changfan), as well as water platforms and suction equipment for dredging in rivers (Crawford et al., 2016; McQuilken and Hilson, 2016). The number of Chinese citizens that have immigrated to Ghana legally and illegally, to engage in galamsey, is hard to estimate accurately. But by some accounts, they are about 50,000 (Hilson et al., 2014; Hausermann et al., 2020; Botchwey et al., 2019), mostly from Shanglin County in Guangxi province. These Chinese immigrants, known in Ghana as the "Shanglin gang."' have settled in rural parts of Ghana, and have created Chinese mining and cultural communities (Burrows and Bird, 2017; Crawford and Botchwey, 2017).

In a feature piece published on Graphic Online, the writer stated forthrightly that "[w]ithout foreign nationals' intervention in illegal small-scale gold mining in Ghana, the damage to the environment would not have been so devastating" (Graphic Online, 2017). The writer had the finger on the pulse of the galamsey menace. However, it is more accurate to say that without the incursion of Chinese nationals into galamsey, the environmental menace it causes would have been less devastating. The mechanization of galamsey and the environmental menace that has accompanied it are, to all intents and purposes, caused by the China-factor: the onrush of the nationals of China into Ghana to seek for gold by engaging in galamsey. It is important to situate this onrush in temporal context. As with the population of Chinese nationals engaged in galamsey, the time they started arriving in Ghana is difficult to state accurately. Based on the literature on this subject, they might have started arriving in Ghana between 2005 and 2008 (Burrows and Bird, 2017; Hausermann et al., 2020; Botchwey et al., 2019).

Crawford and Botchwey's (2017) research into the onrush of Chinese nationals to galamsey is, perhaps, the most revealing of state capture. They posed many poignant questions, which in our view foreshadow the captured Ghanaian state. The rhetorical formulation of the questions illustrates this assertion: where is the Ghanaian state when Chinese nationals are engaged in "out of control" galamsey and with a "culture of impunity?" How did such large numbers of foreign miners, particularly from China, come to be involved in ASM in Ghana, especially given its illegality? How could tens of thousands of Chinese and other foreign nationals be working in an industry that, by law, is restricted to Ghanaian citizens, especially with the introduction of heavy machinery such as excavators and bulldozers, highly conspicuous in rural areas? Further, how could Chinese miners in particular operate in a country that is so different from their own? Most notably, how did they get access to land on which to undertake mining? (Crawford and Botchwey, 2017, 450).

In the mainstream literature on the onrush of Chinese nationals to galamsey, the usual answers to these questions are drawn from theories similar to those used by Crawford and Botchwey: corruption and collusion of state officials, the role of big men (and big women), the role of local patrons, and so on (Crawford et al., 2016; 2017; Hausermann and Ferring, 2018; Botchwey et al., 2019; Ocquaye, 2023). As we argued above, all these theories offer persuasive accounts of the problem at hand. However, the high degree of dysfunctionality of the Ghanaian state in the face of the onrush of Chinese nationals to galamsey means a deeper incapacitation of the Ghanaian state. No such situation of the incapacitation of the state exists in any other sector of the Ghanaian economy, as that conspicuously displayed and witnessed in the case of the open operation of galamsey by the nationals of China.

The extreme incapacitation of the Ghanaian state in the face of the onrush of Chinese nationals to galamsey is demonstrated by the chain of illegal acts they engage in, culminating in their operation of galamsey. They do this with impunity, with the Ghanaian state doing very little to enforce the law banning foreigners from engaging in any form of ASGM in Ghana. For example, the Chinese nationals have moved to Ghana in huge numbers between 2005 and 2016. Some of them came to Ghana illegally, and then bribed immigration officers to enter the country. They even managed to bribe immigration officers to issue them with fake work permits. Also, they managed to import or hire heavy mining equipment and move them to the rural areas, and then acquired land, and mined in broad day light for gold. Furthermore, they have been able to repatriate the gold that they extract back home without getting arrested and prosecuted (Crawford et al., 2016; 2017; Hausermann and Ferring, 2018;

Hausermann et al., 2018; Botchwey et al., 2019; Ocquaye, 2023). Using the concept of "Big Man," Hausermann and Ferring (2018) explain how these illegal acts and crimes are facilitated by the power elite. They defined "Big men" as wealthy and powerful Ghanaian businessmen or government officials, and in some cases, wealthy Chinese nationals.

Based on their research, they describe vividly the role these "Big men'" play in facilitating the operation of galamsey by the nationals of China;

> Big men use connections to obtain official documents and provide capital required for prospecting and licensing procedures. Operating behind the scenes, these individuals also arrange political cover for foreign operations through personal associations. We heard stories of big men shepherding Chinese miners from Accra directly to rural mining sites they (or their political connections) own, moving the Chinese by the busload at night, accompanied by state security vehicles (police and/or military). (Hausermann and Ferring, 2018, p. 1021; see also Hausermann et al., 2018)

What is being described above is state capture. The definition of big men, the high level of power they are connected to, and the state protection they can get for Chinese nationals to engage in galamsey—and doing so with impunity—all point to state capture.

EN (AISHA) HUANG'S EXPLOITS ON GALAMSEY: THIS IS WHAT STATE CAPTURE LOOKS LIKE

En Huang (popularly called Aisha Huang in Ghana) is a Chinese national who symbolizes state capture in the onrush of Chinese nationals to do CMM galamsey in Ghana. Because of her power and influence, as well as the huge galamsey business she operates, she is popularly known in Ghana as the notorious Chinese galamsey queen or kingpin. She is well connected politically to powerful people in both NDC- and NPP-led governments, with whom she exchanges favours for protection of her illegal mining activities from the law enforcement agencies (Ayelazuno and Mawuko-Yevugah, 2019: 248).

Based on official government records, En (Aisha) Huang has been in Ghana since the early 2014. The National Identity Authority (NIA) records show that she applied for and was issued a non-citizen identity card on 26 February 2014. She renewed the card twice: on 31st August

2016 and 8th January 2018, using the same details and Chinese passport number G39575625, with the name En Huang (Graphic Online, 2022a, 2022b, 2022c). It is a reasonable estimation to claim that she has been operating her galamsey business freely since 2014 until 2017 when she was arrested with four other Chinese nationals by the Ghanaian security agencies. Ms. Huang and her accomplices were charged with various mining offences under Section 99 (1) of the Minerals and Mining Act, 2006 (Act 703) and the Immigration Act, 2000 (Act 573) in a Ghanaian court of law (Graphic Online, 2018).

However, the dynamics of state capture revolving on Aisha Huang were activated between 2018 and 2022. Redolent with state capture, the trial of Aisha Huang and her accomplices took a stunning dramatic turn in December 2018. The Ghanaian state—headed by the president who vowed to fight galamsey even at the cost of his political career—asked the court to discontinue the trial. Using its powers to initiate and discontinue criminal processes of crimes committed in Ghana, the State Attorney, filed an application before the trial judge requesting for the trial to be discontinued (known in legal terms as *nolle prosequi*); a request that was made without any plausible reasons. The implausible reason was that the state was no more interested in prosecuting Ms. Huang and her accomplices. The trial judge obliged, and they were set free. However, they were subsequently deported from the country by Ghana Immigration Service (Graphic Online, 2018).

The advocates of the anti-galamsey military operations—for example, members of *OccupyGhana* and *The Media Coalition* against illegal small-scale mining—were dissatisfied, indeed, angry with this surprising turn the case had taken (The Ghana Report, 2019b). *OccupyGhana* contended that the decision of the Government to discontinue with the prosecution of Ms. Huang and the other four Chinese nationals "beggars belief, insults our intelligence, contradicts the President's numerous pledges to fight Galamsey, and is probably the most obvious indicator that the Government's commitment to the anti-Galamsey fight has been at best half-hearted" (Starrfm.com.gh, 2019).

However, one of the highest government officials—the Senior Minister, Mr. Yaw Osafo-Maafo—provided a glimpse of why the government made such a surprising decision to discontinue the prosecution of the Chinese nationals. He justified the decision of the government in words that illustrate state capture:

We have a very good relationship with China. Today, the main company that is helping develop the infrastructure system in Ghana is Sinohydro, it is a Chinese Company. It is the one that is going to help process our bauxite and provide about two billion dollars to us. So, when there are these kinds of arrangements, there are other things behind the scenes. Putting that lady (Aisha) in jail in Ghana is not going to solve your economic problems. It is not going to make you happy or me happy, that's not important, the most important thing is that she has been deported from Ghana ... (Graphic Online, 2019)

Embedded in this quote are nuggets of information on state capture in the onrush of Chinese nationals to do CMM galamsey in Ghana. One can see, for example, that the economic might of China weighed on the government's decision, which means that the power elite in the state capture may include a powerful international actor as the Chinese state. China may be using its soft powers to leverage the decision of the Ghanaian state to stop the prosecution of its nationals (Tsikudo, 2022). And as the theory of state capture suggests, the power elite are connected to the inner sanctum of power to influence decisions. The Senior Minister who was part of the inner sanctum of the power of state is here saying that the decision to free the Chinese nationals was taken at the highest level of government. This was confirmed by the president of Ghana when he admitted in a public forum that his government made the wrong decision; to wit "I think the decision to deport Aisha Huang in hindsight was a mistake and that is why that process and procedure is being stopped" (The Ghana Report, 2019c; Starrfm.com.gh, 2019).

As we argued all along, the existence side-by-side of the formal Ghanaian state and the shadow state is embedded with internal contradictions. The President and his Senior Minister, the first and third most powerful government officials, have literally performed this contradiction with their views on the controversial Aisha Huang's case.

Yet the state capture that Aisha Huang's power and influence demonstrate was yet to be played out more vividly. Ms. Huang returned to Ghana, the date of which is not known, and continued with her galamsey business. Indeed, in a breathtaking act of boldness, she went to a government office, the National Identity Authority (NIA), to renew her non-citizen identity card on 25th August 2022. Surprisingly, she managed to do the renewal even when she was caught by the NIA Foreigner Identification Management System (FIMS) for impersonation and other offences related to misrepresentation of a person's identity. It came to light that her initial purpose for attending the NIA registration centre in Tamale in the northern region of Ghana was to register for a new non-citizen identity card, using a Chinese passport with personal details different from those used for her old card. She presented a different Chinese passport with number EJ5891162; bearing the name Ruixia Huang; whose date of birth is 7th November 1975. The NIA system detected that her biometrics were already in the system and matched with her old card. When she was confronted with this information, she admitted she was the same person, but she has changed her name (Graphic Online, 2022a, 2022b, 2022c). This means that she either managed to outwit the Chinese authorities to issue her a second passport, or elements of these authorities compromised on the integrity of the process of attaining a Chinese passport.

In a state that is not captured by the power elite, she would have been arrested immediately for further investigation. This is because, not only did she try to deceive public officers with a new passport, but even more serious a criminal behaviour, the new passport she presented had a different name and date of birth. One does not need to be a trained police officer or detective to know that her excuse—that she had changed her name—was a lie. Even if she changed her name from En Huang to Ruixia Huang, she could not have changed her date of birth from 7th July 1986 to 7th November 1975. Despite all these pieces of evidence that set the alarm bells ringing about serious crimes that were being committed by En (Aisha) Huang, NIA surprisingly gave her two options. Either to go and bring official certified affidavit and a gazette supporting the change of name, based on which, her application will be processed for a non-citizen identity card with the new name. Or she should renew the old card with the same details. Unsurprisingly, Ms. Huang opted for the latter and NIA renewed her card. All these decisions were taken by senior officers of NIA in Accra, not the junior ones in the Tamale office (Graphic Online, 2022a, 2022b, 2022c).

But En (Aisha) Huang was subsequently arrested again with three Chinese nationals and arraigned before court on 2nd September 2022 for offences of illegal mining and sale and purchase of minerals without a licence. Providing brief facts of the case, the prosecutor told the court that after her deportation, Ms. Huang changed her identity and returned to Ghana illegally, through the Togo border, and then went back to continue mining illegally (Graphic Online, 2022a, 2022b, 2022c).

Ms. Huang's exploits in galamsey planted doubts in the mind of the Ghanaian president about his own government's claim that she was deported. Speaking in an interview with a local radio station in the Volta Region, the president said, and surprisingly so;

> I'm not still sure whether she (Aisha Huang) was in fact deported or whether she fled the country the first time, and has now come back....but whatever, there still seem to be some uncertainty about it, but whichever way it is, she has become some sort of nickname for all that galamsey represents and unfortunately, for the involvement of Chinese nationals in Ghana. (Graphic Online, 2022a, 2022b, 2022c; The Ghana Report, 2019c)

The contradictory actions of the Ghanaian state—as illustrated by the quotes of the president and the lax handling of the mining offences that the state has accused Ms. Huang of—are the morbid symptoms of the captured state. They illustrate the intrinsic contradiction in the symbiotic relationship between the shadow state and the formal state; with the former—made up of a vast network of kleptocratic power elite, within and outside government– exercising power over the decision of the latter. But alas, on 4 December 2023, the Criminal Division of the Accra High Court found her guilty of undertaking a mining operation without a licence, facilitating the participation of persons engaged in a mining operation and illegal employment of foreigners. She was subsequently sentenced to a prison term of four-and-half years plus a fine of GH¢48,000 (Graphic Online, 2023a, 2023b, 2023c, 2023d). This action of the court gives a ray of hope, which is that, even in a captured state, there are fractions of state actors who resist the influence of the power elite, and adhere to the virtues of good governance and the promotion of public good.

Is the Ghana Armed Forces (GAF) also Captured?

The Ghanaian military is highly respected by Ghanaians. A recent survey of Ghanaian's trust in public institutions, Ghana Armed Forces came out tops as the most trusted institution in Ghana (CDD-Ghana, 2022). Hitherto known for its intervention in politics through coup d'états, Ghana's military has transformed over the last three decades to a professional army, disciplined and respectful of the democratic principles, especially those related to military-civilian relations and civilian control of the military (Agyekum, 2019). Ghanaian soldiers have performed excellently in international assignments such as UN peacekeeping missions within and outside Africa (Edu-Afful, 2022; Banini et al., 2020). As a fighting force, the Ghanaian military was ranked by the Global Firepower (GFP) as the 19th most powerful on the African continent (Citionline.com, 2016), and it was rated "perfect" in power index and ranked 96th in strength out of the 142 countries across the world which were assessed in 2022 (GFP, 2022).

Why has such a professional and strong military failed to defeat galamsey, a relatively weak foe? There are others who disagree with the premise of this question—the failure of the militarized fight—as leading members of the Ghana government such as the president and his ministers of defence and lands and natural resources, as well as the military command, have touted the successes of the above-mentioned military operations against galamsey. However, our bar of success is set very high. What are so often cited as successes—such as the arrests of illegal miners and the seizures and burning of mining equipment—do not meet our criteria of success in the fight against galamsey. It borders on mediocrity to associate the success of the military operations just with the arrest of workers at the galamsey sites and the confiscations or burning of pieces of mining equipment. This is the easiest thing that the Ghana police could have done without the military. It would be strange for an army of the calibre of the GAF to be deployed in such large numbers, and with such sophisticated military equipment and weapons, and not be able to arrest mostly unarmed civilians and seize mining equipment that are in plain sight.

Success should be more than this, and should be measured by the elimination of the serious threat to society that necessitated the deployment of the military: in this case, the environmental menace caused by mechanized and semi-mechanized galamsey. In this sense, the above-mentioned military operations should have eliminated mechanized and semi-mechanized galamsey, measured by the absence of mechanized and semi-mechanized mining; at the very least, in forest reserves and water bodies. As documented above, between July 2017 when Operation Vanguard was launched and October 2022 when Operation Halt III was launched, the military has failed to accomplish this. By our criteria of success, the failure of the military to defeat galamsey is palpable; and one need not look further than the successive operations organized by the military over this period, on one hand, and on the other, the enduring existence of mechanized and semi-mechanized galamsey. An enduring existence illustrated by the hundreds of heavy mining equipment that the personnel of these operations continue to seize and the illegal miners they continue to arrest.

Besides this, the high reputation and respect of the GAF and its officers and junior ranks have enjoyed among Ghanaians seemed to be waning because of their involvement in the fight against galamsey. Civilians are beginning to disrespect soldiers deployed in these operations, and in some cases, even violently attacked and killed some of them. A case in point is the lynching of Major Maxwell Mahama Denkyira-Obuasi in the Central Region. Some media reports alleged that he was lynched by an irate crowd who believed that he was among a detachment of military personnel deployed to protect the illegal mining of some people well-connected to the high echelons of power. Other reports claim the military detachment, which he was the commander, was deployed to fight galamsey. The military high command has denied these allegations (The Herald Ghana, 2023; Ghanaweb, 2022). However, a witness in the trial of the murder of Major Mahama, WO II Sabi—who was a member of the military detachment—lent credence to media reports that the detachment was deployed to protect a mining company: C&G Mining Company. Under cross-examination by one of the lawyers of the accused persons, he said "I was sent to go there, but I did not know why. We were told we were going to Diaso to protect C&G Mining Company" (Daily Guide Network, 2018).

Some senior officers and other ranks of the Ghana Army have expressed their concerns over the professional challenges they encounter and the maltreatment they get from civilians when deployed to deal with civil issues (Edu-Afful, 2022). For example, Brigadier General Joseph Aphour, the General Officer Commanding the Central Command of the Armed Forces was reported in the media complaining about the violent attacks on soldiers deployed to fight galamsey in the mining communities. According to him, civilians have pelted soldiers deployed in galamsey operations with stones and other dangerous materials (Ghanaweb, 2022). As one research report on this subject has correctly observed, "[t]he use of soldiers for policing roles in Ghana has a negative impact on the Ghana Armed Forces. It politicises soldiers, undermines their authority in the eyes of the public and has the potential to militarise internal security unnecessarily" (Albrecht et al., 2021).

As in the South African state capture, mechanized and semi-mechanized galamsey happens with impunity because its operators, both within the state and in civil society, are powerful people who have direct or indirect access to the inner sanctum of power to influence decisions in Ghana (Bhorat et al., 2017). They have captured the state, repurposing its institutions to protect their interests. And because of this, galamsey is not an enemy that can be fought with military might, weaponry, and operational strategies. All these are often deployed in the military crackdowns and swoops on some galamsey operators, viewed by the officers and junior ranks as the enemy they have been deployed to fight and defeat. But this misses the complex interplay of forces and acts of state capture that have created, nurtured, and deepened CMM galamsey before the military operations were ordered to fight it. By focusing on the arrest of miners and seizing mining equipment in the field, the military are barking up the wrong tree: they have not identified the enemy they are fighting correctly, let alone fight it. Yet this enemy, the shadow state, is amorphous and difficult to identify and fight.

References

African Eye Report. (2020). *Minister lodges money laundering charge against journalist, security chief and ex-NPP chair*. https://africaneyereport.com/minister-lodges-money-laundering-charge-against-journalist-security-chief-and-ex-npp-chair/ (29 December 2022)

Agyekum, H. A. (2019). *From Bullies to Officers and Gentlemen: how notions of professionalism and civility transformed the Ghana Armed Forces*. New York: Berghahn Books.

Albrecht, P., Aubyn, F., and Edu-Afful F. (2021). *Halt and Vanguard: Two military operations in Ghana and their consequences*. DIIS. https://www.diis.dk/en/research/halt-and-vanguard (Accessed 26 December 2022).

Asaase Radio (2024). *Green Ghana Day: Government to allocate GHC1.5 million*. https://www.asaaseradio.com/2024-green-ghana-day-government-to-allocate-ghc1-5-million/ (Accessed 30 September 2024).

Ayelazuno, J. (2011). Ghanaian elections and conflict management: Interrogating the absolute majority electoral system. *Journal of African Elections*, *10*(2), 22–53.

Ayelazuno, J. A. & Aziabah, M. A. (2023). Making visible the galamsey scandals in Ghana: digital media as new technologies of democratic accountability. *The Extractive Industries and Society*, (16): 101366.

Ayelazuno, J. A., and Mawuko-Yevugah, L. (2019). Large-scale mining and ecological imperialism in Africa: The politics of mining and conservation of the ecology in Ghana. *Journal of Political Ecology*, (*26*), 243–262.

Ayelazuno, J. A., and Mawuko-Yevugah, L. (2021). Between the Africa mining vision and the neo-patrimonial state: The agency gap in Ghana's regulation of artisanal and small-scale gold mining. *South African Journal of International Affairs*, *28*(4), 555–582.

Aziabah, M. A., and Ayelazuno, J. A. (2024). The failure of the militarised fight against 'Galamsey' in Ghana: A critical overview of the class and political dynamics. *Journal of Planning and Land Management*, *3*(2), 31–51.

Banini, D. K., Powell, J., & Yekple, M. (2020). Peacekeeping as coup avoidance: lessons from Ghana. *African Security*, *13*(3), 235–259.

Bhorat, H., Buthelezi, M., Chipkin, I., Duma, S., Mondi, L., Peter, C., ... & Friedenstein, H. (2017). Betrayal of the promise: how South Africa is being stolen. *State Capacity Research Project*, 1–72. https://www.wits.ac.za/media/wits-university/news-and-events/images/documents/Betrayal-of-the-Promise-25052017.pdf (Accessed 19 December 2022).

Botchwey G., Crawford G., Loubere N., and Lu, J. (2019). South-south irregular migration: The impacts of China's informal gold rush in Ghana. *International Migration*, *57*(4), 310–328.

Burrows, E., and Bird, L.—African Arguments (2017, May 30). *Gold, guns and China: Ghana's fight to end galamsey.* https://africanarguments.org/2017/05/gold-guns-and-china-ghanas-fight-to-end-galamsey/ (Accessed 26 December 2022).

CDD-Ghana (2022). *News release, 28 July 2022.* https://www.afrobarometer.org/wp-content/uploads/2022/07/R9-News-release-Corruption-Afrobarometer-28july22.pdf (Accessed 15 September 2024).

Citi Newsroom. (2020). *CID arrests six individuals over missing excavators saga.* https://citinewsroom.com/2020/02/cid-arrests-six-individuals-over-missing-excavators-saga/ (Accessed 29 December 2022).

Citi Newsroom. (2022). *My son is not involved in galamsey—Frimpong-Boateng.* https://citinewsroom.com/2020/02/my-son-is-not-involved-in-galamsey-frimpong-boateng/ (Accessed 30 December 2022).

Citi Newsroom. (2023). *Akonta Mining not engaged in illegal mining—Akufo-Addo.* https://citinewsroom.com/2023/01/akonta-mining-not-engaged-in-illegal-mining-akufo-addo/ (26 August 2024)

Citionline.com. (2016). *Ghana's military ranked 19th most powerful in Africa.* https://citifmonline.com/2016/05/ghanas-military-ranked-19th-most-powerful-in-africa/?fbclid=IwAR2G8UseBYne-MY2tPUpzhYh-sVJXUu2DErdhlNUEcy92wG9gJnZv4QAGy0#sthash.OxcYxhwQ.dpuf (26 August 2024)

Crawford, G., Agyeyomah, C. Botchwey, G. and Mba, A. (2016). The Impact of Chinese Involvement in Small-scale Gold Mining in Ghana. Policy Brief 33110, International Growth Centre, LSE and Oxford University. https://www.theigc.org/wpcontent/uploads/2016/08/Crawford-et-al-2015-Final-Report-1.pdf (Accessed 30 December 2022).

Crawford, G., and Botchwey, G. (2017). Conflict, collusion and corruption in small scale gold mining: Chinese miners and the state in Ghana. *Commonwealth & Comparative Politics*, 55(4), 444–470.

Donkor, E.A., (2022a). Destruction for gold, part 1. https://www.youtube.com/watch?v=8wE8ya-po_c&t=57s (20 May 2023).

Donkor, E.A., (2022b). Destruction for gold, part 2. https://www.youtube.com/watch?v=0NC7ALzpYEM&t=620s (Accessed 20 May 2023).

Donkor, E.A., (2022c). Destruction for gold, part 3. https://www.youtube.com/watch?v=2roPsklYJew (Accessed 20 May 2023).

Edu-Afful, F. (2022). The anatomy of Ghanaian domestic military operations: Exploring operations vanguard and calm life. *Contemporary Journal of African Studies*, 9(1), 39-52. https://doi.org/10.4314/contjas.v9i1.4.

Eduful, M., Alsharif K., Eduful, A., Acheampong, M., Eduful, J., and Mazumder, L. (2020). The illegal artisanal and small-scale mining (galamsey) 'menace' in Ghana: Is military-style approach the answer? *Resources Policy*, (68), 101732. https://doi.org/10.1016/j.resourpol.2020.101732

Ghanaweb. (2020). *315 excavators seized; only 127 left—Galamsey task force.* https://www.ghanaweb.com/GhanaHomePage/NewsArchive/315-excavators-seized-only-127-left-Galamsey-task-force-857680 (29 December 2022)

Ghanaweb. (2022). *Military cautions against attacks on soldiers by galamseyers.* https://www.ghanaweb.com/GhanaHomePage/NewsArchive/Military-cautions-against-attacks-on-soldiers-by-galamseyers-1686368 (25 September 2024).

Ghanaweb. (2024). *Illegal mining activities disrupt work on three bypass projects on Accra-Kumasi Highway—Report.* https://www.ghanaweb.com/GhanaHomePage/NewsArchive/Illegal-mining-activities-disrupt-work-on-three-bypass-projects-on-Accra-Kumasi-Highway-Report-1940790 (Accessed 24 September 2024).

Ghenvironment.com (2023). *Passage of L.I. 2462: The law was passed with well-motivated reasons—Jinapor.* https://ghenvironment.com/Forests_Biodiversity/passage-of-li-2462-the-law-was-passed-with-well-motivated-reasons-jinapor1696327061 (Accessed 15 September 2024).

GIF. (2023). *Ghana Institute of Foresters position paper on L. I. 2462.* https://ghana.arocha.org/wp-content/uploads/sites/15/2023/12/GIF-POSITION-PAPER-ON-LI-2462.pdf (25 September 2024).

Global Fire Power (GFP). (2022) *Ghana Military Strength, 2022.* https://www.globalfirepower.com/country-military-strength-detail.php?country_id=ghana#viewNotes (25 September 2024).

GNA (2023). *NPP Primary: Ekow Ewusi wins Cape Coast North.* https://gna.org.gh/2023/12/npp-primary-ekow-ewusi-wins-cape-coast-north/ (Accessed 30 August 2024)

Graphic Online (2017). *Menace of foreigners in Ghana's illegal gold mining.* https://www.graphic.com.gh/features/opinion/menace-of-foreigners-in-ghana-s-illegal-gold-mining.html (Accessed 17 March 2018).

Graphic Online (2018). *Aisha Huang and four other Chinese illegal miners deported.* https://www.graphic.com.gh/news/general-news/nia-confirms-en-aisha-huang-s-ghana-card-is-authentic.html (28 December 2022).

Graphic Online (2021a). Cameron Duodu writes on how Asantehene exposed galamseyers in a room. https://www.graphic.com.gh/news/politics/cameron-duodu-writes-on-how-asantehene-exposed-galamseyers-in-aroom.html (Accessed 29th December 2022)

Graphic Online (2021b). Simon Mensah: There was no attempt to 'gag' Otumfuo on galamsey 'name and shame'. https://www.graphic.com.gh/news/politics/simon-mensah-there-was-no-attempt-to-gag-otumfuo-on-gal amseyname-and-shame.html (Accessed 29th December 2022).

Graphic Online (2022a). *Aisha Huang sneaks into Ghana, arrested again for illegal mining.* https://www.graphic.com.gh/news/general-news/aisha-huang-sneaks-into-ghana-arrested-again-for-illegal-mining.html (28 December 2022).

Graphic Online (2022b). *NIA confirms renewed En 'Aisha' Huang's Ghana Card is authentic.* https://www.graphic.com.gh/news/general-news/nia-confirms-en-aisha-huang-s-ghana-card-is-authentic.html (30th September 2022).

Graphic Online (2022c). *Sustaining galamsey fight: Lands Ministry to track excavators—Control room ready.* https://www.graphic.com.gh/news/general-news/sustaining-galamsey-fight-lands-ministry-to-track-excavators-control-room-ready.html (Accessed 26 December 2022).

Graphic Online. (2023a). *Missing excavators: Police probe Frimpong-Boateng's allegations.* Graphic Online. https://www.graphic.com.gh/news/general-news/ghana-news-missing-excavators-police-probe-frimpong-boatengs-allega tions.html (Accessed 16 September 2024)

Graphic Online (2023b). *Galamsey allegations: Frimpong-Boateng fails to provide evidence—A-G.* https://www.graphic.com.gh/news/general-news/ghana-news-galamsey-allegations-frimpong-boateng-fails-to-provide-evidence-a-g.html (16 January 2024).

Graphic Online (2023c). *Review law on mining in forest reserves—Stakeholders.* https://www.graphic.com.gh/news/general-news/ghana-news-review-law-on-mining-in-forest-reserves-stakeholders.html (Accessed 15 September 2024).

Graphic Online (2023d). Why Aisha Huang was jailed 4 and half years and why judge wished for longer sentence. https://www.graphic.com.gh/news/general-news/ghana-news-aisha-huang-jailed-for-galamsey.html (Accessed 15 August 2024).

Graphic Online (2024). *Konongo under galamsey siege.* https://www.graphic.com.gh/news/general-news/ghana-news-konongo-under-galamsey-siege.html (Accessed 26 September 2024).

Hausermann, H., Adomako, J., and Robles, M. (2020). Fried eggs and all-women gangs: The geopolitics of Chinese gold mining in Ghana, bodily vulnerability, and resistance. *Human Geography*, *13*(1), 60–73.

Hausermann, H., and Ferring, D. (2018). Unpacking land grabs: Subjects, performances and the state in Ghana's 'small-scale' gold mining sector, 2018. *Development and Change*, *49*(4), 1010–1033.

Hausermann, H., Ferring, D., Atosona, B., Mentz, G., Amankwah, R., Chang, A., Hartfield, K., Effah, E., Asuamah, G. Y., Mansell, C., and Sastri, N. (2018). Land-grabbing, land-use transformation and social differentiation: Deconstructing "small-scale" in Ghana's recent gold rush. *World Development*, *(108)*, 103–114.

Hilson G., Hilson A., and Adu-Darko, E. (2014). Chinese participation in Ghana's informal gold mining economy: Drivers, implications and clarifications. *Journal of Rural Studies*, *(34)*, 292–303.

McQuilken, J. and Hilson, G. (2016). *Artisanal and small-scale gold mining in Ghana: Evidence to inform an 'action dialogue'.* IIED. http://pubs.iied.org/16618IIED (Accessed 14 March 2018).

Metro TV. (2023, January 6). *Good Morning Ghana.* Accra. https://www.facebook.com/OfficialGoodMorningGhana/videos/488931266687127 (Accessed 6 January 2023).

Myjoyonline.com. (2020). *We've started retrieving missing excavators—Operation Vanguard taskforce member.* https://www.myjoyonline.com/weve-started-retrieving-missing-excavators-operation-vanguard-taskforce-member/ (Accessed 30 December 2022).

Myjoyonline.com (2022). *Halt operations in Tano Nimiri Forest Reserve—Lands Ministry tells Chairman 'Wontumi's mining company.* https://www.myjoyonline.com/halt-operations-in-tano-nimiri-forest-reserve-lands-ministry-tells-chairman-wontumis-mining-company/ (Accessed 27 December 2022)

Myjoy.online.com. (2022). *Some government officials and politicians are involved in illegal mining—Asantehene.* https://www.myjoyonline.com/some-government-officials-and-politicians-are-involved-in-illegal-mining-asantehene/ (Accessed 29 December 2022).

Nature and Development Foundation. (2023). *Legal opinion on Legal Status of Environmental Protection (Mining in Forest Reserves) Regulation2022 (L.I.2462).* https://ndfwestafrica.org/wp-content/uploads/2023/12/Legal-Opinion-on-LI-2462-pdf.pdf (Accessed 26 September 2024)

Nature and Development Foundation. (2024). *Background.* https://ndfwestafrica.org/projects/mining-in-forestreserves/#:~:text=Background,the%20impacts%20of%20such%20actions (Accessed 25 September 2024).

Ocquaye, N. (2023). *Explaining the persistence of illegal Chinese mining in Ghana: The efficacious role of local patrons.* LSE GSU Working Paper, 9(1), 1–16.

Pulse.com.gh (2020). *Missing excavators: Minister reports Peace FM journalist to CID.* https://www.pulse.com.gh/news/local/missing-excavators-minister-reports-peace-fm-journalist-to-cid/0sh60y6 (Accessed 30 December 2022).

Pulse.com.gh (2020). *6 arrested over 500 missing excavators.* https://www.pulse.com.gh/news/local/6-arrested-over-500-missing-excavators/pxzk01d (Accessed 29 December 2022).

Pulse.com.gh (2022). *Akonta Mining Company has no permit to mine in Tano Nimri Forest Reserve — Minerals Commission.* https://www.pulse.com.gh/news/local/akonta-mining-company-has-no-permit-to-mine-in-tano-nimri-forest-reserve-minerals/75g8407 (Accessed 5 January 2023).

Starrfm.com.gh (2019). Your 'mistake' on Aisha Huang slap on Ghanaians—OccupyGhana to Akufo-Addo https://starrfm.com.gh/2019/09/your-mistake-on-aisha-huang-slap-on-ghanaians-occupyghana-to-akufo-addo/ (28 December 2022).

TaylorCrabbe and ClientEarth. (2024). *Mining research briefing 4: Mining in forest reserves– Spotlight on L.I. 2462.* https://ndfwestafrica.org/wp-content/uploads/2024/08/ghana-mining-briefing-4.pdf (Accessed 15 September 2024)

The Fourth Estate (2024). *Forest reserves forest invasion: Companies owned by Wontumi, Kumasi mayor & others scramble to mine in Ghana's.* https://thefourthestategh.com/2024/09/forest-invasion-companies-of-wontumi-kumasi-mayor-npp-juaben-parliamentary-candidate-others-scramble-for-mining-in-ghanas-forest-reserves/ (Accessed 15 September 2024).

The Ghana Report. (2019a). *Galamsey fight: 'Higher authority' aids culprits return—Sir John.* https://www.theghanareport.com/galamsey-fight-higher-authority-aids-culprits-return-sir-john/ (Accessed 29 December 2022).

The Ghana Report. (2019b). *Explain Aisha Huang's deportation—Media coalition.* https://www.theghanareport.com/explain-aisha-huangs-deport ation-media-coalition/ (Accessed 28 December 2022).

The Ghana Report. (2019c). *Aisha Huang's deportation was a mistake—Nana Addo.* https://www.theghanareport.com/aisha-huangs-deportation-was-a-mistake-nana-addo/ (Accessed 28 December 2022).

The Ghana Report (2020). *Missing excavators: Frimpong-Boateng appeals to CID to investigate peace FM journalist and others.* https://www.thegha nareport.com/missing-excavators-frimpong-boateng-appeal-to-cid-to-invest igate-peace-fm-journalist/ (28 December 2022)

The Ghana Report. (2020). *Missing excavators: Frimpong-Boateng appeals to CID to investigate Peace FM journalist and others.* https://www.thegha nareport.com/missing-excavators-frimpong-boateng-appeal-to-cid-to-invest igate-peace-fm-journalist/ (Accessed 29 December 2022).

The Herald Ghana. (2023). Ex-Minister reveals gov't & military lied about Major Mahama's murder at Denkyira. https://theheraldghana.com/ex-minister-rev eals-govt-military-lied-about-major-mahamas-murder-at-denkyira/ (Accessed 28 April 2025).

The Minerals Commission—Ghana (2022). *Press Release: Re-alleged operations of Akonta Mining Ltd in Tano Nimri Forest Reserve.* https://www.mincom. gov.gh/wp-content/uploads/2022/10/Alleged-Operations-of-Akonta-Min ing-Ltd.pdf (Accessed 5 January 2023).

The Ministry of Lands and Natural Resources (2021). *No mining in forest reserves—Minister for lands and natural resources directs.* https://mlnr.gov. gh/index.php/no-mining-in-forest-reserves-minister-for-lands-and-natural-res ources-directs/ (Accessed 5 January 2023).

Tsikudo, K. A. (2022). Soft powering the China Water Machine: The Bui Dam and China–Ghana relations. *Canadian Journal of African Studies/Revue canadienne desétudes africaines, 56*(2), 319–339.

Conclusion: Theoretical and Political Praxis

Artisanal and small-scale mining (ASM) in general—and particularly artisanal and small-scale gold mining (ASGM)—is an industry that is widely known to employ hundreds of millions of people across developing countries endowed with natural resources. Especially, those countries which are endowed with mineral resources such as gold, diamonds, copper, lithium, and cobalt. Paradoxically, it is an industry that is characterized predominantly by informal and criminal activities in, otherwise, highly capable states in Africa, South America, Oceania, and Asia. Despite the connection of illegal ASGM to the formal economy of these minerals-rich countries—with the minerals produced by it counted towards accounting the total produced in these countries—operators of informal ASM/ASGM have been stereotyped, stigmatized, and vilified as environmental criminals, as criminal bands, as a nuisance, as inferior, and many more negative representations (see Childs 2014; Ofori and Ofori, 2018; Sojková, 2022; Katz-Lavigne et al., 2024).

Based on this othering of informal ASM operators and the biases against them relative to large-scale capitalist mining—which is viewed as formal and good sources of revenue—the states of minerals-rich developing countries have deployed the military and other security organs to interdict their "othered," stereotyped destructive activities. There are many examples of these military crackdowns across the Global South: in South Africa they were used against the zama zamas in *Operation*

J. A. Ayelazuno and M. A. Aziabah, *State Capture in the Militarized Fight Against Illegal Small-Scale Goldmining in Ghana*,
https://doi.org/10.1007/978-3-031-82673-3

Prosper (Panchia, 2023); in Zimbabwe, they were used against gold panners, miners, and traders—called *Operation Chikorokoza Chapera*—in November 2006 (Spiegel, 2014); the government of Peru authorized a military operation, *Operation Mercury* (*OM, Operación Mercurio* in Spanish), against illegal ASM in the region of Madre de Dios (MDD) in February 2019 (Dethier et al., 2023); the cabinet of the government of Papua New Guinea, in April 2024, authorized a joint military and police operation against illegal ASM in the Porgera Valley; and the Colombian government has since 2012 deployed police and military operations against ASM operators under the Community of Andean Nations (CAN) authority (Benites, 2023, p. 2).

Focusing on Ghana, this book grapples with these intractable governance problems of the ASM industry across Africa, Asia, Latin America, and Oceania. Ghana is a model case of the regulatory failure of the ASM industry by the state, culminating in the predominance of informal activities in the industry—galamsey. This situation has aggravated its negative environmental effects due to the invasion of galamsey by the power elite classes. In response, the Ghanaian state has taken a strongarm, albeit misplaced, approach of deploying military crackdowns, ostensibly to eliminate galamsey. But this approach has yielded insignificant successes, at best, but failed, at worst. As a result, the ASM sector of Ghana is a quintessential example of informality, chaos, and the environmentally and socially ruinous nature of the industry across Africa and the other regions mentioned above. Though a leading member of the Africa Union (AU), this situation illustrates the signal failure of Ghana to implement one of AU's key development policies: the Africa Mining Vision (AMV) (Ayelazuno and Mawuko-Yevugah, 2021).

We are, thus, presented with a vexed conundrum, both intellectual and political; namely, the inability of the Ghanaian state—which is reputed as a model democratic state in Africa—to regulate its ASGM industry. But this book limits its analysis to what it considers as a more baffling aspect of this incapacity of the Ghanaian state between 2017 and 2022—and even to 2024. This period marked a turning point in the history of the Ghanaian state's efforts to regulate the industry and stop illegal mining and the environmental menace it engenders. Three reasons make this period the watershed historical conjuncture in the fight against illegal ASM (galamsey): first, this is the only time that a Ghanaian president and Commander-in-Chief of the Ghana Armed Forces (GAF) vowed to fight galamsey at the cost of his presidency. In his own words: "I have said it in the Cabinet, and perhaps this is the first time I am making this public, that I am prepared to put my Presidency on the line on this matter" (Graphic Online, 2017). Elaborating on this vow—and referring to the stakes of the 2020 Ghanaian presidential elections—he said "Well, this is a choice I have to make as a human being. Do you do what is right or what you think will make you get along? I think you do what is right and what you are required to do" (Graphic Online, 2017). The second reason why this period is unique is the banning of all forms of ASGM, both legal and illegal, for more than a year—between April 2017 and December 2018. Third, is the declaration of war on galamsey by the President and Commander-in-Chief of the GAF in 2017, a battle he marshalled coercive apparatuses of state, led by the GAF, to fight. Yet as illustrated throughout this book, the state abysmally failed to win the battle. Why, despite its overwhelming coercive capacity, did the Ghanaian state fail to win a war with a weak enemy: galamsey operators, who are mostly unarmed civilians, and operating in the plain sight of the security agencies?

Situated in relation to the existing state-theoretical literature explaining this puzzle—informality, neopatrimonialism, and corruption—this book set out to contribute to this oeuvre by drawing on the insights of state capture theory. To date—and to the best of our knowledge—the lens of state capture has not been deployed to unpick this puzzle. To be sure, the existing state-centric theories of the incapability of the Ghanaian state to address the problem of galamsey are insightful conceptually and empirically, as they shed light on the morbid symptoms of a deeply perverted Ghanaian state and its poor quality of governance of the ASGM sector. But these theories do not capture the lowest depth to which the capacity of this state has been hollowed out by these perversions. The state is so hollowed to such an extent that the two most powerful organs of the Ghanaian state, the presidency and the military, have failed to win the war against galamsey. This book is the first to frame this failure in a novel way that illuminates the dysfunctionality and hollowness of the Ghanaian state at the highest level, by throwing light on its highest echelons of power or its most powerful organs: the president/Commander-in-Chief and his military.

Its main intervention is in the intersection of theory, praxis, and methods. Theoretically, the book demonstrates that state capture provides fascinating and fresh insights into the intractable problem of galamsey. The depth and mechanisms of the influence of state officials, as the case of state capture in South Africa illustrates, explains the failed militarized fight despite it was launched and led by the president, his ministers, and commanders of his security forces. For example, the concepts of shadow state and repurposing of the formal state illustrate that commonly cited causes of the problem—often attributed to informalization, corruption, and neopatrimonialism—fail to fully capture the degree to which the state has become dysfunctional as the regulator of ASGM. This book has shown that informalization, corruption, and neopatrimonialism are morbid symptoms of state capture. It then probed below the surface of these symptoms to show that the shadow state is the disease that triggers them. While these symptoms are usually manifest on the formal state—such as the democratic state of Ghana with all the appearance of a functioning state as illustrated by the military swoop—the shadow state is invisible, yet more powerful.

Building on state capture theory, we highlight the immense challenges of praxis—specifically, the complexity of the galamsey problem, its political and class dynamics, all of which defy simple policy interventions such as formalization, good governance, and availability of political will. Drawing on state capture theory, this book argues that solutions to the galamsey problem are far more complicated than often assumed by government, international organisations, and other stakeholders. To address the galamsey problem more effectively will require innovative and sophisticated policies, based on analysis and identification of the power elites that constitute the shadow state and how they operate to capture the state. Without confronting the problem of the shadow state, efforts centred on good governance and formalization are unlikely to succeed. These conventional policies do not address the political root-causes of the galamsey problem—especially CMM galamsey.

From a critical political-economic perspective—and drawing on the class dynamics of CMM galamsey documented in this book—we argue that even the "right" policies addressing state capture are not sufficient. Indeed, given the deep and vast network of kleptocratic actors within and outside the Ghanaian state, these policies may never be designed because of the strong influence of mining policies by the mining-power elite class. This calls forth radical political praxis—struggle and resistance of the subaltern classes against the mining-power elites and their kleptocratic political actors. On this—and unapologetically siding with the subaltern classes engaged in galamsey for survival—we canvass for grass-roots movements in the mining communities to resist the mining-power elites and the complicit organs of the Ghanaian state providing protection for their destructive activities in the mining communities. Public/ activist intellectuals, as the two authors of this book, have a crucial role to play in this political praxis. Beyond providing critical analysis and calling attention to the injustices the subaltern classes are inflicted, they must be in the trenches with the subaltern classes in the struggle against the powerful mining elite. They can do this, for example, by engaging in the sensitization of the subaltern classes to and raising public awareness about the injustices their elected leaders inflict on them. This is essential to build class consciousness among them and overcome their segmentation on partisan political, ethnic, and religious lines. This is a first step to mobilizing a class-based social movement to engage in the liberation struggles against the mining-power elites within and outside the Ghanaian state.

Already, these struggles are beginning to emerge. As of September 2024, civic activism against the government's failure to fight galamsey had started and seemed to be gaining momentum. Incensed by the aggravation of the deleterious environmental and human effects of galamsey documented in this book, a coalition of civil society organizations (CSOs) were up in arms over this dismal failure. The coalition that is made up of various CSOs, concerned about sundry issues, had issued press statements calling on the government to take decisive action to stop galamsey. The CSOs include the following: Ghana Catholic Bishops' Conference (GCBC), the Ghana Association of Medical Laboratory Scientists (GAMLS), Media Coalition Against Galamsey; The Christian Council of Ghana (CCG), the Executive Women Network (EWN), the Office of the Chief Imam, the Trades Union Congress (TUC), Ghana Journalists Association (GJA), University Teachers Association of Ghana (UTAG); The General Agricultural Workers Union (GAWU); The Centre for Climate Change and Food Security (CCCFS); and the Civil Society Organizations (CSOs) Platform on the Sustainable Development Goals. Notably, the Ghanaian workers unions, led by the TUC, had threatened to embark on a nationwide strike by the end of September 2024 should the government fail to take decisive action to address the escalating galamsey crisis.

Another hopeful development on radical political praxis relates to the political agency of Ghanaian youth: the Millennials and Gen Zs. Democracy Hub, a youth-dominated CSO, embarked on a three-day protest dubbed #*OccupyJulorbiHouse demonstration*. The demonstration was aimed at drawing attention to not only the aggravated situation of galamsey, but to other serious problems of governance and socioeconomic issues such as injustice, unemployment, rising poverty, state capture, nepotism, corruption, and the need for judicial independence. Some of them were arrested and detained without bail and are being prosecuted by the Attorney General's (AG) department. As we have argued in this book, the co-existence of the formal state and shadow state is embedded with internal contradictions. The captured state demonstrates both capacity and incapacity, based on which one is required to protect the interests of the power elite class. This is what was on display in this case. While Ghana is facing existential threat from the criminal activities of the mining-power elites, the police and AG department have deployed the might of the state to deal with minor offences. Paradoxically, the power elites who have committed more serious crimes of illegal mining were walking scot-free and actively committing the crime.

Yet reminiscent of the hope in political agency and resistance of Ghanaians noted here, there is public outrage against the government because of this contradictory and discriminatory behaviour. Social media is inundated with campaigns for the release of the protesters, with the hashtag #FreetheCitizens going viral (The Africa Report, 2024).

Methodologically, the book pushes the boundaries of knowledge production on galamsey and the social sciences, generally, in Ghana and beyond. The data analyzed in the book are qualitative, collected from digital and internet sources. This approach is neither a known nor typical social science method; especially, in the Ghanaian academy where traditional methods as the use of survey questionnaires and fieldwork ethnography are dominant. Yet this book illustrates that the ICT revolution of our time has transformed the modes of social interaction and the landscape of ethnographic fieldwork. The technology of digital media makes it possible for people who have access to it (and can use it) to use it to enact actions and interactions with other people across the world and in real time. The digital revolution provides the possibility of mediated interaction in which, for example, the internet makes it possible for a great number of people to meet and interact on online platforms in real time and across space. And by so doing, compressing time and space in unmediated face-to-face interaction; and thus, eliminating the spatial and temporal barriers in face-to-face interaction between people, which requires co-presence of the actors. In the specific case at hand in this book, that is the impunity of the mining-power elite class—encompassing the destruction of the environment and livelihoods of the subaltern classes—and the militarized fight against galamsey, as well as the evidence of state capture and the failure of this fight, and the swirl of political scandals that swept across the fight, were all played out and captured by the digital media. The internet thus served as a vast trove of data for analysis in support of the argument presented in this book.

Indeed, some of the textual evidence gleaned from internet sources—such as mass media news portals and social media sources—would have been nearly impossible through traditional methods such as in-depth personal interviews. The rise of the internet and digital media has transformed the landscape of political communication affording politicians and political parties with communication tools to communicate directly with citizens, and to promote or repair their political brands in real time. As a result, we are able to get their views on sensitive and controversial political issues as the fight against galamsey, not from face-to-face interviews, but from their media engagements: for example, their speeches and interviews published on mass media portals, as well as their tweets and postings on their Facebook walls. (Published in mass media portals.)

REFERENCES

Ayelazuno, J. A., & Mawuko-Yevugah, L. (2021). Between the Africa Mining Vision and theneo-patrimonial state: The agency gap in Ghana's regulation of artisanal and small-scale gold mining. *South African Journal of International Affairs, 28*(4), 555–582.

Benites, G. V. (2023). Natures of concern: The criminalization of artisanal and small-scale mining in Colombia and Peru. *The Extractive Industries and Society*, (13), 101105.

Childs, J. (2014). From 'criminals of the earth' to 'stewards of the environment': The social and environmental justice of Fair Trade gold. *Geoforum, 57*, 129–137.

Dethier, E. N., Silman, M. R., Fernandez, L. E., Espejo, J. C., Alqahtani, S., Pauca, P., & Lutz, D. A. (2023). Operation mercury: Impacts of national-level armed forces intervention and anticorruption strategy on artisanal gold mining and water quality in the Peruvian Amazon. *Conservation Letters, 16*(5), e12978.

Katz-Lavigne, S., Mkodzongi, G., and Nyandoro, M. (2024). 'Bandits' and machete gangs: The criminalization of artisanal and small-scale mining in the Democratic Republic of Congo and Zimbabwe. *The Extractive Industries and Society, 9*(101504), 1–12.

Graphic Online. (2017). *I will put my Presidency on line to stop galamsey—President*. https://www.graphic.com.gh/news/general-news/i-will-put-my-presidency-on-line-to-stop-galamsey-president.html (Accessed 30 September 2024).

Ofori, D. R., & Ofori, J. J. (2018). Digging for gold or justice? Misrecognition and marginalization of "illegal" small-scale miners in Ghana. *Social Justice Research, 31*(4), 355–373.

Panchia, Y. (2023). Unearthing a crisis: South Africa's battle against illegal mining. *Mining Review Africa*. https://www.miningreview.com/gold/south-africas-battle-against-illegal-artisanal-mining/ (Accessed 15 September 2024).

Sojková, I. (2022). Framing illegal artisanal and small-scale gold mining in the Ghanaian media during the# StopGalamsey campaign. *The Journal of Modern African Studies, 60*(3), 371–396.

Spiegel, S. J. (2014). Legacies of a nationwide crackdown in Zimbabwe: Operation Chikorokoza Chapera in gold mining communities. *The Journal of Modern African Studies, 52*(4), 541–570.

The Africa Report. (2024). Public outrage mounts over police crackdown on protesters. https://www.theafricareport.com/363119/ghana-public-outrage-mounts-over-police-crackdown-on-protesters/ (Accessed 2 October 2024).

Index

The manufacturer's authorised representative in the EU is Springer
Nature Customer Service Centre GmbH, Europaplatz 3, 69115 Heidelberg,
Germany. If you have any concerns regarding our products, please
contact ProductSafety@springernature.com

Printed and bound by CPI Group (UK) Ltd, Croydon, CR0 4YY
24/04/2026
02096370-0001